T0320946

UK economy: the crisis in perspective

UK economy: the crisis in perspective

Essays on the drivers of recent UK economic performance and lessons for the future

Editors
**Gabriele Giudice, Robert Kuenzel
and Tom Springbett**

Routledge
Taylor & Francis Group

LONDON AND NEW YORK

First edition 2012
Routledge
2 Park Square, Milton Park, Abingdon OX14 4RN, United Kingdom

Simultaneously published in the USA and Canada
By Routledge
711 Third Avenue, New York, NY 10017, USA

Routledge is an imprint of the Taylor & Francis Group, an informa business

ISBN 978-92-79-19706-2 (hbk)
ISBN 978-92-79-19707-9 (ebk)

Library of Congress Cataloging in Publication Data
UK economy: the crisis in perspective / editors Gabriele Giudice, Robert Kuenzel, Tom Springbett. – 1st ed.
    p. cm.
    1. Great Britain – Economic conditions – 1997–. 2. Financial crises – Great Britain. 3. Great Britain – Economic policy – 1997–. I. Giudice, Gabriele. II. Kuenzel, Robert. III. Springbett, Tom.
    HC256.7.U45 2011
    330.941 – dc23
                    2011027028

Typeset in Times New Roman
by Taylor & Francis Books

Printed and bound in Great Britain by
CPI Antony Rowe, Chippenham, Wiltshire

Contents

Illustrations

Figures

Tables

Acknowledgements

The editors are grateful to the chapter authors and to all of those who attended and spoke at the Directorate General for Economic and Financial Affairs (DG ECFIN) seminar on the UK economy in June 2010, in particular Ken Warwick, Henrik Braconier, Spencer Dale, Stephen King, George Buckley, Willem Buiter, Vanessa Rossi, Geoffrey Dicks and Ajai Chopra. We are grateful to colleagues in the Commission for their active contribution in making the seminar a success and this book a reality, in particular Marco Buti, Matthias Mors, Sean Berrigan, Karl Scerri and Ralph Wilkinson for speaking at the seminar and/or their support in its conception and in producing this book; Christian Weise and Olivia Mollen for helpful comments on the chapters written by the editors; Adriana Reut for the statistical assistance; Ondina Seabra and Stela Dinica for ensuring the smooth running of the seminar; Robert Gangl for support in the co-edition process; the European Commission for funding the seminar, and Kristine de Winter for assistance with the funding process.

Disclaimer

The views expressed in this book are those of the authors and do not necessarily coincide with those of the European Commission.

About the authors

Ray Barrell is a Professor at Brunel University. Between April 1990 and August 2011 he was a Senior Research Fellow at the National Institute of Economic and Social Research, directing macroeconomic modelling and forecasting. He was a university lecturer in economics from 1976 to 1984, teaching at Sussex, Southampton, Stirling and Brunel and specialising in monetary economics and econometrics. He then moved to be an Economic Adviser at HM Treasury from 1984 to 1987 before arriving at the Institute in 1988. In the last 15 years he has examined and supervised PhDs at the European University Institute in Florence and at Bordeaux University, and examined PhDs at York, Exeter, Brunel, Leicester, Loughborough, Imperial College, Birkbeck College and the London Business School. Since arriving at the National Institute Professor Barrell has published over 100 papers.

Rowena Crawford is a research economist in the Pensions and Public Finance sector at the Institute for Fiscal Studies. She is a co-author of the annual IFS Green Budget, and her recent research has included analysis of the UK public finances and of public spending in particular. Her other research interests include pensions policy and retirement saving behaviour.

E. Philip Davis is Senior Research Fellow at the UK's National Institute of Economic and Social Research, and Pastor, Penge Baptist Church. He is also Associate Professor, Brunel University, West London and an Adviser on Macroprudential Policy to the International Monetary Fund (IMF). Davis left the University of Oxford in 1980 and was employed by the Bank of England up to 2000, except for two periods on secondment to the Bank for International Settlements (BIS) and the European Monetary Institute. At the Bank of England he held a number of positions related to financial stability, including Senior International Financial Adviser, Europe and the USA. In 2000–09 he was Professor of Economics and Finance at Brunel, including a spell as Head of Department. Davis has published widely in the fields of financial stability, banking, corporate finance and financial regulation, as well as pensions, institutional investment, euromarkets and macroeconomics, and most recently Christian economics, as listed on his website: www.ephilipdavis.com. His recent work has focused inter alia on optimal regulation of bank capital and the prediction of banking crises in Organisation for Economic Co-operation and Development (OECD) countries, as well as on ethical issues underlying the subprime crisis. He has worked closely with the IMF as a consultant and researcher on financial stability matters, as well as the OECD, European Commission and various central banks and regulators. He runs an annual course on financial stability for 'Central Banking Publications' in Windsor. His books include *Debt, Financial Fragility and Systemic Risk*, published by Oxford University Press in 1995 and *Financial Structure* (with Joseph Byrne) published in 2003 by Cambridge University Press. He runs a discussion group on financial stability with over 900 members: groups.yahoo.com/group/financial_stability.

Carl Emmerson is Deputy Director of the Institute for Fiscal Studies. He is an editor of the annual IFS Green Budget, and—along with co-authors Rowena Crawford and Gemma Tetlow—his research has included analysis of the UK public finances and, in particular, assessing the impacts of state and private pension reforms. The Institute for Fiscal Studies (IFS) is a research institute that exists to promote effective economic and social policies by understanding better their impact on individuals, families, businesses and the government's finances through top quality economic analysis independent of government, political party or any other vested interest. More details of IFS research can be found at www.ifs.org.uk.

Gabriele Giudice is head of the unit responsible for the UK, Estonia and Latvia in the Directorate General for Economic and Financial Affairs (DG ECFIN) at the European Commission. He has a degree in International Economics from Bocconi University in Milan, and a post-degree diploma from ISPI, the Institute for International Policy Studies, Milan. His professional experience is mostly in the European Commission, at DG ECFIN, which he joined in 1994. In 2004–08 he was a member of the private office of the Commissioner for economic and monetary affairs, Joaquín Almunia, advising him in particular on economic and budgetary issues in the European Union (EU) and the Economic and Monetary Union. He returned to DG ECFIN in 2008 taking the position of head of unit for the monitoring of cyclical developments in the EU and co-ordinating the EU programme of harmonized business surveys. Since May 2009 he has been head of the unit carrying out surveillance of the UK, Estonia and Latvia (and until September 2010, also Lithuania). This includes being in charge of the EU financial assistance to Latvia through the Balance of Payments facility. His experience relates mainly to implementing and improving budgetary surveillance in the EU, the functioning of Economic and Monetary Union, and the economic and budgetary monitoring of individual countries. He has contributed several publications on these matters.

Dawn Holland is a Senior Research Fellow at the National Institute of Economic and Social Research (NIESR) in London. She has worked at

NIESR with the Institute's well-known global econometric model, NiGEM, since 1996. Her primary research focus has been on issues related to production functions and supply-side modelling and in particular the role of risk premia in the demand for capital. Recent studies include an analysis of the impact of transitional restrictions on the location decision of EU-8 migrants to the EU-15, and a study of fiscal multipliers under a series of different assumptions. She manages the quarterly production of NIESR's global economic forecast and has been a member of the editorial board of the National Institute Economic Review since 2003.

Dilruba Karim holds a PhD in Economics from Brunel University where she is now a lecturer. She is a member of the Brunel Macroeconomics Group and is currently affiliated with the National Institute of Economic and Social Research where she has researched the effects of banking crises and their prediction. Her main research focus has been on the design of Early Warning Systems for banking crises including linear and non-linear estimators. She has also worked on the housing market in Sweden and its links to macroprudential policy. Most recently she has worked on the costs of crises, leading crisis indicators, calibration of macroprudential policy, the effects of capital composition on bank risk taking and the effects of bank size on risk. She currently holds an ESRC grant for research into the causes of crises in Latin America and Asia.

Robert Kuenzel is an Economist in DG ECFIN. Upon joining the Commission in 2007 he spent three years covering the UK economy before moving to euro-area macroeconomic research. He has previously worked in the UK Treasury and the Department for Business, Innovation and Skills and holds a bachelor's degree in Philosophy, Politics and Economics and an MSc in Public Economics from the University of York.

Iana Liadze is a Senior Research Officer at the National Institute of Economic and Social Research. She joined the Institute's World Economy and Macroeconomic Modelling Team in July 2006. Her research interests include applied economic modelling and forecasting using the National Institute's Global Econometric Model (NiGEM). Her publications assess fiscal spillovers and trade relations in Europe, as well as the impact of EMU on growth. She has also published on the determinants of banking crises in OECD countries as well as Latin America and Asia

Christopher A. Pissarides is Professor of Economics at the London School of Economics and Political Science (LSE) and holder of the Norman Sosnow Chair in Economics. In 2010 he was awarded the Nobel Prize for Economics jointly with Dale Mortensen and Peter Diamond, for their work on frictions in labour markets. Professor Pissarides is the current (2011) President of the European Economic Association, a Fellow of the British Academy and the Econometric Society, and a Foreign Honorary Member of the American Economic Association.

Xavi Ramos is Associate Professor at the Universitat Autònoma de Barcelona and IZA (Institute for the Study of Labor) research fellow. His research interests include income inequality and its implications for government policy. His research has been published in monographs, book chapters and in a variety of journals, including *Economica, Review of Income and Wealth* and *International Tax and Public Finance*. He is currently on the Board of Editors of the *Journal of Economic Inequality* and is Book Review Editor for the same journal.

Dave Ramsden began his civil service career as an economist in 1986 before joining the Treasury in 1988. He has worked on a wide range of macro- and microeconomic policy issues and between 1999 and 2003 Dave led the Treasury's analysis on whether the UK should join the euro. From 2003 to 2006 he worked on the review that led to the creation of HM Revenue & Customs and was the Treasury's Director of Tax and Budget. Since 2008 Dave has been Chief Economic Adviser to the Treasury with director-general responsibilities for economic and fiscal policy advice, analysis and surveillance. Dave is also Head of the Government Economic Service.

Oriol Roca-Sagalés is Associate Professor at the Universitat Autònoma de Barcelona. His research interests focus on the link between quality of government and fiscal and political decentralization and the macro-economic and distributive effects of fiscal policies. He has recently published his research in the *Journal of Urban Economics, Fiscal Studies* and *Environment and Planning C – Government and Policy*, among others.

Tom Springbett is an economist at DG ECFIN. Before that, he worked in the UK Treasury, focusing mainly on financial regulation and European issues. He has a degree in economics with French from Durham University.

Gemma Tetlow is Programme Director of Pensions and Public Finances at the Institute for Fiscal Studies. Her research focuses on the analysis of the UK's public finances and public service spending, and issues relating to pension saving, the health of older workers and retirement decisions. Gemma was educated at the University of Warwick and University College London.

Martin Weale currently serves as an independent member of the Bank of England's Monetary Policy Committee to which he was appointed in 2010. This followed a term of 15 years as Director of the National Institute of Economic and Social Research. Before this he worked as a lecturer in Economics at the University of Cambridge and a Fellow of Clare College and, for two years after graduating, as an Overseas Development Institute Fellow at the National Statistics Office in Malawi. He has researched a large number of aspects of applied economics at both macro- and micro-economic levels. He has recently been working on issues connected with savings and pensions, including the impact of means-tested benefits on retirement behaviour and the adequacy of overall saving. He has also carried out a substantial amount of work on various aspects of economic statistics. Weale was appointed Commander of the Order of the British Empire (CBE) for his services to Economics in 1999 and was elected an Honorary Fellow of the Institute of Actuaries in 2001. In 2006 he was appointed to the Board of Actuarial Standards.

Preface

By Marco Buti[1]

In June 2010 the UK economy was in a dire condition. Over the previous year it had experienced the biggest annual decline in gross domestic product (GDP) since the Great Depression, the virtual nationalization of one the UK's largest banks and the ballooning of the government deficit to record peacetime levels.

At that time, when the European Commission held a seminar bringing together some of the UK's leading economists, analysts and policymakers to discuss the causes, consequences and lessons of the crisis, what struck me was that the mood was still broadly optimistic. While recognizing the clear failings that had helped take the UK economy down this dangerous path, there was acknowledgement of some of the UK's enduring strengths.

Most prominent among these strengths was the UK's flexible labour market, which had allowed a marked reduction in structural unemployment in the years before the crisis but also, through wage flexibility, helped prevent the recession from causing job losses in the numbers seen in the early 1980s and 1990s. Another strength that came out in the discussion was the UK's international openness. The positive commitment of successive UK governments to the EU single market agenda has been a force for good in Europe, and it is pleasing to see evidence from the discussion and in this book that this commitment to openness and unfettered trade within the EU has made a significant contribution to UK growth.

Of course there was also a lot of discussion of what went wrong. With hindsight it is clear that the UK entered the crisis with too large a government deficit and with too great a reliance on cyclical revenues. The fact that this happened in spite of the government having deemed its fiscal position to be compliant with its own fiscal framework suggests that that framework did not do its job. It is encouraging to see progress in this area in recent months which both strengthens domestic fiscal oversight and improves consistency with the Stability and Growth Pact. Financial regulation was another area where there were many lessons learned from the crisis. Again, it is a positive sign that the UK has been taking tough and radical decisions at home since our seminar, although there are clearly further challenges left to confront, as discussed in the remainder of this book.

I am glad that the Commission has generated a deep reflection and analysis on what has been a momentous period in UK economics, which is ultimately reflected in this timely book. The fact that since the seminar took place several of the authors have been awarded high-level recognitions, such as the Nobel Prize for Economics for Chris Pissarides and membership of the Monetary Policy Committee of the Bank of England for Martin Weale, witnesses the quality of the analysis in this book. I am confident that it will prove a useful contribution to the debate.

Note

1 Marco Buti is Director General of the European Commission's Directorate General for Economic and Financial Affairs (DG ECFIN).

Abbreviations

ABCP	asset-backed commercial paper
ABS	asset-backed securities
ADF	Augmented Dickey-Fuller
AME	annually managed expenditure
BBC	British Broadcasting Corporation
BCBS	Basel Committee on Banking Supervision
BIS	Bank for International Settlements
BRC	Budget Responsibility Committee
CBO	Congressional Budget Office
CCE	common correlated effects
CDOs	collateralised debt obligations
CEBS	Committee of European Banking Supervisors
CLG	Communities and Local Government
CPB	Central Planning Bureau
CPFF	Commercial Paper Funding Facility
CPI	consumer price index
CT	corporation tax
DG ECFIN	Directorate General for Economic and Financial Affairs
DELs	Departmental Expenditure Limits
ECB	European Central Bank
EEA	European Economic Area
EFO	Economic and Fiscal Outlook
EIS	Enterprise Investment Scheme
EMIR	European Market Infrastructure Regulation
ERM	Exchange Rate Mechanism
ESM	European Single Market
EU	European Union
EU-27	The 27 Member States of the European Union
FCA	Financial Conduct Authority
FDI	Foreign Direct Investment
FISIM	financial intermediation services indirectly measured
FOMC	Federal Open Market Committee
FPC	Financial Policy Committee

FRO	Financial Risk Outlook
FSA	Financial Services Authority
G7	a group of finance ministers from seven industrialized nations
G20	a group of finance ministers and central bank governors from 20 major economies
GDP	gross domestic product
GVA	gross value added
IFS	Institute for Fiscal Studies
IIP	international investment position
ILAS	individual liquidity adequacy standards
ILO	International Labour Organization
IMF	International Monetary Fund
IZA	Institute for the Study of Labor
LFS	Labour Force Survey
LIBOR	London Interbank Offered Rate
LSE	London School of Economics and Political Science
LTV	loan-to-value
MFIs	monetary financial institutions
MiFID	Markets in Financial Instruments Directive
MLD	Mean Log Deviation
MPC	Monetary Policy Committee
NAIRU	non-accelerating inflation rate of unemployment
Neths	Netherlands
NHS	National Health Service
NIESR	National Institute of Economic and Social Research
No.	number
OBR	Office for Budget Responsibility
OECD	Organisation for Economic Co-operation and Development
OLS	ordinary least squares
OMOs	open market operations
ONS	Office for National Statistics
OPEC	Organization of the Petroleum Exporting Countries
PBRs	Pre-Budget Reports
PPP	Purchasing-power parity
PRA	Prudential Regulation Authority
PSNB	public-sector net borrowing
QE	quantitative easing
R&D	Research and development
RHPG	real house price growth
RMBS	residential mortgage-backed securities
SBA	Small Business Administration
SGP	Stability and Growth Pact
SIVs	Special Investment Vehicles
SMEs	small and medium-sized enterprises
SMP	Single Market Programme

TALF	Term Asset-Backed Securities Loan Facility
TFP	Total Factor Productivity
UK	United Kingdom
US(A)	United States (of America)
VAR	vector autoregressive models
VAT	value-added tax
Vol.	Volume
WTO	World Trade Organization

1 Introduction and overview

Gabriele Giudice, Robert Kuenzel and Tom Springbett

In the decade between 1997 and 2007, the UK enjoyed strong and stable growth. Gross domestic product (GDP) grew by an average of 3.2% per year, peaking at 4.5% in 2000. Unemployment fell from its peak of 10.4% in 1993 to 5.3% in 2007. The same year, government debt was 44.5% of GDP and the deficit was 2.7% of GDP. However, this strong growth performance masked emerging imbalances, in particular: (i) greater-than-average reliance on household consumption growth to propel GDP, leading to an increasing current account deficit;[1] (ii) a large increase in household debt linked to the housing boom and falling saving rate; and (iii) a fiscal position which, although within the limits for deficit and debt set in the Stability and Growth Pact, failed to take into account the large cyclical revenues which were flattering the overall balance.

After many years of persistent and exuberant growth in the so-called Noughties, the correction that arrived was much tougher than expected. UK GDP first contracted by 1.1% in 2008 and then by 4.4% in 2009. The trigger was the international financial crisis to which the UK was particularly exposed because of its large, globally integrated and highly leveraged financial sector and high levels of household debt, particularly in the form of mortgages.

A prominent feature of the pre-crisis decade was the rapid expansion and globalization of the UK financial sector. The seeds of this success had been sown in 1986 with the Big Bang reform of regulation of the City of London. In the following 20 years the City vied consistently with New York for the position of the world's leading financial centre. UK banks also became much more leveraged than in the past. Between December 2000 and December 2007 median leverage[2] of British banks rose from 21 to 35. Between 1960 and 1999 it had averaged 19, peaking at 25 in 1984.[3] This high leverage, coupled with their reliance on short-term funding and exposure to risky repackaged loans, left the banks vulnerable to financial market disturbances.

The crisis triggered serious liquidity and solvency problems for several UK banks. The UK government intervened decisively to support the sector, nationalizing Northern Rock, taking large equity stakes in Royal Bank of Scotland and Lloyds Banking Group, breaking up Bradford and Bingley and providing extraordinary additional liquidity to the whole sector, mainly through the Bank of England. The Bank also implemented unprecedentedly loose monetary policy, reducing the main policy rate to 0.5% and engaging in a £275bn (19% of GDP) programme of quantitative easing. After the nadir of the crisis, banking solvency ratios recovered sharply, assisted significantly by government support.

Private-sector debt in the UK was also very high, especially by European standards, reflecting in particular the indebtedness of the household sector, at 107% of GDP vs. 70% in Europe in 2008. By contrast, UK non-financial corporation debt was, at 132% of GDP, close to the European Union (EU) average of 126%. High household indebtedness was mainly due to a high stock of mortgage debt: in 2009 household loans secured on dwellings were 78% of total loans to households. This high level of indebtedness made households vulnerable to unexpected falls in income and in the value of their collateral. When the crisis hit, the rapid growth in household consumption, which had done so much to drive pre-crisis growth, went into reverse.

Both the financial and the household sector were very exposed to the housing market, a factor that exacerbated the UK's crisis experience. Average nominal house prices doubled between 2000 and 2007. While the UK's strict planning laws prevented this price increase from causing a construction boom it did help drive a large increase in household debt as first time buyers were forced to take on more debt to buy houses and some existing owners borrowed more against their increased housing equity.

There was a clear link between rising house prices and rising household debt since the majority of the increase in debt was in the form of mortgages. The link between house prices and the UK's domestic consumption boom is less certain. It could be that both were caused mainly by strong consumer confidence and access to cheap credit, as consumers found themselves more able to borrow for house purchases or current consumption and less worried about a job loss or other negative financial event making them unable to service their debt. The Bank of England (2001) provided a useful examination of the theory and early empirical evidence from the early days of the house price boom. It pointed out that UK households cannot, in aggregate, realize an increase in housing wealth by selling housing assets because, unlike financial assets, UK houses are not widely traded on international markets. However, households can take advantage of increased housing equity to increase their secured borrowing, which is typically cheaper than unsecured borrowing. A model can be defined under which this phenomenon allows rising house prices to feed into increased housing investment and household consumption. As such, it seems likely that rising house prices did at least reinforce the UK's pre-crisis consumption boom.

The interaction between the financial and household sectors through the housing market also had significant implications for the public sector. After years of strong revenues from property transaction taxes and corporate taxes on the financial sector, the near-collapse of the banking sector and the sudden drop-off in property transactions had a dramatic impact on the public finances. The government deficit rose by 8.5 percentage points in two years to 11.2% of GDP in 2009.

In the external sector, UK net exports deteriorated steadily throughout the pre-crisis decade, with a surplus in (mainly financial) services more than offset by a large and growing deficit in goods. This decline appears to have been due partly to the strength of domestic consumption and partly to the persistent strength of sterling, with demand for the pound kept high by the UK's relatively high interest rates. Over the course of 2008 and 2009 sterling depreciated 25% on a nominal effective basis as the interest rate differentials with the rest of the world evaporated and investments in the UK banking sector became less attractive. However, this did not deliver an immediate improvement in UK net exports. Nevertheless, the impact of the depreciation was felt through high imported inflation, which helped push inflation well above the official target of 2% for a long period.

Quarterly growth returned in the final quarter of 2009, though with some volatility, to an average annualised rate of around 1.6%. However, the level of GDP looks likely to remain well below its pre-crisis trend for the foreseeable future. For the UK economy to adapt sustainably to the post-crisis world implies a number of challenges both for the public and private sector.

Consolidation of the public finances is the most pressing. While the UK entered the crisis with low government debt, the high deficit will soon take debt above the EU average. The crisis revealed the unsustainable nature of some pre-crisis tax revenues. The government must now meet the challenge of returning the public finances to balance with output significantly lower than pre-crisis expectations and a particular weakness in previously tax-rich parts of the economy.

The crisis also clearly exposed the weakness in the fiscal framework, which had been considered during the golden decade by many UK politicians and commentators as superior to the European Stability and Growth Pact. While decisive steps have been taken to define a new fiscal mandate and set up the Office for Budget Responsibility to provide the official forecast independent of political influence, the effectiveness of the new UK fiscal framework remains to be tested over a full economic cycle.

In addition, as part of the fiscal consolidation, public investment will suffer cuts in real terms of around 28% by 2014–15 compared to its 2010–11 level. UK public investment has been significantly below the EU average throughout recent history. This has been reflected in relatively poor UK infrastructure, particularly as regards transport. The investment gap closed significantly during the last decade. While it was not realistic to avoid cutting investment given the need for such significant cuts in overall spending, persistently low government investment could constitute an obstacle to growth in the future. Thus, there appears a good case for attaching high priority to public investment, research and development (R&D) and other forms of growth-enhancing expenditure in future spending rounds.

A second challenge for the UK is to ensure financial stability and avoid the formation of new bubbles. While the triggers of the crisis were global, two factors that exacerbated the situation in the UK were the large, globally integrated and highly leveraged financial sector and the overheating housing market. In the financial sector a particular problem, not unique to the UK, was a failure to identify and mitigate risks that were common to the business models of most or all banks, as opposed to idiosyncratic risks associated with any one given institution. Key examples were UK banks' reliance on short-term funding and implicit underwriting of off-balance sheet vehicles, which were excluded from regulatory capital calculations in spite of banks *de facto* standing behind them. There were also failures in individual firm supervision. Reducing the risk of such failures in the financial sector in the future and strengthening the economy's ability to cope if they do happen are thus key challenges for the UK.

Concerning the housing market, a number of issues stand out. First, house price swings have a big impact on household balance sheets. Second, banks providing mortgages are vulnerable to swings in the housing cycle, increasing its economic impact. Third, public finances are vulnerable to swings in housing tax revenues. Fourth, high house prices help explain the large share (around 25%) of the population living in state-subsidized accommodation and the high expenditure (around 1.5% of GDP) of housing benefit for poor households. Reducing the UK economy's vulnerability to the housing cycle is thus another important challenge.

The UK has already announced reforms in this area. On the supply side, central control of local planning decisions will be largely abolished and replaced with a system of financial incentives to local authorities to allow new house building. On the demand side, the rules governing sales of new mortgages will be tightened to try to do more to prevent lenders from granting mortgages that borrowers cannot afford. This could potentially rein in demand peaks driven by easy credit availability. The new Financial Policy Committee of the Bank of England could also use tools such as increased capital charges on mortgage lending for banks to lean against the building-up of new housing bubbles. An area of housing policy that remains largely unreformed is taxation. Problems with the UK housing tax system, including its regressivity, the volatility of its revenues and its discouragement of transactions have been highlighted by a number of commentators, including the Organisation for Economic Co-operation and Development (OECD 2011) and the Joseph Rowntree Foundation (2011). Reflecting the importance of housing issues to all sectors of the UK economy, there is a case to build on these measures to develop a more comprehensive package of reforms including in the mortgage market and property taxation.

In the labour market, overall post-crisis performance has been much better than might have been expected given the severity of the recession. Unemployment rose from 5.3% in 2007 to 7.8% in 2010. By mid-2011, two years after the most serious UK recession in recent history, unemployment had still not risen above its 1990s average. A number of factors contributed to this apparent paradox, including wage flexibility, which allowed average real wages to fall, labour hoarding by firms, a concentration of job losses in sectors with the highest output per worker, and the success of labour market reforms in the 1990s and early 2000s which reduced structural unemployment.

However, some groups were hit harder than others. Youth unemployment increased disproportionately. Between Q4 2009 and Q4 2010, unemployment of more than two years duration among the 18–24 age category increased by 43.4% compared to 37.2% for the working-age population as a whole. The 16–24 year old age group accounted for 56% of the total decline in employment between the peak in Q2 2008 and trough in Q1 2010, despite representing only 15% of total employees in 2008. A further challenge comes from the approximately 400,000 public-sector job cuts required to implement the government's challenging fiscal consolidation. While private-sector job creation in aggregate is likely to generate sufficient vacancies to accommodate those losing their jobs in the public sector, their skills may not be appropriate to the areas of the economy growing most quickly, notably manufacturing.

Some longer-standing problems in the labour market also remain to be resolved. Weak work incentives have been a long-running problem for the UK, with high marginal withdrawal rates for those moving off benefits into low-paid jobs and a complex benefits system which makes it hard for benefit recipients to assess how much benefit they would lose if they took a job. These issues can be particularly acute for single parents and second earners. This contributes to the high rate of jobless households with children, which is the highest in Europe at 17.5% compared to 10.2% for the EU as a whole. Combating poverty and promoting social inclusion represents hence a key concern. People in the UK also face a higher risk of poverty than the EU average (17.3% against an EU average of 16.3% in 2009).

Another long-standing issue in the UK that was brought out by the crisis is the low rate of business investment. In the decade to 2007 private-sector fixed capital formation averaged 15.6% of GDP in the UK compared to 17.8% in the EU. During the crisis an unprecedented drop-off in investment brought the ratio down to 11.9% in 2009 compared to 16.2% in the EU. While the UK's relatively large services sector partly explains its low historical investment record, the differences do not appear big enough to explain the entire gap. A period of strong investment growth could therefore offer a significant boost to the UK economy, both in the short-to-medium term as a support to weak domestic demand and, over the longer term, to help drive productivity gains.

One key driver of this investment weakness during the crisis has been tight credit supply, as banks demanded higher spreads reflecting their desire to deleverage and reduced risk appetite. Whilst it is impossible to split out the effects of lower credit demand and reduced availability reliably, as the Bank of England (2010) points out, the fact that spreads increased[4] and that some borrowers substituted corporate bond finance for bank credit suggests that tighter supply was the main explanatory factor. Improving credit availability could therefore help significantly in fostering an investment rebound.

Another critical support to final demand in the post-crisis period could be net exports. The external sector subtracted around one percentage point from GDP growth in 2010 as imports rebounded faster than exports. This was surprising given sterling's significant depreciation in 2008 and 2009. As the majority of UK exports go to the USA and the euro area, it did not benefit from the much more dynamic developments in emerging markets, pointing to the need to rebalance the composition of its destination markets. Restricted credit availability could also have played a role here as banks reduced their provision of trade finance. The government has since decided to broaden the range of products offered by the Export Credits Guarantee Department, which should alleviate this problem. Firms may also have been waiting to see whether sterling would remain at its lower level before deciding whether to increase capacity or to invest time in building an overseas client base. As such, the weakness in net exports since the depreciation is not in itself evidence that a net export rebound will not come eventually, although its timing remains uncertain.

In sum, the UK's recent economic experience has raised a number of questions, some of them short-term, others more fundamental. Interpretation of this vast boom and bust has focused the minds of the UK's leading economists, sometimes with the aim of finding a culprit in policy decisions. The extent to which UK policy and institutions were direct causes of its crisis should not be exaggerated. As an open economy and leading participant in financial globalization, the UK could never have come through the crisis unscathed. However, there are aspects of the UK's crisis experience, and of its strong pre-crisis performance, which yield valuable insights for those who seek to understand the UK economy and to define optimal policies for the future.

A good place to start this assessment is with a detailed analysis of the components of UK growth in the pre-crisis decade. Examining a breakdown of the UK's main growth drivers in Chapter 2 of this book, Ray Barrell, Dawn Holland and Iana Liadze find that it was productivity gains, rather than growing labour and capital input, that were the most important contributor to UK growth in the decade to 2007, resulting from more integrated and competitive markets. While financial services did play a part in this, their contribution was only around one-eighth of total productivity growth for the period, implying that while the UK benefited more than most from the rapid expansion of the financial sector, it was not utterly reliant upon it. Policy does seem to have played a significant part in driving the UK's golden decade, with European integration and strengthened competition policy prevalent. This points clearly to key priorities looking forward to secure sustained growth supported by the remaining scope for further integration at European level.

Another important pillar of UK growth was steadily falling unemployment. In Chapter 3, Christopher Pissarides points out that this strong performance was all the more unusual for coming without accelerating inflation, which had always accompanied UK employment booms in the past. This step forward in labour market performance was built on several factors, particularly the better anchoring of inflation expectations provided by inflation targeting, China's expansion which provided cheap imported goods, harder-to-get and less generous unemployment benefits and finally an increase in labour supply from net immigration from the new EU members and commonwealth countries. Although net migration and imported deflation from China are likely to fade as supporting factors for the UK labour market, better control of inflation and better work incentives look likely to provide enduring benefits.

On the demand side of the equation, we have already mentioned the much larger role played by consumption growth in UK GDP in the decade to 2007 compared to the euro area. Rapid growth in private consumption alongside persistent government deficits implied sustainability problems, particularly as ageing populations and diminishing environmental resources increased the importance of preparedness for the future. Once the house price boom, which increased household wealth with no corresponding increase in the real productive assets of the economy, is taken into account, the picture becomes even more concerning. In Chapter 4, Martin Weale shows that UK consumption growth in the decade to 2007 was indeed unsustainable: it implied a substantial decline in the ratio of produced wealth to GDP in the UK and therefore a transfer of wealth from future generations to the current one. In this context, the sudden jump in the saving rate that accompanied the crisis appears to have been an inevitable correction, supporting the conclusion that UK growth in the decade to 2007 was indeed unsustainable over the long term. Subsequently, households were forced to smooth the impact of weak real income growth on consumption by reducing saving. The Commission forecasts the saving rate to remain low for a while as households prioritise maintaining reservation levels of consumption over restoring depleted savings, but thereafter they would use a larger proportion of any real wage gains for saving. While this would help the level of household indebtedness slightly, it is likely to remain well above the EU average, implying that consumption growth may remain weak over the medium term.

Its high degree of international financial integration has meant that the UK has for a long time been subject to major in- and outflows of funds. However, during the crisis concerns surrounding the health of the UK's external balance sheet rose, accompanied by falls in the pound sterling. In Chapter 5, Robert Kuenzel examines the underlying changes in financial flows and the UK's international investment position (IIP) in order to assess the extent of the correction and revaluation of the UK's external position in the face of the financial crisis, and explain the recent disconnect between current account flows and net foreign asset stocks. The chapter finds little evidence of unsustainable trends in UK net financial flows but highlights the vulnerabilities linked to the UK's large gross international investment position.

Often forgotten in discussions of economic aggregates are distributional issues. Much of the increase in government spending in the decade to 2007 was aimed at reducing inequality, for example the introduction of new benefits for the poorest pensioners and tax credits for poor and middle-income working families. The vast increases in public healthcare spending were also probably redistributionary since the rich have the option of paying for private health-care. In Chapter 6, Xavi Ramos and Oriol Roca-Sagales show that higher government spending does tend to reduce inequality but that it also significantly reduces growth. This highlights the tough trade-offs faced by the UK government, as it tries to address difficult issues around poverty and social exclusion within a very tight fiscal envelope and in a context of broad economic weakness.

Among the many challenges facing the UK mentioned earlier, two of the most immediate are putting the financial sector back on a sustainable and independent footing, through effective regulatory reforms and a timely and fair withdrawal of the government's unprecedented support for banks; and addressing the high fiscal deficit to preserve the country's credibility in nervous and fragile global capital markets. These questions are dealt with in Chapters 7, 8 and 9.

In the pre-crisis decade UK banks were indeed succeeding in world markets, but also financing a major leveraging of consumer balance sheets. In Chapter 7, Tom Springbett looks at the changing relationship between the UK economy and its banking sector after the financial crisis took hold in 2008, and assesses how much the role and position of the UK banking sector has really changed and how much it needs to change in the future. He also considers the future policy agenda, discussing the need for a new system of macroprudential regulation and the government's plans, finding that the new policy framework is indeed likely to deliver stronger safeguards against financial crises in the future. In Chapter 8, Philip Davis and Dilruba Karim catalogue and assess the UK government's many and various interventions in the financial sector. One important aspect of these interventions is that they have made more explicit the implied obligation on governments to prop up their countries' banking sectors when financial stability is seriously threatened. This observation demands not only better regulation of the banks to reduce the frequency and seriousness of crises but also greater consideration of the compensation tax-payers should expect to receive from banks in exchange for this support. The UK government has set out plans to impose a levy on banks but its level is low relative to most estimates of the financing cost savings banks enjoy as a result of their implicit state guarantee. As such, the discussion on the appropriate relationship between the banking sector and taxpayers clearly still has further to run.

On the fiscal side, Rowena Crawford, Carl Emmerson and Gemma Tetlow set out in Chapter 9 the anatomy of the UK's fiscal crisis, which has broken records both for the size of its deficits and the severity of the spending cuts planned to address it. The impact of the consolidation on UK growth will only be known after the fact, but there are clear risks involved. While consolidation was essential given the UK's fiscal position—and indeed in the UK's long-term interests given the additional confidence it offers to firms and external investors—it remains an open question whether the Keynesian or the non-Keynesian effects of such consolidation will prevail, and thereby what the sign and size of its impact on domestic demand and GDP growth will be in the short-to-medium term. Longer term, there are clearly lessons to be learned, particularly the importance for governments of being able to distinguish between permanent and temporary tax revenues and of making fiscal hay while the sun shines, something that indeed is at the core of the European fiscal governance framework. With the introduction of the new Office for Budget Responsibility, the new government has taken a step forward on this and it should remain a priority.

Finally, concluding the review of the problems that built up in the UK economy before the crisis and of the challenges ahead, in Chapter 10 Dave Ramsden sets out the UK Treasury's analysis of such developments and of the action the government is taking to draw on the lessons of recent history. Facing circumstances that at times seemed daunting, the government has begun a programme of radical reforms to the whole of economic policy, including a huge fiscal consolidation, a new fiscal framework, a new system of financial regulation and macroprudential oversight, and a microeconomic policy agenda aimed at rebalancing the economy away from consumption and towards exports and investment. He outlines an agenda of the first UK coalition government in decades which is ambitious by all standards, the implementation of which is delivering promising results and which needs to be pursued carefully and with determination over the coming years to make the UK stronger and steadier than before.

The long journey of the UK through the Noughties, a golden ride which let many in the country and abroad think that 'this time was different' and allowed the development of perilous imbalances, ended with a cold bath. The British economy and society have started to recover from this large and unexpected reverse. Drawing the lessons from this experience is important to set the stage for sustained but also sustainable and socially balanced growth over the next years. This book, with the many authoritative academics and practitioners who have provided their insights on how the boom and the crisis unfolded, and how the challenges are being addressed, aims to contribute to this endeavour.

Notes

1 Whereas domestic consumption accounted for one-half of euro area growth in the pre-crisis decade, in the UK it was three-quarters.
2 Leverage is defined as total assets divided by total equity.
3 Source: Bank of England *Financial Stability Report* June 2010 and Commission calculations.
4 In a simple model of supply and demand for credit where demand increases and supply decreases proportionately with the spread, a negative demand shock would lead to a decrease in the market-clearing spread whereas a negative supply shock would lead to an increase in the market-clearing spread.

References

Bank of England (2001) 'Why House Prices Matter', *Quarterly Bulletin* Winter 2001, available at www.bankofengland.co.uk/publications/quarterlybulletin/qb010406.pdf.
——(2010) 'Understanding the Weakness of Bank Lending', *Quarterly Bulletin* Q4 2010, available at www.bankofengland.co.uk/publications/quarterlybulletin/qb100406.pdf.
Joseph Rowntree Foundation (2011) 'Tackling Housing Market Volatility in the UK', available at www.jrf.org.uk/publications/tackling-housing-market-volatility-uk.
OECD (2011) 'Economic Survey of the United Kingdom', available at www.oecd.org.

2 Accounting for UK economic performance 1973–2009

Ray Barrell, Dawn Holland and Iana Liadze[1]

Introduction

Up until the onset of the financial crisis, UK performance looked better than that of many other European countries. There are many ways to decompose the factors behind this better performance, and we compare two approaches, both of which are related to an evaluation of input quantity and quality. The first involves the use of growth accounting, and the second the estimation of a cross-country panel regression. We have combined these approaches previously in Barrell, Holland, Liadze and Pomerantz (2007, 2009), but for a different set of countries over a shorter period, and hence our work extends our previous discussions.

Both approaches start with the assumption that output growth depends upon the growth of labour and capital inputs and on the rate of growth of technical progress. However, it is useful to separate labour input (or the level of technical progress) into a quantity and a quality component. Barrell, Holland, Liadze and Pomerantz (2007) undertook a preliminary version of this using data on skill composition and skill rewards across a number of countries. We adopt a similar approach for a sample of 12 Organisation for Economic Co-operation and Development (OECD) countries, covering the 35-year period to 2007. Our choice of countries was determined by data availability, especially in relation to skills indicators.

Growth accounting on basic price income data is performed for labour hours, labour quality and capital inputs, and hence a true Total Factor Productivity (TFP) residual is calculated. This allows us to decompose growth into a component driven by capital deepening, one by raw labour input, and another by labour quality as measured by a Tornqvist-based measure of workforce skills. The residual is attributed to total factor productivity growth. This analysis allows us to make a first evaluation of the impact of reforms in education and training in the UK over the last 20 years and to discuss the relationship between the timing of TFP changes and policy innovations such as competition legislation and product and labour market reforms. We also investigate in passing the potential impact of the growth of financial services in the run up to the crisis. Growth accounting allows us to separate out the impact of capital deepening on labour productivity from skills and TFP effects. A more formal analysis of the factors affecting TFP is needed and this is undertaken in the second approach.

The second approach is essentially a variant of the cross-country panel regression framework developed by Barro (1991). The cross-country panel regressions relate output per person hour to our measure of workforce skills and a series of factors that are thought to drive the rate of technical progress, such as research and development, openness to innovations from abroad through trade and foreign direct investment, as well as heightened competition brought about by the removal of trade barriers. We also look at the impact of banking crises on labour productivity. We address the issue of the impact of financial crises on the sustainable level of output, and note that only for around one in four crises is there any evidence that there has been a permanent scar. However, the current crisis is likely to leave a permanent scar on almost all advanced economies.

All estimation extends to 2007, and we then analyse the response to the banking sector-induced recession and the impact on output in order to evaluate the robustness of institutions against a strong downturn. This must be undertaken in a comparative context, and we use the same group of countries throughout. It is not clear that institutions in the UK have been robust against the crisis, although we must distinguish between the short- and the long-term impact. In particular the fiscal and monetary response could have been more robust, but there are many factors that pattern the short-term response to the crisis. We draw on Barrell and Holland (2010) to help explain differences in the depth of the crisis. Labour market institutions in the UK appear to be more able to absorb this shock than in the past, as Holland, Kirby and Whitworth (2010) suggest. The financial sector is likely to shrink in all economies, and the impact on the UK may be larger than in most other countries, as it has a larger share in activity. However, apart from this, there is no strong reason to suggest that the long-term impact on the UK will be particularly larger than other countries, although the recession has been more severe than in many. The crisis has been global, and risk premia are likely to rise by similar amounts everywhere, and impacts on sustainable output will also be similar, and we suggest that output per person hour in the UK will be permanently 3% lower than we had anticipated in early 2008.

Overview of the UK growth performance

Up until the onset of the financial crisis, output growth in the UK exceeded that in many other European countries. Gross domestic product (GDP) at basic prices increased at an average annual rate of 2.4% per annum in the thirty years from 1978 to 2007, with somewhat stronger growth in the final decade. Figure 2.1 illustrates the UK growth performance relative to the other 11 OECD economies covered in this study. UK growth has not been as rapid as in the North American economies, although these differences

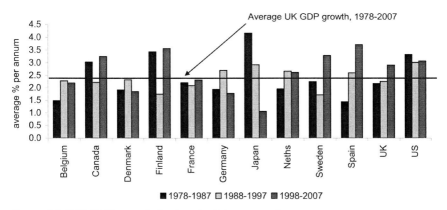

Figure 2.1 UK GDP growth (basic prices) in perspective

narrowed sharply in the final decade of our sample to 2007. Within the European Union (EU), growth has recently been faster in Finland and Sweden, and for the last two decades also in Spain, while the UK growth performance compares favourably to the rest of the countries in the sample. Over the last period growth accelerated in the UK, Sweden, Spain, Finland and Canada noticeably, and it was approximately constant in the USA, the Netherlands, Belgium and France, whilst it decelerated in Denmark, Germany and Japan. Our objective is to evaluate the factors that may have driven this relative improvement in UK economic growth.

There are many reasons why growth might accelerate in some countries and not in others. Structural reforms that increase efficiency of factor use, improvements in technology and increases in the quantity or quality of factors of production are the three obvious categories to look at. We should also examine the level of productivity per person hour to see how far countries are from the efficiency and technology frontiers, and we do that in Figure 2.2, which plots productivity in 2005 purchasing-power parity (PPP) relative to the USA for each of our start or end years. In no year does any country in our sample (and with our PPP base in 2005) have productivity per person hour higher than that in the USA, and hence we can regard this as our frontier. We would expect other countries to generally catch up with the USA, but it is not clear that this has been happening.

In 1977 UK productivity per person hour, which is the dependent variable in our second approach, was lower than in most of the other countries studied here, and higher only than in Finland and in Japan[2.] The UK and Finland are the only countries where productivity relative to the USA rises over each interval, and productivity in the UK, Finland and Sweden rises relative to the USA over the last period we consider. On the basis of growth and improvements in the level of productivity, UK performance looks better than most countries we consider in the decade from 1997 to 2007, and we can evaluate the reasons for this.

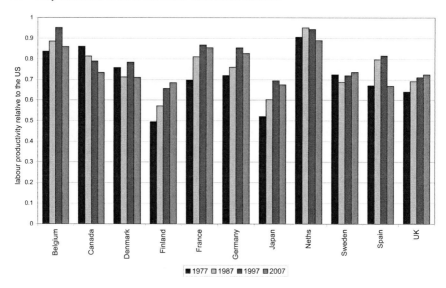

Figure 2.2 Relative levels of productivity (USA = 1.0, 2005 PPPs)

It is common to describe the productive capacity of an economy through the use of an aggregate production function, which describes the interaction between factor inputs, such as labour and capital, the state of technology, and any other factors that may affect the quality or efficiency of the production process. Growth may vary across countries because factor input growth differs over time and space. Labour supply depends on institutions, preferences and demographics, and its equilibrium will change when the structures of these institutions, preferences and demographics change. Capital input growth may also differ over time either because investment growth changes or because the rate of depreciation of the existing capital stock changes. The productive capacity of factor inputs depends on their innate quality, for example driven by the skill level of the workforce, and on the technology used to combine factor inputs, which may depend on the domestic research base as well as access to innovations developed abroad.

Factor inputs

Labour market reforms and their effects on participation and equilibrium unemployment are likely to increase equilibrium output, but they are not necessarily drivers of technical progress, except to the extent that they change rent-seeking behaviour. These reforms mainly affect the supply of labour, and it is difficult to separate out their effects in our growth accounting and econometric work. Output also depends upon the quantity of capital available, and increased competition and the reduction of barriers may increase the efficiency with which capital is used, and there may be capital flows from low-return to high-return regions. In addition, the quantity of capital may increase if savings globally rise or the user cost of capital displays a downward trend, and these two factors may be related. The user cost of capital may trend down because increased saving puts downward pressure on real interest rates, because policy and innovation reduce risk premia, or because financial innovation reduces the cost of intermediation and hence the margin between borrowing and lending rates. All of these are discussed in Barrell, Gottschalk, Kirby and Orazgani (2009). Trends in user cost and other factors affecting capital deepening may continue for a long period, but the gains may be illusionary, as we may have discovered in the recent financial crisis. Specific effects of financial crises are hard to track down, but they will sometimes induce a re-evaluation of risk premia on investment and reduce the equilibrium capital stock and hence the equilibrium level of sustainable output.

Market efficiency and technical progress

There are a number of factors that affect overall productivity, and these may be grouped into the efficiency with which factors are used, the level of scientific knowledge available to complement capital and labour, and the skills and training of the workforce. General purpose technical progress may be a common pool resource driven by public good scientific research and general innovation, and it is likely to be similar across countries. However, institutions may speed up or even prevent the absorption of new ideas.

Openness to trade is thought to have important effects on productivity growth. The ability to trade enables a country to specialize in more efficient production processes, raising the aggregate growth rate temporarily. Endogenous growth models have also pointed to the possibility that contacts with the outside world may potentially raise the growth rate permanently (see, for instance, Coe and Helpman 1995; Proudman and Redding 1998). There is evidence that increases in competition brought about by the removal of trade barriers raise output, and we draw attention to the single market programme (European Single Market—ESM) as a factor affecting a number of our countries, which would capture both the increase in trade as a result of the changing nature of goods and also the conscious attempts to increase competition by removing barriers. There may also be country-specific competition policy factors that we should take into account, and country-specific policies toward research may be important in explaining differences in growth.

Endogenous growth models have been developed by Aghion and Howitt (1998) and others where research and development (R&D) expenditures or the number of researchers drive the growth process. Griffith *et al.* (2004) discuss the two faces of R&D. Not only does R&D increase the innovation rate in the technology frontier country, but it also raises the absorptive capacity of an economy to new ideas. Hence in our econometrics below we use an estimate of the stock of R&D as an indicator of usable knowledge, based on the accumulation of flows of R&D onto a depreciating stock.[3]

Skills

Our growth decomposition and regression studies separate the quantity of labour input into the production process from the quality of labour input. Quantity measures of the level of employment and average hours of working time per employed person are readily available. However, quality measures are more difficult to estimate, as for our purposes skills cannot be measured independently of their usefulness. We need to be able to distinguish broadly comparable types of labour across countries, with differing levels of education. In addition we need to be able to estimate their value in the production process, and perhaps the best way to do this is to use relative wages as an indicator of the relative productivity of the workforce. We would want skills in the economy to increase with an increase in the proportion of those with a higher skill level. We would also want the quantum of skills to increase if the skills acquired became more productive, either because the skills had improved, or technical change had made them more useful. We therefore choose to measure skills by wages (marginal products) relative to the unskilled. This is perhaps problematic as the unskilled are not completely unskilled in any of our countries, and they have degrees of numeracy and literacy that change over time, changing their productivity. However, setting them to 1.0 is the least bad option we have to index skills.[4]

We adopt a Tornqvist discrete time version of a Divisia index to construct an indicator of workforce skills. The EU KLEMS[5] database contains information on the skill mix of a large group of the OECD member countries. In particular, data on hours worked by persons engaged and compensation of the workforce in low-, medium- and high-skill category groups are available. First, a relative compensation for each skill group over time was calculated.[6] Based on the assumption that relative wages reflect relative marginal product, skill premiums for medium- and high-skill groups are calculated relative to the low-skill category. A Tornqvist index[7] is then calculated as:

$$LN(TQ) = \sum_{J=1}^{3} S_{j,t}(\ln x_{j,t} - \ln x_{j,t-1})$$

$$\text{with } S_{j,t} = 0.5(S_{j,t} + S_{j,t-1})$$

(1)

where TQ is the Tornqvist index, $S_{j,t}$ is the share of the wage bill directed to skill category j at time t and $x_{j,t}$ is the share of hours worked by the skill group. Once the Tornqvist index is created, it is applied to the initial value of total hours worked and the skill index is calculated as a relative value in each year as compared to the first available year of observations.[8] Given our assumption that wage differentials reflect underlying productivity differentials we constructed an index of efficiency units of labour for each country, with a higher value of the index implying a higher level of knowledge embodied in workers, which raises productivity of labour.[9]

There are common trends across all countries in both compensation shares and hours worked by less-skilled workers, with an increasing share of hours worked and compensation received by highly skilled employees. However, the relative speed and size of the change in shares lead to different time patterns of skill indices in the countries. The Tornqvist skill index increases over time in all countries, with the largest increases in the UK and the USA, followed by Spain, as we can see from Figure 2.3. Skills have risen least rapidly in Germany, Canada and Sweden. In all countries, to a different extent, we have seen a change in the skill mix of the workforce over the sample period. The share of hours worked and total compensation of high-skilled workers have risen, with an increase in the share of compensation for high-skilled workers outstripping the growth in the hours worked. The middle-skilled group on average maintained a constant share in both hours worked and compensation, while the low-skilled group has seen both shares falling. Increases in compensation for high-skilled workers resulted in a rise in the high-skill premium. This has a positive effect on our indicator of skills which is based on the assumption that higher wages indicate higher productivity.

Growth accounting

Robert Solow (1957) is generally attributed with the introduction of the theoretical framework for growth accounting. Solow's framework specifies an explicit model of potential output as a function of factor inputs, such as capital and labour, and an efficiency indicator termed total factor productivity (TFP).[10]

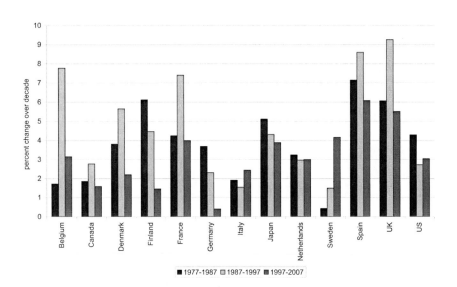

Figure 2.3 Growth in skills
NIESR calculations based on EU KLEMS

This approach assumes a general underlying production function that maps the factor inputs to final output, thereby representing the productive capacity of an economy. With two factors of production this can be expressed as:

$$Y = f(K_t, L_t, T_t) \tag{2}$$

where Y is the final output good, K is the capital stock, L is labour input and T indicates the state of technology, or TFP. Totally differentiating this equation with respect to time, and assuming perfect competition in factor markets and a homothetic production function, the partial derivatives of the production function may be rearranged to obtain a decomposition of the growth rate of output into the sum of the growth rates of each input, weighted by their relative factor share, plus the growth in TFP.

$$d \ln(Y_t) = \theta_{K_t} d \ln(K_t) + \theta_{L_t} d \ln(L_t) + dA_t \tag{3}$$

Where θ_{K_t} is the share of output accruing to capital, θ_{L_t} is the labour share and dA_t is the growth rate of TFP, defined as:

$$dA_t = \frac{f_{T_t} T_t}{Y_t} d \ln(T_t) \tag{4}$$

We have assumed constant returns to scale, and hence $\theta_{L_t} = (1 - \theta_{K_t})$. Growth accounting exercises based on measures of physical units of capital and labour do not allow us to say whether changes in TFP capture efficiency gains in the production process achieved thanks to the implementation of technological innovations or whether they reflect changes in the quality of capital or labour. More can be learned from growth accounting using measures of the quality of the capital and labour input. Skills-adjusted labour input (L) can be expressed as:

$$L = E^* Hours^* S \tag{5}$$

where E is total employment, *Hours* is average hours worked and S is a measure of workforce skills or human capital. The basic growth accounting decomposition can then be expressed as:

$$d \ln(Y_t) = \theta_{K_t} d \ln(K_t) + (1 - \theta_{K_t}) d \ln(E_t^* Hours_t) \\ + (1 - \theta_{K_t}) d \ln(S_t) + dA_t \tag{6}$$

A common growth accounting practice is to subtract the growth rate of (unadjusted) labour input from both sides of (6), to derive a decomposition of labour productivity into its components:

$$d \ln\left(\frac{Y_t}{E_t^* Hours_t}\right) = \theta_{K_t} d \ln\left(\frac{Y}{E^* Hours}\right) + (1 - \theta_{K_t}) d \ln(S_t) + dA_t \qquad (7)$$

The equation above indicates that output per person hour can be decomposed into the contribution from skills accumulation, a contribution from capital deepening, which is the units of capital per hour worked, and the residual category, total factor productivity. In Table 2.1 we use the simple relationship between output, labour input and labour productivity:[11]

$$Y = (E^* Hours)^* \frac{Y}{(E^* Hours)} \qquad (8)$$

in order to decompose GDP growth into the contribution from labour input (E*Hours) and labour productivity, defined as output per person hour. We then decompose labour productivity growth into the contribution from capital deepening, the contribution from skills accumulation and the residual component, total factor productivity growth. We look at three ten-year time periods from 1978–2007 in order to assess whether the contributions of various components have shifted over time.

Averaged over the full 30-year sample period, GDP growth (calculated at basic prices in order to abstract from the impact of indirect taxes and subsidies on the measured level of income) was highest in the USA, closely followed by Finland, Canada, Japan and Spain. GDP growth in Belgium, Denmark, Germany and France has been less robust on average. The average growth rate for Japan is biased by very strong growth in the earliest decade, while average annual growth in the 1998–2007 period was lower in Japan than in any other country in this sample. Conversely, the strong growth in Spain is driven by the very strong growth averaging 3.7% per annum in the most recent decade, while earlier periods were less impressive.

Of the faster growing economies, the performance in the USA, Canada and Spain can be largely attributed to strong growth in labour input, while labour productivity growth in these economies was closely in line with (or lower than in the case of Canada) the others in the sample. Japan and Finland, on the other hand, can attribute their strong growth performance to rapid growth in labour productivity. France, Germany and the UK have also exhibited relatively strong growth in labour productivity on average.

Capital deepening has contributed more towards growth in France, Japan and Spain over the last 30 years than elsewhere, while it has been of less importance in Denmark and the USA. Over the most recent decade, capital deepening played a more important role in the USA, possibly reflecting the low costs of borrowing for investment in the period leading up to the global financial crisis. In most of the other countries in our sample and especially in Spain and Japan, on the other hand, the contribution of capital deepening to growth diminished relative to the previous two decades.

Table 2.1 Growth decomposition

		Belgium	Canada	Denmark	Finland	France	Germany	Japan	Neths	Sweden	Spain	UK	USA
		Percentage point contribution to average annual GDP growth											
GDP at basic prices (% change)	1978–87	1.5	3.0	1.9	3.4	2.2	1.9	4.2	2.0	2.2	1.4	2.2	3.3
	1988–97	2.3	2.2	2.3	1.7	2.1	2.7	2.9	2.7	1.7	2.6	2.3	3.0
	1998–2007	2.2	3.2	1.8	3.6	2.3	1.3	1.1	2.6	3.3	3.7	2.9	3.1
of which													
Hourly labour input (unadjusted)	1978–87	-0.7	2.0	0.9	0.3	-0.9	-0.2	1.0	-0.1	1.2	-1.9	-0.2	1.7
	1988–97	-0.1	0.9	-0.3	-1.3	-0.2	-0.1	-0.2	1.1	-0.4	0.7	0.3	1.4
	1998–2007	1.2	1.9	0.8	1.0	0.4	0.1	-0.7	1.1	1.0	3.7	0.6	1.0
Output per person hour	1978–87	2.2	1.0	1.0	3.1	3.1	2.2	3.1	2.1	1.1	3.4	2.4	1.6
	1988–97	2.4	1.3	2.6	3.0	2.3	2.8	3.1	1.5	2.1	1.9	1.9	1.6
	1998–2007	1.0	1.3	1.0	2.5	1.9	1.7	1.8	1.5	2.3	0.0	2.2	2.0
of which													
Skills accumulation	1978–87	0.1	0.1	0.3	0.4	0.3	0.2	0.4	0.2	0.0	0.4	0.4	0.3
	1988–97	0.5	0.2	0.4	0.3	0.4	0.1	0.3	0.2	0.1	0.5	0.6	0.2
	1998–2007	0.2	0.1	0.1	0.1	0.2	0.0	0.2	0.2	0.2	0.3	0.3	0.2
TFP (excluding skills)	1978–87	1.2	0.4	0.4	1.8	1.4	1.0	1.6	1.1	0.7	1.3	1.4	1.0
	1988–97	0.9	0.5	1.8	1.9	0.7	1.7	1.2	1.0	1.1	0.1	0.8	1.1
	1998–2007	0.5	0.8	0.8	2.2	0.9	1.1	1.0	0.9	1.8	-0.6	1.2	1.2
Capital deepening	1978–87	0.8	0.5	0.3	0.9	1.5	0.9	1.1	0.8	0.4	1.7	0.6	0.3
	1988–97	0.9	0.6	0.5	0.9	1.2	1.0	1.6	0.4	0.9	1.2	0.6	0.3
	1998–2007	0.3	0.4	0.2	0.2	0.8	0.6	0.5	0.4	0.2	0.3	0.7	0.6

We can decompose the remaining component into skills and underlying labour productivity growth. Over the whole period the impact of skills has been largest in the UK, Spain, Japan and France. Residual productivity growth over the whole period has been particularly rapid in Finland, and has also been high in Japan, Germany and Sweden. In the most recent decade, TFP, after accounting for skills, has increased at an average rate of 1.2% per annum in the UK, which has been performing better than most of the other countries in this sample. Only Sweden and Finland had higher TFP growth in this period, reflecting the pace of technical change in specific industries such as telecommunications, in which these small countries specialize. They also underwent extensive product market reforms in the early 1990s and may have gained from membership of the EU in 1995. The improvement in UK performance is clear over this period, and we can turn to look at developments in more detail.

The rise in productivity growth in the last decade may be the result of the process of attempting to improve the efficiency of factor use in the UK over our time period. The first was the start of the privatization programme in 1984, which was based on a belief that private-sector ownership was sufficient to ensure that productivity would improve because the threat of takeover, or an actual takeover, would improve productivity, without any concern for the regulatory framework or competition environment in which privatized firms were placed. As a result, private-sector monopolies with inflexible pricing rules were set up, and efficiency did not improve as much as might have been expected. The second was the beginning of the Single Market Programme (SMP) in 1986, which was a programme that removed barriers to competition in Europe. Its impact is discussed at length in Barrell, Gottschalk, Kirby and Orazgani (2009), and it is clear that it had an impact on sustainable output by improving competitive forces. The first electricity privatization in 1990 was better designed to raise productivity, with some recognition that competition mattered, but it was only with the restructuring of the gas industry in 1995 that the benefits of privatization were beginning to be available.

The gradually changing attitude to competition became clear by 1998, with a new competition act (effective from 2000), where for the first time cartels became illegal, and it was clear that the framework was designed in the interest of the consumer. This approach to market-based regulation was almost certainly a factor behind the increase in TFP growth from the mid-1990s, and it can be considered a success. However, 'light-touch' regulation had its problems, and it was certainly a factor behind the growth of the financial services sector from the mid-1990s, and probably contributed to the crisis we have seen in the last three years.

The change to the competitive environment in the UK had been largely completed by 2002, with only minor improvements thereafter. Part of the changed environment for competition involved reduction in the complexity and stringency of regulation, and this included financial regulation. It was widely believed that light-touch regulation in this sector would enhance the

UK's attractiveness as a location for financial intermediation, and hence enhance output and productivity growth. The contribution of the financial services sector to productivity growth is analysed further in Table 2.2 for the last decade, as data are not easily available for earlier periods for all countries. We calculate productivity growth in this sector (on the assumption that trends in hours were the same as elsewhere) and compare it to the implied productivity growth in the rest of the economy outside this sector. The weighted average of these two growth rates gives whole economy growth.

The impact of the financial sector on overall productivity growth is taken to be the excess (or in two cases shortfall) of the sector's productivity growth as compared to the rest of the economy multiplied by the size of the sector. In the UK productivity growth outside financial intermediation was 2.07% a year, whilst it was 5.54% a year inside the sector. Excess productivity growth in the sector was 3.47% a year, and in 2000 the sector represented 5.1% of the economy. Hence the contribution to growth was 0.18 percentage points (3.47*0.051).

Growth in the financial sector contributed most in Spain, the USA, the UK and Denmark, and in most countries productivity growth was more rapid in this sector. The additional contribution to productivity growth from the sector averages 0.1% per annum across all countries and was almost 0.2% per annum on average in the UK, hence it is a partial explanation of why productivity in the UK grew more rapidly. However, removing this addition from all countries leaves rankings unchanged, as the deduction is lower in Finland and Sweden, the only countries ahead of the UK. Germany moves toward the UK.

Our growth accounting work suggests that capital deepening and skills improvements were only a part of the set of reasons for the improvement in hourly productivity performance in the UK over the period 1997–2007. The same might be said of the impact of financial services. The majority of the improvement came from factors affecting the level of technology and the efficiency of factor use. The period between 1997 and 2007 was unusual in that the most productive country in our group in terms of output per person hour, the USA, actually began to pull further ahead of other countries, excepting the UK, Sweden and Finland. Although convergence of productivity levels has not been uniform, there is a slow tendency for it to happen as Lee, Pesaran and Smith (1997) show. The decade to 2007 was an exception to this pattern, whereas the previous decade had clearly confirmed it, with the USA having the third lowest level of labour productivity growth in Table 2.1. The literature on this topic is extensive, but there is an emerging consensus that the nature of the information and communications technology and bio-technology revolution was particularly suited to the US economy. The reasons for that reflect also on the performance of the UK, Sweden and Finland during the decade.

Over the last two centuries it is possible to describe the growth process as a sequence of product innovation cycles where new products such as the electric motor, the internal combustion engine or the computer are developed, followed by process innovation cycles where those products are improved (see Freeman

Table 2.2 Growth decomposition 1998–2007

		Belgium	Canada	Denmark	Finland	France*	Germany	Japan**	Neths	Sweden***	Spain	UK	US
	Percentage point contribution to average annual GDP growth												
GDP at basic prices (% change)		2.2	3.25	1.85	3.56	2.1	1.77	0.8	2.62	3.2	3.71	2.9	3.06
of which													
	Contribution from financial intermediation	0.24	0.24	0.34	0.01	0.18	0.01	0.10	0.25	0.19	0.45	0.39	0.40
	Contribution from other sectors	1.95	3.01	1.51	3.55	1.92	1.76	0.7	2.36	3.01	3.26	2.51	2.66
Growth in production in financial intermediation		3.95	3.92	6.43	1.16	3.69	0.1	1.46	3.7	4.06	9.46	6.13	5.17
of which													
	Employment	2.23	1.99	0.73	0.61	1.77	0.17	-1.52	0.97	0.58	3.54	0.88	1.53
	Output per person	1.69	1.89	5.66	0.55	1.88	-0.07	3.02	2.71	3.45	5.72	5.2	3.58
Share of financial intermediation (2000)		0.060	0.060	0.047	0.045	0.051	0.042	0.058	0.061	0.045	0.046	0.051	0.076
Hourly productivity growth in financial intermediation		1.70	2.08	5.22	0.90	2.50	0.45	3.64	2.87	3.74	6.31	5.54	3.79
Whole economy productivity growth		1.02	1.31	1.05	2.49	1.65	1.71	1.82	1.45	2.28	0.04	2.24	2.04
Implied productivity growth in rest of economy		0.97	1.27	0.84	2.57	1.61	1.76	1.71	1.36	2.22	-0.26	2.07	1.90
Financial sector contribution to productivity		0.04	0.05	0.21	-0.07	0.05	-0.05	0.11	0.09	0.07	0.30	0.18	0.14

Note: * Sample period for France is 2000–07; ** Sample period for Japan is 1997–2005; *** Sample period for Sweden is 1999–2007.

and Soete 1997 for a discussion). Product innovation has often best been done in flexible labour markets with high levels of scientific skills. It depends upon a sound knowledge base and on entrepreneurial activity. Process innovation has often best been done in labour markets that have long attachments between firms and individuals where on-the-job training and firm-specific skills are perhaps more important than high levels of scientific knowledge. The archetypes of these are the flexible US labour market where 25% of the workforce change jobs each year (see OECD 2010: chapter 3, where adjustments are made for industrial composition of the workforce), as compared with the core Europeans, where only one-sixth of Germans, for instance, change jobs each year. In 1997 only 8% of the German workforce were highly skilled, whereas 28% of the US workforce were in this category.[12] The period from the mid-1970s to the early 1990s was a period of process innovation when German (and other continental) firms improved ways of doing (see Prais 1995 for a discussion). During this period hourly productivity growth in the USA was noticeably below that in Germany and France, as we can see from Table 2.1.

The last decade we look at was a period of innovation in bio-technology and information and communications technology, as well as in finance. This is just the period where we would expect the USA to pull ahead, much as it did. These industries have involved university-based research and have required small company start-ups to initiate growth. The latter is best done in labour markets with low attachment rates such as the USA. As we discuss above, some of the improvement in performance in the USA and elsewhere may have been illusory, in that some of the innovations in finance transferred rents rather than increased output, but much of the improvement elsewhere were real.

The performance and structure of the UK labour market is closer to that of the USA than to the core Europeans in many ways. Job turnover is only 2% lower than in the USA and is 5% higher than in Germany. Skills are increasingly obtained through off-the-job education in the UK, with 13.5% of the workforce with higher-level skills in 1997, noticeably higher than in Germany, but below that in the USA. These factors may be part of the explanation of the improvement in productivity performance in the UK in the last decade in our study. The growth of higher education-related skills in the UK in the last two decades, as measured by the increased proportion of the workforce with those skills, exceeded that of all other countries in our sample, as we can see from Figure 2.4. Finland, Japan, Sweden and Spain came close to the rate of increase in high-skilled workers seen in the UK. The first three are the amongst the best performers in the last decade, with productivity per person hour both before and after allowing for capital deepening growing most rapidly in Finland and Sweden. The impact of the growth of labour with high skills in Spain is masked by the scale of immigration into the economy in that decade. Highly skilled immigrants tend to take lower-level jobs than their skills would suggest, and often their skills, which were obtained in another country, may not be transferrable. It is clear that the countries with the highest levels of

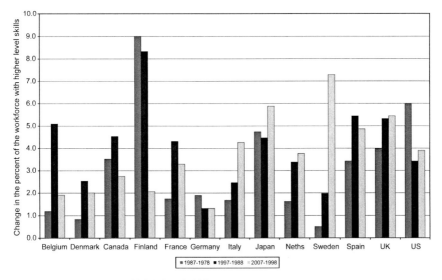

Figure 2.4 The growth of high-level skills
EU KLEMS

high-skilled workers—the USA with 28% in 1997, Finland with 33% and Japan with 20%—were able to benefit from these skills during a period of product innovation. The level of high skills in Sweden is relatively lower than in Finland (although recent growth has been strong, as we can see from Figure 2.4), although the rate and nature of productivity growth in both has been similar, with a very strong science base. This leads us to a distinction between quality and quantity to which we turn next.

There are other dimensions to the bio-technology, information and communications technology revolution that make it different from some previous product innovation waves. Both the products in bio-technology and the processes in computer development are more closely linked to university-level research and innovation than were the development of the internal combustion engine or the construction of an electrical equipment-based economy.

Universities, like individuals, come in many guises: some are centres for elite education others for frontier research, whilst the majority may be neither of these. There are also many ways of grading universities in terms of their teaching or their research.[13] Our group of countries contains 80 of the 100 best universities in the world, with the remaining 20 being in Australia (five), Switzerland (four), China and Hong Kong (three and two, respectively), Ireland (two), Republic of Korea (two), and Norway and Singapore (one each). Figure 2.5 plots the number of elite universities in each country in our sample both in terms of absolute numbers and per million of population. The USA, the largest country here, has 53 elite universities, whilst the UK has 14.[14] These countries have the highest number per million of population along with Sweden, which has two elite institutions. Hence the combination of indicators

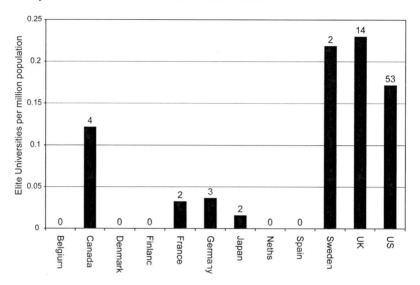

Figure 2.5 Distribution of the top 100 universities in the world
Data are from the *Times Higher Education Supplement* and NIESR database

of the volume of higher education in the workforce and the quality of the output of universities appears to be an important structural factor in explaining why the UK, the USA, Sweden and Finland have moved ahead of others in the last decade.

Clearly, elite universities may be one factor behind the pattern of productivity growth in our sample in the last decade. The number of such institutes per million of population has a correlation of 0.37 with productivity performance in the last decade, both as measured by overall TFP growth and by TFP growth less the contribution of skills. The UK, Finland and the USA have benefited from their relatively high number of high-skilled workers, whilst the UK, the USA and Sweden have benefited by being important centres for scientific research.

Product innovation cycles are often followed by periods of process innovation when leadership changes hands, and we might expect this to happen again. It is of course impossible to know where the next wave of scientific innovation might come from, but it would be reasonable to suppose that over the next two decades we will see another period of product innovation to deal with the causes and consequences of climate change. De-carbonizing the economy is likely to be a knowledge-intensive activity based on the frontiers of science, and hence countries such as the UK, the USA and Sweden may be in a good position to pull further ahead. Of course, this depends upon the continued existence of scientifically excellent universities and research institutions as well as other factors affecting productivity growth. We next consider an approach that will allow us to look at the factors that have affected this improvement in underlying TFP.

Regression analysis

In the previous section we used a growth accounting approach to look at the decomposition of annual GDP growth and its components. We discussed factors affecting change in labour productivity, which we were able to split into growth in skills, TFP and capital deepening, and the contribution from financial services. In this section we analyse in more detail the forces driving change in labour productivity and specifically consider breaking down the determinants of TFP further into possible components, and we attempt to identify two groups of factors associated with improvements in technology and improvements in the efficiency of factor use.

In the section above we discussed the determinants of labour productivity, which we may denote as $y = Y/(E*Hours)$ where Y is output in basic prices, E is employment and Hours are average hours per person in employment. We can separate the determinants into capital deepening, which we may denote k, skills, which we have denoted as S, and the two factors driving TFP, technology which we denote as t, and efficiency which we denote as x. We can then write and evaluate (9) which is the relationship between labour productivity and the factors driving it through their impact on capital and technology. Labour productivity per person hour can be expressed as:

$$Ln(y) = F(k, S, t, x) \tag{9}$$

We use a number of different indicators and drivers of technology and efficiency. We avoid econometric estimation using the capital stock because of measurement problems, and instead look for effects from factors determining capital deepening as well as those that affect the cost of capital, such as risk premia driven by financial crises and the user cost of capital.

The technical progress term t may depend on a number of factors, including R&D and openness and competition indicators. Furthermore, foreign direct investment (FDI) as a proportion of GDP can reflect the creation of knowledge and/or ease of absorption of technical progress via direct import of frontier technology by foreign firms that local firms can imitate. There are also a number of indicators of the potential effects of more effective competition policy. The variable for the ESM mirrors the official timing of the programme and starts in 1986 at 0 and gradually rises to 1.0 in 1993. Membership effect dummies (EU95, EU86) are introduced as well (which increase from 0 to 1 over a three-year period) to capture the gradual process of integration of a country into membership of the EU. We also use a direct indicator of openness (OPEN) as measured by the sum of the volumes of imports and exports of goods and services as a ratio of real output. We can write an equation that is linear in logs that includes these variables as the determinants of labour productivity

$$
\begin{aligned}
ln(y_t) = {} & d_1 + d_3^* ln(k)_t + d_4^* ln(FDI/Y)_t + d_5^* ln(R\&D/Y)_t \\
& + d_6^* ESM_t + d_7^* ln(OPEN)_t + d_8^* ln(S)_t \\
& + d_9^* EU86_t + d_1 0^* EU95_t + error_t
\end{aligned}
\tag{10}
$$

We substitute out k and replace it with its determinants, which we take to be the user cost of capital and banking crisis-related risk premium indicators. We capture the long-run impact of banking crises by introducing crisis dummies (which are 0 prior to the crisis occurrence and 1 thereafter). We include dummies only for systemic crises, although we test this assumption subsequently. The long-run relationship can be written as follows:

$$
\begin{aligned}
ln(y_t) = {} & d_0 + d_3^* ln(user)_t + d_4^* ln(FDI/Y)_t + d_5^* ln(R\&D/Y)_t \\
& + d_6^* ESM_t + d_7^* ln(OPEN)_t + d_8^* ln(S)_t \\
& + d_9^* EU86_t + d_1 0^* EU95_t + d_1 1^* CRIS_t + error_t
\end{aligned}
\tag{11}
$$

In order to establish whether there is a long-run relationship between the variables, we run tests to find a co-integrating set for each country and then use it in the construction of a dynamic panel. The sets with the minimum number of variables are chosen based on the stationary properties of the variables. Augmented Dickey-Fuller (ADF) tests with an intercept[15] and a lag length of one (as data series are annual) are used to check for both the order of integration of variables and the presence of a unit root in the residuals from the estimated long-run equations. ADF test results for variable stationarity reported in Table 2.3 illustrate that we can treat all our variables as integrated of order one (I(1)) and thus use an error correction approach for productivity analysis.

A minimum co-integrating set is derived separately for each country. All relevant variables are included with output per person hour as the dependent variable. All insignificant variables were eliminated. The residuals of the resulting equations were checked for the presence of a unit root. If the unit root test is not passed then different combinations of the variables were checked until a stationary set was found. Results from the co-integrating analysis in Table 2.4 show that all equations for all countries in the sample co-integrate, implying that we have an acceptable specification. In no country is the user cost of capital a significant variable in the co-integrating set.

$$
\begin{aligned}
Dln(y_t)_t = {} & d_1 + d_2^*((ln(y))_{t-1} + d_3^* ln(user)_{t-1} \\
& + d_4^* ln(FDI/Y)_{t-1} + d_5^*(R\&D/Y)_{t-1} + d_6^* ESM_{t-1} \\
& + d_7^* ln(OPEN)_{t-1} + d_8^* ln(S)_{t-1} + d_9^* EU86_{t-1} \\
& + d_1 0^* EU95_{t-1} + d_{11}^* CRIS_{t-1}) \\
& + d_{12}^* Dln(y_{t-1}) + error_t
\end{aligned}
\tag{12}
$$

We then use the minimum co-integrating set in the context of a simple error-correction framework as in (12). We use the Common Correlated Effects

Table 2.3 ADF test results of variable stationarity

	DLn(Y)	Ln(Y)		Ln(R&D/Y)		Ln(FDI/Y)		Ln(SKILLS)		Ln(OPEN)	
	level	level	1st diff	level	1st diff	level	1st diff	level	1st diff	level	1st diff
Belgium	-3.882	-3.413	-2.697	0.267*	-2.848	-2.788	-3.391	-0.715*	-5.284	0.432*	-6.041
Canada	-3.996	-0.445*	-3.923	-1.563*	-2.922	-1.982*	-3.609	-1.205*	-3.309	-0.441*	-3.413
Denmark	-3.134	-1.635*	-3.814	0.02*	-3.541	0.566*	-3.758	-1.425*	-3.807	2.482*	-3.628
Finland	-4.984	-0.535*	-4.967	-1.572*	-3.841	-1.606*	-4.966	-1.068*	-2.443	0.901*	-3.879
France	-4.208	-2.759	-3.931	-2.31*	-2.358	-0.517*	-3.896	-1.374*	-4.102	0.652*	-4.167
Germany	-2.916	-2.018*	-2.661	-2.195*	-3.213	0.317*	-4.083	-1.469*	-3.285	1.725*	-3.748
Japan	-3.235	-2.852	-2.954	0.315*	-3.443	1.884*	-4.268	-0.681*	-3.832	2.067*	-4.407
Neths	-4.701	-2.149*	-3.648	-1.476*	-3.837	-1.728*	-4.063	0.461*	-1.521*	1.332*	-4.653
Spain	-2.046	-2.498*	-3.363	-0.898*	-2.556*	-3.37	-3.378	-1.071*	-1.967	-0.366*	-3.179
Sweden	-2.042	0.417*	-1.728	-2.581*	-3.622	0.028*	-3.966	-1.537*	-3.05	1.473*	-4.234
UK	-5.026	-0.862*	-5.024	-1.431*	-3.577	-2.288*	-4.939	-0.984*	-3.318	1.038*	-3.917
US	-4.372	-0.247*	-3.635	-0.899*	-3.755	-1.25*	-3.286	0.623*	-4.128	0.275*	-4.06

Note: * indicates less than 90% significance level. The first two columns are for productivity per person hour.

Table 2.4 Co-integration of the long run

Belgium	Canada	Denmark	Finland	France	Germany	Japan	Neths	Sweden	Spain	UK	US
-6.232***	-3.915*	-4.624***	-5.633***	-3.811**	-4.055*	-4.224**	-3.702*	-3.554*	-3.496*	-4.014*	-3.577*

Note: *, **, *** represent significance at 90%, 95% and 99% levels correspondingly; data period 1973–2007.

(CCE) (Pesaran 2006) method for estimation, where Ordinary Least Squares (OLS) is applied to the system of error correction equations, with cross-section averages of the independent variables as well as the dependent variable added to each country's specification. The CCE method is employed given the possibility of heterogeneity in our group of countries and probable existence of common unobserved factors omitted from the panel causing parameters to be biased. Of particular relevance is the inclusion of productivity per person hour, the long run-dependent variable, as a common factor. This is calculated in PPP units to ensure comparability across countries and it should pick up any common productivity trend.

The general to specific approach is applied to the panel of variables, where the least significant variable was eliminated and the regression is then repeated. The exclusion process continued until only variables significant at least at the 90% level were left. The results from general-to-specific estimation with the variables to be included in the long as well as short run are reported in Table 2.5.

We organize the variables into three groups, along with skills and banking crisis indicators. We can see FDI and R&D as indicators of knowledge-based technical progress that are specific to each country, whilst openness and the European indicators can be seen as efficiency pressures that are country specific. The common factor (CCE) variables capture the average level and average growth rate of productivity in our sample, and represent common trends in knowledge and efficiency as well as other common factors that might affect productivity per person hour. They are both highly significant in all countries, and have co-efficients that are not significantly different from each other.

The different nature of technical progress and market competition across different countries is illustrated by each country except the two largest, the USA and Japan, having at least one indicator of technical progress that is significant in addition to the common 'trend' variable. FDI is significant and has a positive impact in 7 out of 12 countries in the sample. Increased globalization and trade between countries facilitates FDI and through it the spread of technology and knowledge. R&D is significant in Denmark, Finland, Japan and Germany, and is marginally significant in France, where its significance may be clouded by the presence of an FDI effect as France is the only country where both have an independent role. In all cases R&D has a positive sign, indicating that higher R&D enables these countries to introduce technical advancements more readily. The magnitude of the effect of R&D varies, with Finland showing the highest significant effect and Denmark the lowest. The USA and Japan undertake a lot of R&D, but this appears to be absorbed in the common trend.

Efficiency indicators are present in all countries except France and the two largest economies, Japan and the USA. Global integration (OPEN) is the most significant in the UK, followed by Canada, Finland and then by Sweden and Germany. The European integration variables have a positive effect in Germany, Belgium, Denmark and the Netherlands, and the EU membership

Table 2.5 Estimation results

	Belgium	Canada	Denmark	Finland	France	Germany	Japan	Neths	Sweden	Spain	UK	USA
Error correction	-0.19 (0)	-0.248 (0.01)	-0.538 (0)	-0.568 (0)	-0.16 (0.004)	-0.213 (0.012)	-0.183 (0.001)	-0.256 (0.003)	-0.378 (0)	-0.205 (0)	-0.375 (0)	-0.255 (0.015)
Ln(FDI/Y)	0.013 (0.045)	0.126 (0.017)	–	–	0.096 (0.033)	–	–	0.081 (0.011)	0.074 (0.01)	0.032 (0)	0.048 (0.001)	–
Ln(R&D/Y)	–	–	0.255 (0)	0.468 (0)	0.425 (0.056)	0.33 (0.04)	–	–	–	–	–	–
Ln(Open)	–	0.182 (0.008)	–	0.099 (0.003)	–	0.159 (0.056)	–	–	0.246 (0.054)	–	–	0.297 (0.001)
European Single Market	0.123 (0.004)	–	0.112 (0)	–	–	0.132 (0.001)	–	0.068 (0.032)	–	–	–	–
EU membership 1986	–	–	–	–	–	–	–	–	–	0.115 (0.008)	–	–
Ln(SKILLS)	–	–	–	–	–	–	4.7 (0)	–	–	–	2.066 (0)	1.848 (0.019)
Long-run crisis effect	–	–	–	-0.029 (0.048)	–	–	-0.143 (0)	–	–	–	–	-0.061 (0.054)
Crisis date	–	–	–	1991	–	–	1997	–	–	–	–	1988
DLn(Y/EH(−1))	–	–	–	0.413 (0.001)	–	–	–	–	0.458 (0.001)	0.435 (0.001)	0.288 (0.062)	–
AvLn(Y/EH)	0.078 (0)	0.078 (0)	0.078 (0)	0.078 (0)	0.078 (0)	0.078 (0)	0.078 (0)	0.078 (0)	0.078 (0)	0.078 (0)	0.078 (0)	0.078 (0)
AvDLn(Y/EH)	0.737 (0)	0.737 (0)	0.737 (0)	0.737 (0)	0.737 (0)	0.737 (0)	0.737 (0)	0.737 (0)	0.737 (0)	0.737 (0)	0.737 (0)	0.737 (0)

Note: Ln(FDI/Y) – natural log of the ratio of inward foreign direct investment to output; Ln(R&D/Y) – natural log of the ratio of stock of research & development to output; Ln(OPEN) – natural log of the ratio of sum of exports and imports to output; Ln(S) – natural log of Tornqvist-based skills index; DLn(y) – difference of the natural log of output per person hour; AvLn(y) – unweighted average of the natural log of output per person hour; AvDLn(y) – unweighted average of the difference of the natural log of output per person hour; probabilities in parentheses; estimation period 1974–2008.

indicator suggests that joining the EU raised productivity levels in Spain by more than 10%. While there is no evidence of an R&D effect on productivity in the USA and the UK, and no openness effect in the USA, there is a strong and positive impact from the skills indicator. This result reflects our growth accounting finding that skills effects were clearly present in these countries.

We included seven systemic banking crises in the initial sample and in our final results only three had a significant long-run negative impact: these were Finland in 1991 (at 90% significance level), Japan in 1997 (at 95% significance level) and the USA in 1988 (at 90% significance level). Out of the four remaining systemic banking crises, three (Spain 1977, Japan 1991, Sweden 1991) were found insignificant at the first stage and hence were unnecessary in the minimum co-integrating set. The crisis in the UK in 1974 was included in the initial long-run equation with a negative and significant parameter, but in the dynamic equation there was no explanatory power left for it once the effect from all other variables was taken into account. This may reflect its timing, as it occurred at the same time as a significant increase in oil prices, which had an effect on sustainable output in the UK and elsewhere. The oil price effect on productivity is one of the common factors covered by the CCE variables and, hence, once we put the UK into the panel the independent impact of the crisis disappears.[16] The initial effect in the co-integrating vector can therefore be seen as spurious.

In Table 2.6 we analyse the effects that factors behind technical progress played in the growth rate of productivity in each country. We break down the change in productivity into the contribution from the components in Table 2.5 over ten-year intervals from 1977 to 2007,[17] so that it is comparable to Table 2.1 above. We can partition the factors driving productivity loosely into three groups: knowledge, competition and skills.

The first group involves the creation and absorption of knowledge through R&D and FDI. There is a core group of knowledge creators identified in our analysis, which along with the USA and Japan produce information, and it is at least in part disseminated through the port of FDI. This factor is present in all countries except the USA and Japan, but it is lower in the UK in the first period than in all countries with the exception of Canada, and only Germany is lower in the second period. Over the period 1997 to 2007 there was a minor improvement in the UK's relative and absolute performance driven by these knowledge factors, with Belgium, Spain and Germany having a lower contribution. The second factor based on external market pressure effects from openness and regional integration is more important as a driver of labour productivity in Germany than in other countries, except in Spain at around the time it joined the EU. The remaining component of overall productivity growth might be seen as domestic market pressure, and this is stronger in the UK in the last period than in all countries except France and Belgium.

Skills accumulation contributes to productivity growth only in the UK, Japan and the USA, albeit for different reasons.[18] The decomposition analysis shows that the impact of the accumulation of skills has been more rapid in

Table 2.6 Contribution to the change in productivity

		Belgium	Canada	Denmark	Finland	France	Germany	Japan	Neths	Sweden	Spain	UK	USA
		Percentage point contribution to average annual growth in productivity											
Knowledge	Output per person hour												
	1978–87	2.2	1.0	1.0	3.0	3.1	2.1	3.0	2.1	1.1	3.3	2.4	1.6
	1988–97	2.3	1.3	2.5	3.0	2.3	2.8	3.0	1.5	2.1	1.8	1.9	1.6
	1998–2007	1.0	1.3	1.0	2.5	1.9	1.7	1.7	1.4	2.2	0.0	2.2	2.0
	of which												
	Foreign direct investment (as a % of GDP)												
	1978–87	1.0	0.3	—	—	0.3	—	—	1.0	0.8	1.1	0.4	—
	1988–97	0.1	0.1	—	—	0.9	—	—	0.4	0.8	0.2	0.1	—
	1998–2007	0.1	0.6	—	—	0.9	—	—	0.9	1.0	0.3	0.4	—
	Research & development (as a % of GDP)												
	1978–87	—	—	0.9	2.5	0.9	1.0	—	—	—	—	—	—
	1988–97	—	—	0.9	2.3	0.6	0.0	—	—	—	—	—	—
	1998–2007	—	—	0.9	1.7	-0.2	0.3	—	—	—	—	—	—
Competition	Openness												
	1978–87	—	0.2	—	0.1	—	0.3	—	0.4	0.4	—	—	0.7
	1988–97	—	0.8	—	0.4	—	0.6	—	0.8	0.8	—	—	1.4
	1998–2007	—	0.1	—	0.3	—	0.8	—	0.7	0.7	—	—	0.7
	European single market												
	1978–87	0.0	—	0.0	—	—	0.1	—	0.0	—	—	—	—
	1988–97	1.2	—	1.1	—	—	1.3	—	0.6	—	—	—	—
	1998–2007	0.0	—	0.0	—	—	0.0	—	0.0	—	—	—	—
	European union (1986)												
	1978–87	—	—	—	—	—	—	—	—	—	1.1	—	—
	1988–97	—	—	—	—	—	—	—	—	—	0.0	—	—
	1998–2007	—	—	—	—	—	—	—	—	—	0.0	—	—
Skills	Skills accumulation												
	1978–87	—	—	—	—	—	—	2.3	—	—	—	1.2	0.8
	1988–97	—	—	—	—	—	—	2.0	—	—	—	1.8	0.5
	1998–2007	—	—	—	—	—	—	1.8	—	—	—	1.1	0.6
	Domestic market pressure (a residual)												
	1978–87	1.2	0.5	0.1	0.4	1.9	0.7	0.7	1.1	-0.1	1.1	0.8	0.1
	1988–97	1.0	0.4	0.5	0.3	0.8	0.9	1.0	0.5	0.5	1.6	0.0	-0.3
	1998–2007	0.9	0.6	0.1	0.5	1.2	0.6	-0.1	0.5	0.5	-0.3	0.7	0.7

the UK and Japan relative to the USA, and while in the USA skills were playing an increasing role in productivity growth, in the UK their contribution peaked in the middle decade, although it continued to contribute to productivity growth strongly in the last ten years.

Recent performance

Some of the improved UK performance seen in the last decade we study may have been lost in the recent financial crisis. If financial liberalization contributed to productivity growth outside the financial sector as well as in it, the crisis could have effects throughout the economy. Some of the gains in productivity were clearly illusionary, but we have argued that these will have contributed no more than 0.2 percentage points per annum to UK productivity growth over the period as compared to an average of 0.1 percentage points in our sample. However, if the crisis has led to a deeper recession or a larger scar in the UK, growth could be weaker in the coming decade.

The financial market crisis that started in the summer of 2007 and worsened in the autumn of 2008 has led to a sharp short-term decline in output that exceeds its longer-term impact. We estimate that the permanent scar on output per person hour might be around 3%. The scar is largely driven by a presumed 300-basis point rise in risk premia along with a structural deterioration in the budget balance, which is no worse in the UK than in other countries on average. The risk premium effect is, as far as we can see, likely to be common. The size of the scar differs between countries and, as Barrell (2009) discusses, it will depend upon the relative size of the capital stock as compared to GDP. The UK has a relatively low capital output ratio and a relatively high user cost and hence the rise in the risk premium will have more effect in countries such as Germany, as is suggested in Barrell (2009).

There are, of course, other factors to take into account for the impact of the scar to output as opposed to productivity. Barrell, Gottschalk, Kirby and Orazgani (2009) suggest that there could be up to 1% more reduction in output as a result of increased outward migration. This is in part because the major migrant source countries in recent years have included Poland and Australia, the only OECD countries not to face a recession in 2008 and 2009, and the Indian subcontinent, where performance has remained strong. Hence migrants from these countries will find the UK less attractive both in the short and long run. In addition, as the European economy revives, the temporary barriers to Polish migration introduced in the rest of Europe upon its accession to the EU will have been removed.

Conclusion

Economic performance in the UK clearly improved between 1997 and 2007 as compared to other countries in the OECD. Only a small part of this can be attributed to the growth of financial services, as this sector expanded in other countries as well. The contribution of skills to the improved performance was quite large, as might have been expected given the increase in the proportion of the workforce with higher education, although the skill premium declined in the face of large increases in skilled workers. Major improvements appear also to have come through increases in the efficiency with which factors are used, and these improvements can be associated with policies toward domestic aspects of competition such as the Competition Act of 2000, which have focused more clearly on competition and efficient regulation than had the earlier reforms and privatizations. In addition, the quality of UK higher education institutions appears to have contributed also to good performance during a product innovation period based on bio-technology and computing. This strength may be particularly important going forward as the need to reduce carbon emissions is likely to be addressed only with a major investment in research in the area. Although UK institutions do not appear to be robust to the downturn, and performance has not been good, there are reasons to believe that the scar from the crisis on output per person hour (but perhaps not output) will be around the average for the group of countries we consider.

Appendix: data description and sources

CRIS	Introduced to capture the long-run impact of banking crises and modelled as 0 prior to the crisis occurrence and 1 thereafter. Only systemic crises are included (Finland 1991; Japan 1991, 1997; Spain 1977; Sweden 1991; and the USA 1988). Data source IMF Financial Crisis Episodes database and World Bank database of banking crises.
E	Total employment (thousands). Data source NiGEM database.
EMU	Is introduced to capture the impact of the European Monetary Union, which equals 1 from 1999, in line with the official introduction of single currency in Europe and is 0 prior to 1999.
ESM	Describes the establishment of the European Single Market, which is defined as 0 prior to 1987 and then gradually increases to 1 in 1992, the formal completion of the Single Market Programme.
EU86 and EU95	Are meant to take an account of the impact on a country upon joining the EU, and modelled to be 0 before the country joins the EU and 1 thereafter.
FDI	Stock of foreign direct investment in the country (in constant prices and national currencies). Source UNCTAD, unstats.un.org.
HOURS	Hours worked per employee per quarter. Data source NiGEM database.

OPEN   Is a measure of the openness of the economy and defined as a share of volumes of exports and imports of goods and services in GDP. Data source NiGEM database.

R&D   Stock of research and development. We benchmark the stock in 1973, in the first year of our data period, as flow divided by the average growth rate and the depreciation rate, and we cumulate flows onto this stock with a depreciation rate of 15% per annum. The data source is OECD Main Science and Technology Indicators 2009–2 (1981–2008) and Research and Development Expenditure in Industry database, 1973–1998, www.sourceoecd.org.

S   Tornqvist-based measure of workforce skills. It is a compound skill indicator which uses indicators of relative compensation for each of three (high, medium and low) skill groups to construct index of efficiency units of labour for each country, with a higher value of the index implying a higher level of knowledge embodied in workers. Data come from EU KLEMS database, www.euklems.net.

Y   GDP in basic prices. Data source NiGEM database, except USA and Japan where they are NIESR estimates using indirect taxes and subsidies and the GDP deflator.

Notes

1 We would like to thank seminar participants at the European Commission on 28 June 2010 for their comments. We have had numerous discussion on this topic, and in that context we would like to thank Mary O'Mahony, Martin Weale, Chris Pissarides and our colleagues at the National Institute of Economic and Social Research (NIESR). Rachel Whitworth also gave us detailed comments on the paper.

2 It is likely that hours worked were systematically under-reported in Spain over this period, and it also has a much lower participation rate than other countries included here, and hence only the most productive workers are recorded as in employment.

3 We use OECD data on gross expenditures on R&D for the whole economy. We benchmark the stock before the beginning of our data period as the flow divided by the average growth rate and the depreciation rate, and we cumulate flows onto this stock with a depreciation rate of 15%.

4 We measure skills by their market value, as it allows skill destruction as well as acquisition. Hargreaves' Spinning Jenny destroyed the market value of the skills of hand spinners, much as Cartwright's power loom destroyed the market value of the skills of hand loom weavers.

5 The EU KLEMS database was the result of a large-scale collaborative project between European researchers on productivity financed by the European Commission, and is available at www.euklems.net.

6 The relative wage is the share of total compensation received by a skill category divided by the share of total hours contributed by the same group.

7 This is a weighted sum of the growth rates of the various components, where the weights are the components' shares in total value.

8 Where the skill premium is absent or unreliable we have calculated it by applying the average annual change over the nine preceding years to the previous year's data. A number of countries lack data in 2006 and 2007, and the UK and France have data from 2004 and 2003, respectively, that we consider unreliable.

9 Where data are absent we assume constant shares of skill categories.

10 Other terms for the indicator are Solow residual, measure of ignorance, or rate of technical change.

11 Details of sources are included in an appendix at the end of the chapter.

12 We use EU KLEMS definitions of skills in order to be consistent with our growth accounting work. These individuals have the equivalent of a degree. OECD (2010) suggests that the disparity for tertiary education was less, with 23% of Germans and 34% of US workers having a qualification at this level.

13 We use the 2010 version of the *Times Higher Education Supplement* world university rankings, which uses a combination of research, citations and teaching to rank the top 100 universities in the world. See www.timeshighereducation.co.uk/world-university-rankings.

14 There is an English-language bias in the evaluation of elite universities, as the core language of science is English and, for instance, if universities in France have policies to promote French-language journals then their ranking will be affected. This bias does affect our overall conclusion.

15 There are several cases when variables are difference stationary without an inclusion of an intercept.

16 In particular, we should stress that for the UK there is no evidence that any banking crisis since the Second World War has had a significant and negative impact on productivity per person hour.

17 We take geometric mean of annual changes both in the dependent and independent variables.

18 In the USA both the number of graduates and their skill premium has risen, whilst in the UK the number of graduates rises continually but the skill premium begins to decline just before 2000.

References

Aghion, P. and P. Howitt (1998) *Endogenous growth theory*, MIT Press.

Barrell, R. (2009) 'Long term scarring from the financial crisis', *National Institute Economic Review* articles, No. 210.

Barrell, R., S. Gottschalk, S. Kirby and A. Orazgani (2009) 'Projections of migration inflows under alternative scenarios for the World Economy', *Department of Communities and Local Government economics paper* No. 3.

Barrell, R., D. Holland, I. Liadze and O. Pomerantz (2007) 'EMU and its impact on growth and employment', in M. Buti, S. Deroose, V. Gaspar and J. Nogueira Martins (eds), *EMU at 10*.

——(2009) 'Volatility, Growth and Cycles', *Empirica* vol. 36: 177–92.

Barrell, R. and D. Holland (2010) 'Fiscal and financial responses to the economic downturn', *National Institute Economic Review* articles, No. 211.

Barro, R.J. (1991) 'Economic Growth in a Cross Section of Countries', *Quarterly Journal of Economics* 106, 2 (May): 407–33.

Coe, D. and E. Helpman (1995) 'International R-and-D spillovers', *European Economic Review* Vol. 39, No. 5: 859–87.

Freeman, C. and L. Soete (1997) *The Economics of Industrial Innovation*, third edition, MIT Press.

Griffith, R., S. Redding and J. Van Reenen (2004) 'Mapping the two faces of R&D: Productivity growth in a panel of OECD industries', *Review of Economics and Statistics* Vol. 86, No. 54: 883–95.

Holland, D., S. Kirby and R. Whitworth (2010) 'A comparison of labour market responses to the global downturn', *National Institute Economic Review* articles, No. 211.

Lee, K., M.H. Pesaran and R. Smith (1997) 'Growth and Convergence in a multi-country empirical stochastic Solow model', *Journal of Applied Econometrics*: 357–392.

OECD (2010) *OECD Employment Outlook 2010*, Paris.

Pesaran, M.H. (2006) 'Estimation and inference in large heterogeneous panels with a multifactor error structure', *Econometrica* 74(4): 967–1012.

Prais, S.J. (1995) *Productivity, Education and Training: An International Perspective*, Cambridge: Cambridge University Press.

Proudman, J. and S. Redding (1998) *Openness and growth*, Bank of England.

Solow, R. (1957) 'Technical Change and the Aggregate Production Function', *Review of Economics and Statistics* 39(3): 312–20.

3 British labour market performance before the crisis, 1993–2007

Christopher A. Pissarides

Starting in 1993, the British labour market moved steadily upwards to a steady state with high male and female employment, low unemployment, low inflation and relatively high productivity growth. Male and female employment in the five years prior to the Great Recession (2003–07) were 79% and 70%, respectively, unemployment rates were 5.6% and 4.8%, inflation averaged 3% and labour productivity growth averaged nearly 2%. Moreover, these rates were virtually constant during this period, and there had been very little change in them since 1993.

To obtain this state of affairs there must be a rise in the effective supply of labour relative to capital. By effective supply we mean the supply of 'efficiency units' of labour, effort, as the demand for labour varies. If this did not happen wages would have increased as unemployment fell, eventually causing inflation as firms passed on to prices the higher wage costs. Inflation resulting from higher wage costs was the typical bottleneck that checked growth in the British economy prior to the 1990s. The wage inflation that resulted from the falling unemployment was typically followed by restrictive monetary and fiscal policy and recession. This did not happen in the 1993–2007 period.

One cause of the increase in the effective supply of labour is an increase in numbers through induced changes in labour force participation or migration, to satisfy an ever-increasing demand. However, this does not have to be the only, or even main, reason, and since unemployment rates decreased, it cannot be the only reason.[1] It could also be the result of policy reform that removed the incentives that labour has, either directly or through unions, to hold back supply in order to gain higher wages. The causes of the increase in the effective supply of labour relative to capital in the 15 years prior to the 2008 crisis is the core question investigated in this paper.

Domestic labour force participation did not show any unusual patterns during this period, so this cannot be a cause. Migration, however, increased substantially, especially from the new European Union (EU) members in the more recent period. We argue that it could have contributed to the absence of inflationary pressures over the recent period, and that it was especially important for professional jobs.

Britain also experienced substantial labour market policy reforms, both prior to 1993 and after. Reform since the early 1980s has focused mainly on the relaxation of strict regulation on employers and on placing more emphasis on privately run market production (see Card, Blundell and Freeman 2004). Trade union power was substantially reduced with legislation in the 1980s. The privatization of large state enterprises and the decline of manufacturing, taking place at about the same time, also contributed to the decline of union power by eroding their membership base. Employee dismissal legislation was relaxed and the legal process for handling complaints simplified. It was also made harder to claim unemployment benefit, leading up to the replacement of unemployment benefit by the job seeker's allowance in 1996. These reforms contributed substantially to the absence of bottlenecks in the British labour market in the face of rising demand. They weakened the power of workers to artificially hold back the supply of effort to gain higher hourly wages.

Some other arguments have also been put forward for the absence of inflationary pressures in the 1990s and 2000s. The changes in the operational procedures of the Bank of England that took place after 1993 had an impact on inflation expectations (Johnson 2002; Benati 2004). We argue that this had an important effect on the labour market. By bringing down inflation expectations it reduced wage demands, and made workers less dependent on unions to protect their incomes against inflation.[2]

Whatever the causes of the British economic successes of the pre-crisis era, the question still remains whether the British free-enterprise model caters sufficiently for the disadvantaged groups in the population. For example, has unemployment been kept low by impoverishing the unemployed? Income inequality has risen substantially in Britain since the early 1980s, and Britain is one of the most unequal countries in Europe. Moreover, low-skilled groups in the population have not participated in the benefits of the post-1993 expansion, until much more recently and mainly through the tax system. We briefly discuss these issues and the alternatives, given the EU objective of high employment rates for both men and women.

Section one documents the policy reforms that took place in Britain, mainly in the pre-1993 era. Section two describes macroeconomic trends in 1997–2007, and section three discusses the reasons for the absence of wage pressures in the face of falling unemployment. Sections four and five dwell at greater depth on two of these reasons, unemployment insurance policy and immigration. Finally, section six discusses the implications of the 'British model' for social protection, and section seven briefly concludes.

Section one: policy reforms

The British labour market functioned poorly in the 1980s, reacting to shocks like a rigid market unable to adapt to new levels of aggregate demand or improve productivity performance. The reaction of unemployment to the anti-inflationary macro policy of the new Conservative government elected in 1979 was the typical reaction of a rigid labour market, with unemployment rising quickly when the deflationary shocks hit, and then staying high for a long time, allowing the build-up of substantial long-term unemployment (see Layard, Nickell and Jackman 1991, for a full discussion). At the end of the decade, and before the start of the 'golden years' of 1993–2007, both unemployment and inflation were still very high, at unemployment rates substantially above the ones inherited in 1979 and still plagued by inflationary pressures.

However, the 1980s was also a decade of reforms. Before the reforms took place the economy was characterized by large nationalized industries (producing 12% of gross domestic product—GDP) and poor industrial relations. The nationalized industries were a source of strong unions and strikes were frequent. Overall economic activity was highly regulated with unions objecting to labour market reforms. In terms of the Organisation for Economic Co-operation and Development (OECD) measures of economic regulation, Britain at this time was somewhere in the middle of the pack.

The reforms that were started by the new Conservative government were designed to get rid of the rigidities and restore British economic pre-eminence, which was lost to Germany, France and gradually to other countries a decade earlier. Following the reforms, by the late 1980s the British OECD measures of regulation were at the flexible end of the range, closer to the USA than to the less flexible end of the four European countries, where they were in the 1970s (see, for example, OECD 1999a). Although the reforms were started by the first government of Margaret Thatcher, governments that followed, up to the present, continued with similar market-oriented policies. Briefly, the policy reforms of the 1980s and 1990s can be summarized as follows (Card, Blundell and Freeman 2004).

Large, nationalized industries were privatized and broken up. Several other government functions were passed on to the private sector. This policy produced a smaller public sector and gave more initiative to the private sector. It coincided with the decline in power of trade unions, some of which relied on the large public sector for members and support.

Policy towards unemployment and the labour market switched from out-of-work 'passive' support to more active labour market measures and in-work benefits, mainly in the form of tax incentives. This change coincided with academic work that showed that passive policies were having an adverse effect on unemployment, especially long-term unemployment. It also coincided with pressure from the OECD and the EU on all member states to make the switch from passive to more active policies.[3]

The most highly publicized reforms in the labour market, perhaps because of the industrial conflict that they caused, were legislative reforms to curb union powers. This policy was accompanied by curbs in leadership powers within unions. It is not completely clear whether the decline of union power was caused mainly by legislative reforms or by changes in the industrial structure. They most likely both contributed. There is no doubt, though, that the decade of the 1980s ended with the unions having much less power to influence labour market outcomes than they had had at the end of the previous decade.

Several other reforms encouraged more activity in the private sector (e.g., with respect to pension financing and education), but they are less important for the macroeconomic performance of the economy, which is the main theme of this paper.

Section two: macroeconomic performance

The policy reforms as a whole had a large impact on the microeconomic performance of the economy. They increased productivity, especially in previously unionized firms and in firms that adopted large-scale employee share ownership, and encouraged the influx of foreign capital. Restrictions on employment were lifted almost entirely and product market regulation was relaxed, in some cases even more so than in the USA (see Nicoletti, Scarpetta and Boylaud 1999; Conway, Janod and Nicoletti 2005). The macroeconomic performance of the British economy changed dramatically. How much did the reforms contribute and how much was due to other factors?

Up to the early 1990s, the British economy was one characterized by frequent fluctuations. A typical scenario is one of demand expansion with some output gains, followed by union pressures for more wages. Employers would concede and pass on the higher wages to prices, and the Bank of England, operating under strict government control, would accommodate the higher prices. Inflation would ensue, with depreciation of sterling, economic 'crisis' and restrictive macro policy. The main impediment to smooth growth was that the economy was hitting inflation bottlenecks (or, in the earlier fixed exchange rate period, balance of payments deficits) that forced contraction and fluctuations.

In the late 1980s and up to 1992 macro policy was targeting the exchange rate vis-à-vis the German mark, with a view to controlling inflationary expectations and ending the inflation-unemployment cycle that constrained demand expansions in the past. This policy ended in late 1992, with exit from the European Exchange Rate Mechanism (ERM) in September of that year. Following ERM exit, the Bank of England was given more independence than it previously had. It was required to target inflation without direct controls on the exchange rate. This change had a dampening influence on inflationary expectations. Four years later, in 1997, the Bank was given full operational independence with the control of inflation as its only policy objective. This further dampened inflationary expectations, with important consequences for the labour market.

The key labour market aggregates—employment, unemployment and wages—fluctuated a lot in the 1980s, in response to both exogenous shocks and to macro policy changes. However, from 1993 to the recession of 2008, there was a long period of stability, with both employment and unemployment converging to virtually constant rates halfway through this period. Figure 3.1 shows the employment rates for both men and women since 1991, and Figure 3.2 shows the respective unemployment rates. Both figures provide evidence that the economy turned in 1993, and by 2000 both rates stabilized at steady-state values.

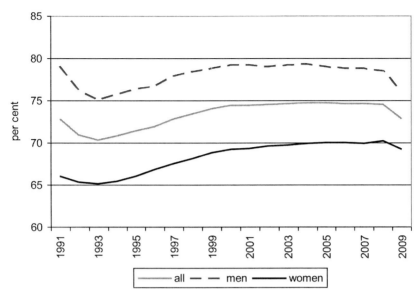

Figure 3.1 Employment rates among the working-age population
Source: Office for National Statistics

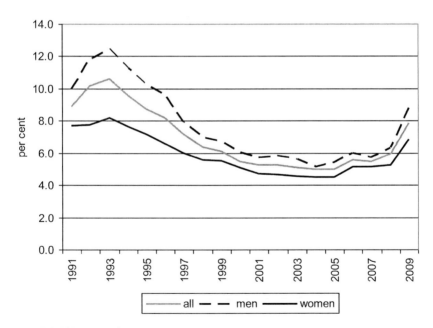

Figure 3.2 UK unemployment rates
Source: Office for National Statistics

For all workers these were 74.5% and 5.2% for employment and unemployment, respectively.

The Phillips curve, shown in Figure 3.3, provides further evidence that the labour market turned in 1993 and reached a steady state in 2000. Whereas before 1993 changes in inflation and unemployment followed the usual downward-sloping path, starting in 1993 unemployment was falling alongside virtually constant and low inflation. At about 2000 unemployment stabilized and small changes in inflation traced a vertical Phillips curve, confirming the unemployment rate of 5.4% as the NAIRU (non-accelerating inflation rate of unemployment) of the British economy.

That inflation remained constant in the face of falling unemployment is a 'puzzle' that needs to be explained. Before attempting an explanation I show the Beveridge curve for this period, the relation between vacancies and unemployment. Information on the behaviour of vacancies may shed light on the causes for the change in unemployment, in particular whether they are due to aggregate shocks, demand or supply, or structural shocks.

The Beveridge curve for Britain at this time shows an economy approaching steady state through an expansion of aggregate demand and then staying on it (Figure 3.4). The upward path in 1993–2000 is the typical path of an economy that expands because of aggregate positive shocks. In 2001 the measurement methods for job vacancies changed to a more reliable survey-based method, similar to the one used to measure unemployment. There is a break in the figure, but it shows that the vacancy rate (the ratio of job vacancies to

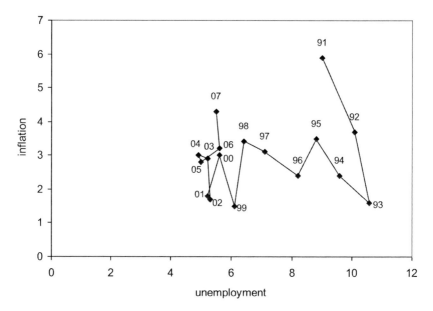

Figure 3.3 The Phillips curve, 1991–2007
Source: Office for National Statistics

employment) was practically constant between 2002 and 2007, at 2.1%–2.3%. The economy was practically on a point on the Beveridge curve, with about 2.5 the 'equilibrium' ratio of vacancies to unemployment. This contrasts with the earlier period. In the earlier period the only vacancy series available is the series notified to job centres, which is incomplete, but it still picks up dynamic changes. The points plotted in Figure 3.4 show an economy that turned from recession to recovery in 1993 and converged to a steady state in 2000.[4]

Given this dynamic behaviour of the UK labour market, what are the interesting questions to ask about the pre-crisis period? Put differently, are there any 'puzzles' that need to be explained? It seems that the most interesting fact in need of explanation is the one that is evident in both the Phillips curve in Figure 3.3 and the Beveridge curve in Figure 3.4. In particular, given the past tendency of the British economy to exhibit inflationary pressures when unemployment was falling, why was inflation not rising during the boom years of 1993–2007? Or, asking the question from the labour market perspective, why did unemployment fall and employment rise beyond expectation, given previous experience, for both men and women, without creating wage pressures? The Phillips curve in previous decades was of the textbook downward-sloping kind, although it became flatter over time, as the British economy became less inflation-prone. However, it has never been completely flat as in the 1993–2000 period, and never vertical as in the 2000–07 period, and this needs explanation.[5]

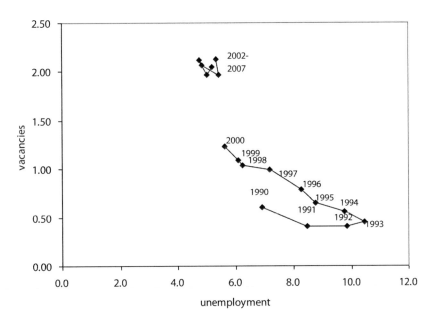

Figure 3.4 The Beveridge curve, 1990–2000
Source: Office for National Statistics

Before attempting an explanation, we note a rather interesting behaviour of unit labour costs and pose a counter-factual question. In the seven years prior to 2000 unit labour costs were rising at about the same rate as output per job, but after 2000 they started rising faster (see Figure 3.5). Between 1993 and 2001 the ratio of output per job to unit labour costs was virtually unchanged, after a small rise, but from 2001 to 2007 it deteriorated by about 3.5%. Moreover, this deterioration was due almost entirely to the non-wage component of costs. The corresponding ratio of output per job to unit wage costs fell by only 0.5%. This opens up the question of whether, had there been no crisis, the British economy would have been able to sustain the low inflation, full employment regime for much longer, given that costs had been rising faster than productivity for a few years. Answering this question became irrelevant by the turn of events, however, since following the onset of the Great Recession in 2008, the productivity-to-cost ratio deteriorated very rapidly, making it unsustainable in the absence of direct support from the government.

Section three: wage pressures

The period since 1993 has been a period of steady expansion of aggregate demand, driven mainly by the private sector. Housing and stock market prices were rising fast and international trade was growing very rapidly. What

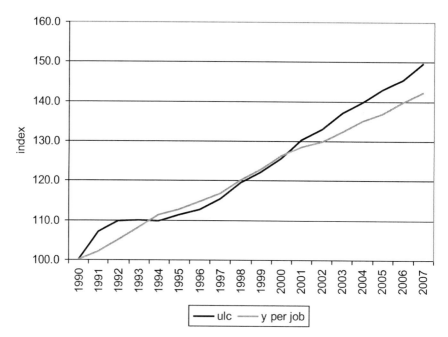

Figure 3.5 Unit labour cost and output per job
Source: Office for National Statistics

are the usual wage pressures created in this situation? The most popular model of wage determination used in the British context is one of bargaining, possibly with trade unions, driving up the wage in some key industries. The rest of the economy then follows suit, either through more bargaining, or though private decentralized agreements.

The usual scenario in the past was that with rising employment and falling unemployment, inflation expectations would build up and unions would bargain for higher wages. Employers would grant them because demand was rising, and this created inflation and depreciation of sterling. The government would then intervene with anti-inflation policy, which checked the rise in demand and employment. This did not happen at conventional rates in the 15 years prior to the crisis of 2008.

Both changes in expectations and the decline of union power contributed to this. Inflation expectations changed fundamentally when the Bank of England changed its policy in 1993 to inflation targeting, and even more so when it was granted operational independence in 1997. This played an important role in reducing the urgency of wage demands, from fear that inflation would erode their real value before the next negotiating round. Union power was eroded both by legislation changes in the 1980s and by the decline of large, state-owned industries that provided a strong membership base. The decline of union power was very important in this process because as employment was rising and unemployment falling, unions were not demanding wage rises with the militancy that they were demanded in the 1970s and 1980s.

Two measures of union power are frequently used in econometric studies, and both show a substantial decline in the 1990s (see Figure 3.6). Union density measures the fraction of workers who are union members, and union coverage those covered by union agreements. Usually union density is considered to be a more accurate measure of union power. This measure falls from 50% in the early 1980s to 30% in the late 1990s. The alternative measure, union coverage, falls even more dramatically, from more than 70% in the early 1980s to about 30% in the late 1990s. These dramatic falls must have had a big impact on wage behaviour in the 1990s and 2000s. The absence of strikes and other militant union activity throughout this period is further evidence that unions became too weak to influence labour outcomes to the extent that they used to do in the past.

Even in competitive markets, however, when unemployment falls to very low levels bottlenecks develop and wage pressure builds up. Something else must have been happening in the British labour market that led to the relaxation of bottlenecks at unemployment rates that were too low by historical standards. These other factors, if indeed they were present, have to be factors that relaxed the supply of labour constraint compared to the supply of capital, namely, factors that made labour more abundant relative to capital.

We can identify three such factors, which, through different channels, led to an effective increase in the supply of labour relative to capital. The first is trade with more labour-abundant countries. China is the prime example here.

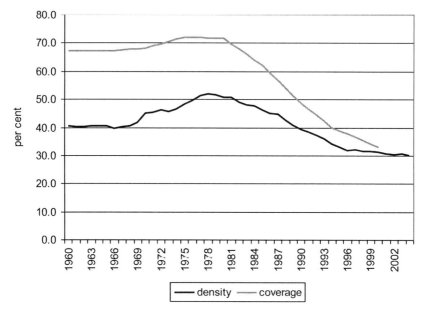

Figure 3.6 Measures of union power
Source: OECD

Following its accession to the World Trade Organization (WTO), China became a major trading partner in highly labour-intensive manufactured goods. This has the same impact on the labour market as an increase in the supply of labour, since imported goods can satisfy the increase in the demand for final goods without wage rises.

Second, the provision of unemployment insurance became more strict, pushing up the effective supply of labour. Unemployment insurance has two types of effect on the labour market, and both contribute to lower wage pressures. The generosity of unemployment compensation is a main determinant of the opportunity cost of employment to the worker. When the opportunity cost is lower, workers are prepared to work for a lower wage. The easiest way to see this is in a bargaining situation. If the level of unemployment benefit is cut workers are in a weaker bargaining position and agree to negotiate a lower wage rate. Also, the generosity and duration of unemployment benefit is an important influence on the intensity of job search and the duration of unemployment. When job search is less generously subsidized and the subsidy is expected to end, unemployed workers feel more urgency to get back to work and accept on average lower wages.

Finally, immigration has a direct impact on labour supply. The timing of the potential build-up of bottlenecks in the British labour market coincided with the timing of the expansion of the EU to the east. Britain allowed immigration from the new member states from the time of accession, and it benefited in large numbers from it. New immigration responds quickly to changes in the domestic demand for labour, effectively increasing the elasticity of labour supply in response to job availability and wages.

I examine here changes to unemployment compensation and immigration rates during the 10 years prior to the recession.

Section four: unemployment insurance

There are a number of measures that can be used to proxy the generosity of the unemployment insurance system. The level of unemployment benefits relative to the wage, known as the replacement ratio, is the main one, but the duration of benefits is also important. By this we mean the number of weeks that an unemployed worker is allowed to claim benefit before it is terminated, or some other sanction becomes effective, such as participation in an active policy measure. Finally, eligibility, or coverage, is obviously important. If the eligibility criteria change and it becomes tougher to claim benefit, fewer people would be entitled to it and so wage pressure would be less.

Figure 3.7 shows the OECD measure of the generosity of unemployment insurance benefits in Britain. It is the average replacement ratio for three earning levels, three family situations and three durations of unemployment. It declines monotonically from the early 1980s, but its biggest falls took place before 1993. In 1993 it stood at 18%, and remained at that level until the end

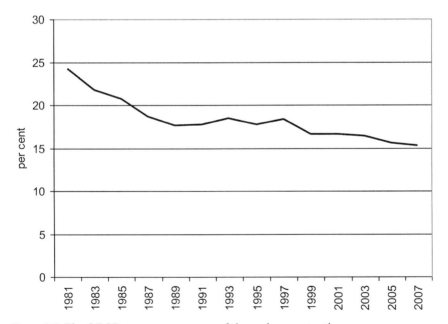

Figure 3.7 The OECD summary measure of the replacement ratio
Source: OECD

of the decade, after which it fell to 15%. It is questionable how much this kind of decline can affect wage pressure, especially since other OECD evidence shows that most of the decline is due to a fall in the replacement ratio available to workers in the first year of unemployment, and not to the duration of benefits. In such cases it is not expected that the fall by 3 percentage points would have much impact.

Of more concern, however, is the change in entitlements that seems to have taken place in the 1990s. The claimant count series of unemployed is an administrative series that reports the number of workers claiming unemployment benefit, whereas the Labour Force Survey (LFS) series, which is the one discussed here, follows the conventional International Labour Organization (ILO) definition of unemployment. There is an overlap between the two—active job seekers who are entitled to benefit and are collecting it belong to both. There are workers who are unemployed and searching for a job, though, who are not entitled to benefit, and workers who, although eligible for benefit and claiming it, are not active job seekers.

Before 1996, when job search was not a strict criterion for eligibility, the claimant count included many workers who claimed benefits to which they were entitled, although they were effectively not in the labour force. With the introduction of the job seeker's allowance in 1996, at least in principle the vast majority of workers on the claimant count should be active job seekers as well. There are, of course, other criteria for entitlement to the job seeker's allowance, in particular the person either has to have made contributions to the national insurance fund for at least two years, or have low income. The criteria for entitlement to the job seeker's allowance are a lot tougher than those that existed before 1996 for claiming unemployment benefit.

Figure 3.8 shows the relation between the claimant count of unemployment and the LFS definition. For men, the number on the claimant count normally exceeded the number actively looking for work up to about 1997. From then on the number on the claimant count decreased relative to the number actively looking for work, until in 2008 the ratio between the two was down to 64%. For women, the number on the claimant count was always less than the number actively looking for work because fewer met the other eligibility criteria, but it was rising up to the 1990s. It was at a high point of 62% in 1996 and then declined monotonically to 33.5% in 2008. These are large changes in eligibility for unemployment benefit, and they could have a big impact on wage pressure and unemployment durations.

Further evidence is provided in Figure 3.9, which shows the percentage of LFS unemployed claiming benefits. In the early 1980s the vast majority of LFS unemployed claimed unemployment benefit, but this fraction declined quickly. By 1996 only 60% of LFS unemployed were receiving benefits. The introduction of the job seeker's allowance brought further declines, and by 2007 the fraction halved to 30%. In 1998, and in view of the fast decline in the fraction of LFS unemployed claiming benefit, the authorities introduced a supplementary question in the LFS, which asked all unemployed if they were

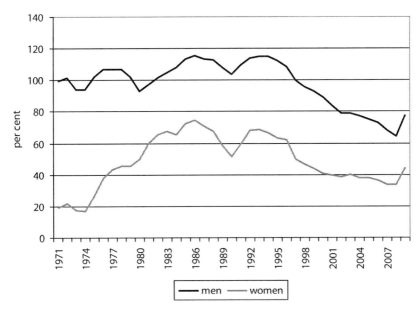

Figure 3.8 Ratio of claimants to labour force survey unemployed
Source: Office for National Statistics

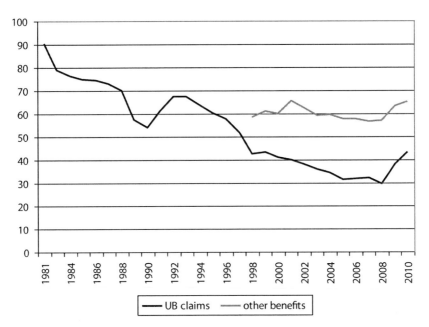

Figure 3.9 Percentage of LFS unemployed claiming benefits
Source: Office for National Statistics

claiming any other kind of benefit. About 60% of them said they were, and this fraction fell only very slightly by 2008. The fall in the fraction of unemployed claiming benefits was not compensated by a rise in other welfare payments.

Section five: immigration

Immigration flows increase the responsiveness of the supply of labour to job availability and wage changes. In an upswing they are potentially important means for breaking bottlenecks that might cause wage pressures. In the downswing they reduce the impact of recession on unemployment. Britain has been traditionally a net recipient of immigrants but the question is how large are the flows involved? Are they large enough to make a real difference to the labour market responses of labour supply and wages?

Figure 3.10 shows total net immigration excluding students, children and adults over the retirement age of 65 for men and 60 for women. There are clear cycles that show the responsiveness of immigration to economic conditions. Not surprisingly, net immigration is higher when the economy is doing well and lower when there is recession. Net immigration starts an upward trend at about 1997, and peaks in 2004, the first year that the citizens of the new members of the EU were allowed to come to Britain. Assuming that adult immigrants of working age join the labour force, the cumulative net addition to the labour force in the 10 years 1998–2007 is just under 1 million people. This is about 3.2% of employment, which is substantial enough to

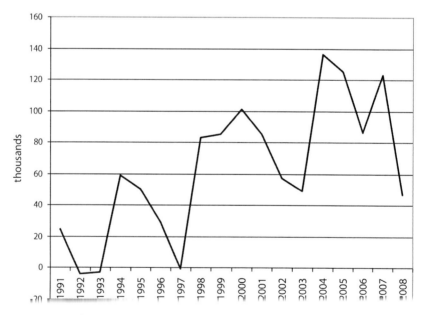

Figure 3.10 Net immigration, adults of working age
Source: Office for National Statistics

make a difference to wage pressures, given the size of the unemployment pool. In the extreme case where job creation is independent of immigration flows, and due, for example, to domestic demand conditions, without this inflow of immigrants firms would be competing more aggressively for domestic workers (unemployed or out of the labour force) and forcing wages up.

There are, however, some strong assumptions underlying the argument that immigration reduced firms' competition for new labour to the full extent of the immigration of working age adults. Some of the persons coming in over this period were accompanying adults, mostly spouses who were not necessarily seeking work. A number for accompanying persons is given in the immigration statistics and it adds up to about 300,000 (out of 1 million) over this period. Of course, many of the accompanying persons eventually join the labour force, so not all of these should be treated as out of the labour force.

A second assumption is that job creation in Britain was independent of immigration flows. Modern labour market theory emphasizes that an increase in the supply of labour in boom times encourages more job creation, irrespective of the wage rate, giving rise to multiplier effects (Pissarides 2000). If this mechanism were strong, it would imply that for wage determination purposes the number of immigrants coming in should not be treated as a net addition to the labour force for a given number of jobs, but because of the multiplier effects that this mechanism implies it also implies that the rise in net immigration brought a stronger growth of jobs over this period than otherwise would have been, again irrespective of wage developments.

Another factor that plays a role in the contribution of immigration to labour market outcomes is the occupation of immigrants. Figure 3.11 reports the net immigration of three different occupational groups, professional and managerial, manual and clerical, and all other. The biggest group is the professional and managerial one. The manual and clerical flows were big in only two years, 2004 and 2005, associated presumably with the expansion of the EU. This can be seen more clearly in Figure 3.12, where two series are shown, net immigration from the old Commonwealth and from the EU.

Net EU immigration is virtually non-existent until 2004, when it increases rapidly over the following two years; however, immigration from the old Commonwealth is still a stronger force than immigration from the EU. In view of these data, it is unlikely that net immigration played a role in holding wage pressures down before 1997, because of the small numbers involved. Numbers built up after 1997 and immigration could have played a role over the period 1997–2003. Given that most immigration over this period was of professional people from the old Commonwealth, the main contribution of immigration was in relieving bottlenecks in professional occupations. The influx of manual and clerical workers from the new member states of the EU after 2004 is also very likely to have contributed to holding down wage pressures for these types of workers. This impact of immigration is potentially more important for the macroeconomic outcomes because prior to the early 1990s it is in these occupations that wage pressures were building up as unemployment declined.

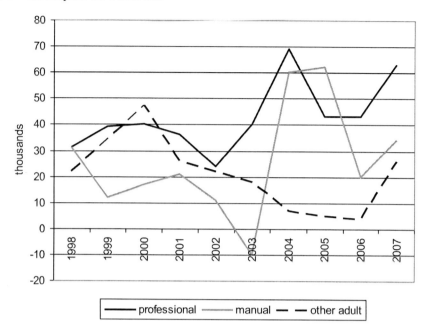

Figure 3.11 Net immigration by occupation
Source: Office for National Statistics

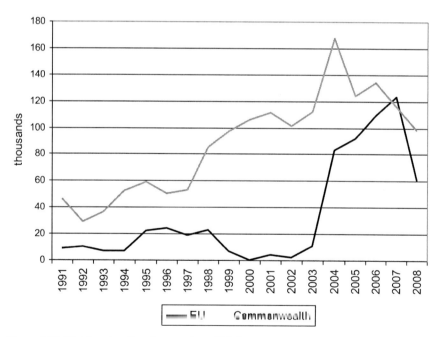

Figure 3.12 Net immigration by country of birth
Source: Office for National Statistics

Section six: social protection

The key dilemma of labour market policy in Europe is how to encourage higher employment of both men and women with adequate social provision for lower-income groups and the unemployed (see for example European Commission 2000, 2003). The trade-off is that the provision of generous welfare support for lower-income groups gives rise to work disincentives. There is a risk that policies aimed at the fulfilment of the social objectives jeopardize the economic objectives of high employment, especially of lower-skilled workers and demographic groups without strong attachment to the labour force.

It is clear that economic policy in Britain since the 1980s has shifted emphasis from the social to the economic objectives. There has been a shift from out-of-work to in-work benefits, such as lower transfer payments associated with lower taxes, especially at the higher end of the wage distribution. Income support for the unemployed became more difficult to obtain and less generous. The outcome is an employment level for both men and women that easily satisfies the EU's Lisbon targets (70% for men and 60% for women). Durations of unemployment are short compared with other European countries and labour force participation for marginal groups, such as single mothers, is also relatively high.

At the same time, however, inequality has increased substantially since the early 1980s (see Card, Blundell and Freeman 2004). The increase has come from above-trend growth in the incomes of high earners, driven mainly by a booming financial sector and by lower marginal rates of taxation at the top end. This increase is a general phenomenon in industrial countries (OECD 2008), but inequality in Britain is amongst the highest. In the EU, where comparable statistics exist, Britain has the highest level of income inequality among comparable countries. The bigger inequality in Britain is partly due to its faster growth during the 1980s. The shift from public to private production and from out-of-work to in-work benefits contributed to this faster increase in inequality. At the same time, though, the USA experienced an even bigger increase in inequality, driven both by faster increase in high incomes and a fall in the real incomes of low-income groups. Card, Blundell and Freeman (2004) claim that British low incomes did not fall (a feature that also characterizes other European countries) because of the bigger income support provided to low-income workers in Europe than in the USA.

Of course, the choice of whether to put more emphasis on income support for poorer households, or more emphasis on achieving high employment, is a political one. It could be argued that the shift of policy emphasis in Britain in the 1980s is the main driver for the growth of the financial sector and the influx of foreign capital and labour, which have undoubtedly been beneficial to the economy. The question is whether there is an alternative to this policy, namely, whether high inequality and poverty for those without a job is a price that has to be paid if the high employment rates needed to satisfy the EU's objectives are to be achieved.

The much-discussed alternative is the Nordic, or Scandinavian, model. Under this group of policies high taxation is levied to finance an extensive programme of income support for low-income groups and an equally extensive programme of policies aimed at getting the unemployed back to work. This set of policies achieves both the high-employment objectives of the Lisbon treaty and alleviates poverty through government transfers and subsidized employment. Scandinavian countries have the lowest levels of inequality amongst OECD countries (OECD 2008), but they also have the highest tax rates (marginal and average) and the highest state-subsidized employment levels.

There is no doubt that the headline figures of the Nordic approach to labour market policy are impressive: the social objectives are achieved without jeopardizing the economic objectives. However, the government-financed programmes of labour market policies needed to achieve these objectives are expensive and the impact on the distribution of employment is also very large.[6] These are policy options that many nations may not find easy to implement.

Section seven: conclusions

The 'British model'—a market-based economy with limited welfare transfers and labour market policies driven mainly by the objective to provide incentives for market work—had phenomenal success in the 15 years prior to the Great Recession of 2008. Policy reforms that started in the 1980s have shifted emphasis from out-of-work welfare benefits to in-work benefits and incentives, and moved public production to either totally or partially private ownership. Trade union powers were curbed, the Bank of England was given more independence to tackle inflation, and foreign capital and workers were welcomed with limited formalities and low taxation. The result was virtual steady growth starting in 1993.

However, this policy also caused more inequality and the unemployed are not as well supported as in other European countries. The alternative policy regime that produces similar headline employment figures, the Nordic model, goes to the other extreme, of high taxation used to finance extensive welfare programmes, designed to give assistance through the market. The choices are ultimately political. Standards of living are comparable across the countries that practise each model, but the distribution of income and work across individuals and between the market and the home are very different.

Notes

1 The employment rate used domestic population as the denominator, so it could increase when more people join the labour force; however, the unemployment rate uses the labour force as denominator, so it cannot fall by increasing the number of workers through labour force entry (unless the new entrants have higher employment rates than the incumbents, which is implausible).

2 Globalization is another frequently cited reason for the absence of inflationary pressures. The growth of trade ensured a supply of manufacturing goods from abroad at steady low prices, and could have the same effect as an increase in domestic labour supply. We do not address the impact of globalization in this paper, focusing instead on labour market issues.

3 Academic work focused mainly on the impact of policy measures on the duration of unemployment. The consensus is that passive support increases duration but only if it is of long duration. Short duration support gives incentives for more active job search. See, for example, the summary in Layard, Nickell and Jackman (1991) and Layard and Nickell (1999). The main OECD publication, which has been extremely influential, is the *Jobs Study* (OECD 1994), followed by updates, such as OECD (1999b) and other shorter publications in the annual OECD *Employment Outlook*. The main EU publication making the case for more active policies is the *Delors Report* (European Commission 1994), followed by other publications that led to the Lisbon strategy in 2000 (European Commission 2000).

4 There is a big contrast between the behaviour of the Beveridge curve in the period shown in Figure 3.4 and the previous decade. In the 1980s the rise of unemployment after the initial period of the negative shocks was one taking place at virtually constant vacancies, indicating that there was also something 'structural' going wrong with the British economy, and not just a contraction of aggregate economic activity. See Jackman, Layard and Pissarides (1989).

5 See Pissarides (2006) for more discussion of the period up to 2002.

6 The literature on the Scandinavian model is extensive. See, for example, Lindbeck (1997) for a general discussion and evaluation, Calmfors, Forslund and Hemström (2004) for a discussion of the impact of different labour market policies, and Ngai and Pissarides (2009) for the impact of taxes and subsidies on employment.

References

Benati, L. (2004) 'Evolving Post-World War II U.K. Economic Performance', *Journal of Money, Credit and Banking* 36: 691–717.

Calmfors, L., A. Forslund and M. Hemström (2004) 'The Effects of Active Labor-Market Policies in Sweden: What is the Evidence?', in J. Angell, M. Keen and J. Weichenrieder (eds), *Labor Market Institutions and Public Regulation*, Boston, MA: MIT Press.

Card, D., R. Blundell and R. Freeman (2004) *Seeking a Premier Economy: The Economic Effects of British Economic Reforms, 1980-2000*, NBER Books, National Bureau of Economic Research, Chicago: Chicago University Press.

Conway, P., V. Janod and G. Nicoletti (2005) 'Product Market Regulation in OECD Countries: 1998 to 2003', *Economics Department Working Papers* No. 419, Paris: OECD.

European Commission (1994) *Growth, Competitiveness, Employment: The Challenges and Ways Forward into the 21st Century*. Luxembourg: Office for Official Publications of the European Community.

——(2000) *The Lisbon Strategy*, see for example, ec.europa.eu/archives/growthandjobs_ 2009.

——(2003) *Jobs, Jobs, Jobs: Creating More Employment in Europe*, Report of the Employment Taskforce chaired by Wim Kok, Brussels.

Jackman, R.J., R. Layard and C.A. Pissarides (1989) 'On Vacancies', *Oxford Bulletin of Economics and Statistics* 51: 377–94.

Johnson, D.R. (2002) 'The Effect of Inflation Targeting on the Behavior of Expected Inflation: Evidence from an 11 Country Panel', *Journal of Monetary Economics* 49: 1521–38.

Layard, R. and S. Nickell (1999) 'Labor Market Institutions and Economic Performance', in O. Ashenfelter and D. Card (eds), *Handbook of Labor Economics*, vol. 3C, Amsterdam: North-Holland.

Layard, R., S. Nickell and R. Jackman (1991) *Unemployment: Macroeconomic Performance of the Labour Market*, Oxford: Oxford University Press.

Lindbeck, A. (1997) 'The Swedish Experiment', *Journal of Economic Literature* 35: 1273–379.

Ngai, L.R. and C.A. Pissarides (2009) *Welfare Policy and the Distribution of Hours of Work*, London School of Economics, Centre for Economic Performance Discussion Paper 17.

Nicoletti, G., S. Scarpetta and O. Boylaud (1999) 'Summary Indicators of Product Market Regulation with an Extension to Employment Protection Legislation', *Economics Department Working Papers* No. 226, Paris: OECD.

OECD (1994) *The OECD Jobs Study*, Paris.

——(1999a) 'Employment Protection and Labour Market Performance', *Employment Outlook*, Paris.

——(1999b) *Implementing the OECD Jobs Strategy: Assessing Performance and Policy*, Paris.

——(2008) *Growing Unequal? Income Distribution and Poverty in OECD Countries*, Paris.

Pissarides, C.A. (2000) *Equilibrium Unemployment Theory*, second edition, Boston, MA: MIT Press.

——(2006) 'Unemployment in Britain: A European Success Story', in M. Werding (ed.), *Structural Unemployment in Western Europe: Reasons and Remedies*, CESifo Seminar Series, Cambridge MA, London UK: MIT Press.

4 Unsustainable consumption

The structural flaw behind the UK's long boom

Martin Weale

Introduction

In the 1960s and 1970s a substantial gap developed between gross domestic product (GDP) per head in Britain and in its neighbouring countries. Both Germany and France overtook the United Kingdom, and after a revision to its national accounts in the 1980s it seemed that Italy had also done so. After Britain recovered from the depression of the early 1980s, however, the gap with its neighbours stopped widening and, by the first decade of the 21st century, most indicators suggested that Britain once again out-performed them.

While it is too early to say what the relative standing of the major European countries will be once they have recovered from the current depression, it is not too early to ask whether there were features of Britain's economic performance that were unsustainable. Was the relatively rapid growth a consequence of, if not sound economic management, at least a failure to impede a run of good luck? Or was it based on an approach to economic management which, if not certain or even likely to lead to a sharp economic contraction, was at least inherently bound to lead to disappointment? In other words, was Britain's economy operating in a way that was eventually likely to require some sort of uncomfortable adjustment? Notoriously, in the government's successive Budget Statements a table showing data and forecasts for government borrowing included a section titled 'Fairness and Prudence?' Was the economy run in a way that was i) prudent, and ii) fair to future generations? Was it *ex ante* unsustainable?

This paper examines these questions. It begins by discussing the concept of sustainability and its relationship with saving and wealth. It then presents data on wealth, consumption, income and saving for the United Kingdom. This is followed by a discussion of sustainability in time-series models and an analysis of how the UK aggregate data are consistent with notions of sustainability. Notions of sustainability and fairness are then discussed further with explicit reference to intergenerational transfers and a means of identifying fair levels of consumption and saving is discussed. The importance of land and other natural resources in this analysis is considered. Estimates are presented of the extent to which consumption in the UK ahead of the crisis was consistent with notions of fairness and sustainability and the effects of the recent crisis on these calculations are considered. Finally, conclusions are drawn.

Sustainability as an economic concept

The concept of sustainability is widely used in economics, even if suffering from being used in different ways in different circumstances. Much analysis focuses on the stock of resources available to the economy, with environmentalists giving particular attention to some components of the natural capital stock. Concern about the sustainability of the fiscal position looks at avoiding unaffordable liabilities, however defined, and much the same approach can be applied to an analysis of the external position or, indeed, to the private sector. Obviously, the overall focus of attention depends on the question being addressed.

Perhaps the simplest concept of sustainability is the notion of maintaining consumption. As Sefton and Weale (2006) showed, net saving makes it possible for future consumption to be higher than current consumption, even in the absence of technical progress; in an economy enjoying Harrod-neutral growth, however, saving is necessary simply to ensure that consumption grows in line with income and one might instead define as sustainable a level of consumption which can be expected to grow in this way.

In an intergenerational context, the notion of sustainability could be used to mean that each generation pays its own way. This means that: i) to the extent that it decumulates environmental capital, it leaves behind enough produced capital to compensate for this loss; ii) it does not sell environmental capital to its successors for more (in real terms appropriately adjusted for growth) than it paid for it; and iii) it does not exploit other mechanisms such as pay as you go transfers to move resources from future generations for its own enjoyment.

These arguments suggest that a focus on external debt as an indicator of national sustainability is incomplete. It is logically possible for an economy to borrow from abroad in order to invest profitably at home.[1] An economy that does this may be more at risk of funding crises than one where all investment is domestically financed. However, an external deficit does not, on its own, indicate a weakening or low capacity of the economy to sustain consumption, while a combination of an external deficit and low domestic investment, reflected in a low rate of national saving, does.

Sectoral sustainability is less clear as a concept than is national sustainability, because ultimately all economic activity is undertaken on behalf of households. For this reason a sectoral analysis might be regarded as creating an artificial distinction between some activities undertaken on behalf of households and other activities undertaken on behalf of households. In fact, fiscal policy could be described as unsustainable if it were to lead to a situation where the government accrued debt on a scale so large that it found it difficult to raise the tax revenue to service that debt. Sargent and Wallace (1981) drew attention to the fact that the disincentive effects of taxation mean there is a maximum possible share of the economy that can be collected in taxation and used this to identify a maximum possible debt to GDP ratio. However, public expectations of service provision by government mean that questions of afford-ability of the debt burden arise at a much earlier stage than the limit identified by Sargent and Wallace (1981).

The sustainability of private-sector behaviour receives rather less discussion than that of the government. In part, this is because of its heterogeneity; it may also be because resolution regimes such as bankruptcy are institutionalized in a way that they are not for governments. Nevertheless, seeing the economy as a combination of private-sector economic agents and the government, it is clear that an analysis of national sustainability, combined with an analysis of government sustainability implies, as a matter of accounting, an analysis of private sustainability.

A conventional analysis of government sustainability may fail to allow for the pressures arising on government spending as a result of private-sector behaviour. For example, the private sector may not bother to make adequate provision for retirement, in the expectation of generous state benefits. The government may not intend to provide these, but once a substantial cohort of people reaches old age, the political pressures may mean that the government has little choice but to pay up, turning what had looked like a sustainable fiscal position into an unsustainable one. Similarly, expectations of provision of health services and social care may run ahead of what the government intends to provide, with the government having no mechanism for making its policy credible. Even if these sorts of pressures do not arise, there might be considerable political risks associated with a situation where private-sector expectations were disappointed whether or not those expectations were in any inter-temporal sense affordable. An overall picture of the robustness of the economic position can be obtained only by looking at private or national sustainability in addition to government sustainability.

There are, nevertheless, two reasons for focusing on national sustainability rather than private-sector sustainability. First of all, the calculations are sim-pler because transfers between the sectors are netted out. Second, international comparisons are facilitated because the results are robust across different prac-tices in different countries whereby some types of service are provided privately in some countries and publicly in other countries. As a precursor to further discussion we next turn to present data on consumption income, saving and wealth in the UK.

Consumption, income and saving in the whole economy

The simple notion of sustainability in the context of Harrod-neutral progress implies that the ratio of produced wealth to income should be reasonably stable. In order to minimize valuation effects, we compute this as the value of the produced net domestic capital stock measured at current market prices plus the value of net foreign assets. Only the latter component is sensitive to the effects of changes in prices of financial assets.

Figure 4.1 shows estimates of the ratio of produced wealth as a multiple of GDP going back to 1920. The data for the period before 1988 are computed from the sum of the estimates of the domestic capital stock and net foreign assets provided by Feinstein (1972) for 1920. This is increased by net national saving in each subsequent year and revalued using the GDP deflator, with both series taken from Sefton and Weale (1995) up to 1945 and from the national accounts from then on in order to provide a time series up to and including 1987. The figures for 1988 onwards are taken from the Office for National Statistics (ONS) national balance sheets and capital stock data.

The pattern shown by these data is of considerable interest. The Second World War led to a large decline in the nation's wealth relative to its income, reflecting the reality that the war was financed by dis-saving. Following the end of the war, wealth was built up again, reaching its 1938 value in 1975 and rising to a peak in 1981 (when GDP was affected by the recession of the early 1980s). Since the late 1980s the ratio of produced wealth to income has declined sharply again, falling below its 1945 value in 2006. A slight rise in 2008, the last year shown on the graph, is a consequence of valuation effects associated with the financial crisis, and the sharp decline of the exchange rate that happened then. However, the picture is that since the late 1980s the impact of economic decisions on the value of the country's produced wealth has been broadly similar to that of the Second World War, and on the face of it consumption in recent years has been higher than is consistent with the idea of sustainability in a Harrod-neutral world.

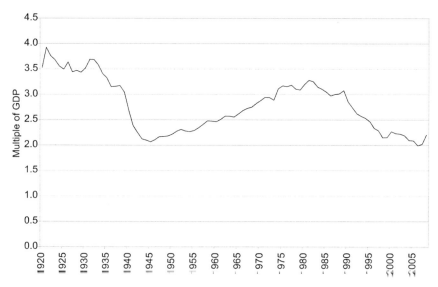

Figure 4.1 Produced wealth in the UK as a multiple of GDP
Source: See text for explanation

The savings pattern underlying this can be seen from Figure 4.2. This shows net national saving as a proportion of GDP. The savings rate rose steadily in the period from the end of the Second World War until the early 1970s. It was particularly low between 1980 and 1995, but since 1995 it has averaged 4.8% of GDP. The average rate of growth of real GDP during the period was 2.8% and, if i) this were maintained, and ii) the price of produced capital rose in line with the GDP deflator, then the ratio would eventually settle at 1.72, or not much more than one-half the value of the ratio at its 1981 peak.

None of this analysis answers the question of how much saving the country needs. One might think that with a population that is ageing as a result of the decline in fertility after the peak of the baby boom in the 1960s and the separate effect of declining mortality rates faced by old people, the country's required level of wealth would have increased rather than fallen in the last 15 years or so. However, the wealth level of the early 1980s may have been much too high on an absolute basis. In principle, the life-cycle model is consistent with low or even negative holdings of aggregate wealth. However, for this to happen the bulk of labour income must accrue fairly late in working life. We defer the question of what level of wealth the country might be expected to hold and explore in further detail how the dynamics of wealth accumulation have changed over the post-war years, looking at them from a macro-economic perspective.

Sustainability in time-series models

In a traditional analysis of sustainability of the public sector one would be concerned about whether government debt, *D*, measured in real terms after deflation by the aggregate consumption deflator for government and household consumption combined, satisfies the transversality condition

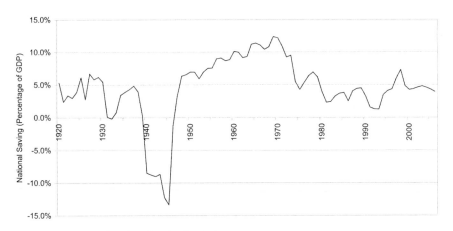

Figure 4.2 Net national saving in the UK
Source: Sefton and Weale 1995; Office for National Statistics

$$\lim_{t\to\infty} D_t e{-rt} = 0 \tag{1}$$

The analogous condition for produced national wealth, W_t is[2]

$$\lim_{t\to\infty} W_t e{-rt} = 0 \tag{2}$$

Provided that the long-run rate of return is higher than the rate of growth of the economy, these equality conditions rule out both government and the economy as a whole acquiring stocks of net assets which become infinitely large relative to the size of the economy, as well as ruling out insolvency.

As Bohn (2007) points out, if w_t follows a time-series process that does not change over time, then this condition is satisfied provided that differencing w_t any finite number of times results in an I(0) process. In practice, working with a finite dataset, one can show that the transversality condition is accepted but not that it is rejected; it is rare to find time series that do not pass stationarity tests after being differenced once or twice. Thus a test based on the order of integration of W_t is not very informative.

The problem that governments face is that debt levels may rise to a point at which it becomes, for practical purposes, impossible to collect the tax revenue needed for debt service; rapid increases of debt from low levels are less of a problem than rapid increases of debt from high levels. Thus the issue is one of non-linearity and Bohn (1999) suggests that a more fruitful approach is to examine the relationship between debt levels and budget deficits (which is, of course, a consequence of policy decisions made by governments). If this appears to stabilize debt at a level at which service will not be a problem, then the government is solvent, while if it stabilizes debt at a level at which debt service is impossible, then the transversality condition will eventually be breached. The debt level at which debt service is affordable is, of course, a matter for political judgement. With reference to the UK, we simply note that concerns are expressed about solvency despite projections showing that, in the aftermath of the crisis, debt levels relative to GDP are likely to be lower than the average for the 19th and 20th centuries.

The analogous question with wealth levels is whether wealth stabilizes at a level so low that the needs of the retired population have to be met substantially by transfers from people of working age or by means of selling non-produced assets such as land to them. As with national debt it is not clear at what level such issues become important without some sort of micro-economic analysis. However, we can begin by exploring in reduced form the relationship between consumption, income and wealth and use this to identify the implied long-term relationship between income and wealth.

Using c and y_t to denote log aggregate consumption and log aggregate net national income, both also deflated by the consumption deflator, we estimate a reduced form relationship explaining log consumption in terms of log income and log wealth denoted w_t. This can then be used to derive the steady-state relationship between income or consumption and wealth on the assumption that all are growing at the same real long-run rate.

We begin by testing the time-series properties of the series; we can accept the hypothesis that all three are I(1) processes, when tested over the period 1950 to 2008. We then use Johansen's trace test (Johansen 1988) to establish the number of co-integrating vectors and can accept the hypothesis that there is one co-integrating vector present in the data. Given that there is only one such vector, we can estimate an equation explaining the first difference of consumption in terms of the lagged first differences and the lagged levels of the three variables.

The general form we adopt is

$$
\begin{aligned}
\Delta c_t = {} & \alpha_1 \Delta c_{t-1} + \alpha_2 \Delta c_{t-2} + \beta_0 \Delta y_t + \beta_1 \Delta y_{t-1} + \beta_2 \Delta y_{t-2} \\
& + \gamma_1 \Delta w_{t-1} + \gamma_2 \Delta w_{t-2} + \theta_c c_{t-1} + \theta_y y_{t-1} + \theta_w w_{t-1} + \phi + \varepsilon_t
\end{aligned}
\tag{3}
$$

We have followed a general to specific methodology and present the results of the estimation for the two periods 1952–80 and 1981–2008 separately in Table 4.1 and Table 4.2.

For the period 1952–80 it is not possible to identify any long-run wealth to income ratio. Consumption grows in response to growth of income in the current year and over the previous three years; it also responds to the growth of wealth two years earlier. In the restricted equation the additional restriction that consumption is homogeneous of degree one in income and in wealth is strongly rejected. The hypothesis that wealth and income enter with equal and opposite signs (with the implication that consumption responds to the wealth to income ratio) is also strongly rejected. During this period, therefore, there was no long-run wealth to income ratio to which the economy was tending.

From 1981 to 2008 the situation is quite different, as the restricted regression in Table 4.2 shows. The dynamics reduce to a much simpler structure with produced wealth playing no direct role as an influence on consumption, and with a steady-state relationship between consumption and net income, implying also, of course, a steady-state savings ratio.

We can extract the implied long-run ratio of wealth to income in the following way. We assume that the steady-state rate of growth of consumption, income and wealth is g and s_t is the savings ratio in year t with $log(1 - s_t) = log(c_t/y_t)$. In the steady state, and dropping the time subscript to indicate steady-state values, the restricted consumption equation implies

$$
g = \beta_0 g + \theta_c log(1 - s) + \phi
\tag{4}
$$

Making the approximation that $log(1 - s) = -s$

$$
g = \beta_0 g - \theta_c s + \phi
\tag{5}
$$

giving

$$\frac{s}{g} = -\left(\frac{[1 - \beta_0] - \phi/g}{\theta_0}\right) \tag{6}$$

which is equal to the steady-state ratio of wealth to income. With the parameters of the restricted equation we find that this gives a long-run ratio of wealth to income of 1.78 with a standard error of 0.17. On average over the period 1980 to 2008 net national income was 87.2% of GDP, although the share has risen to 90% recently. Using the average figure, the implication is that the long-run ratio of wealth to GDP is only 1.55.[3] This suggests that without some change in behaviour the decline since the early 1980s has some way further to run.[4] In other words, a key feature of the UK's economic renaissance was a long consumption boom rather than a sustainable relationship between consumption and income.

Table 4.1a Influences on total consumption, 1952–80

Number of obs	29	Number of obs	29
F (13, 15)	7.21	F (7, 21)	11.31
Prob > F	0.000	Prob > F	0.000
R-squared	0.862	R-squared	0.790
Adj R-squared	0.742	Adj R-squared	0.720
Root MSE	0.008	Root MSE	0.009

Table 4.1b

	Coef.	Std. Err	t	P>t	Coef.	Std. Err	t	P>t
α_1	0.242	0.390	0.620	0.544				
α_2	0.042	0.299	0.140	0.890				
α_3	−0.185	0.236	−0.780	0.445				
β_0	0.446	0.100	4.450	0.000	0.567	0.083	6.870	0.000
β_1	0.228	0.339	0.670	0.511	0.382	0.137	2.790	0.011
β_2	0.381	0.229	1.670	0.116	0.445	0.118	3.770	0.001
β_3	0.304	0.182	1.670	0.115	0.233	0.104	2.240	0.036
γ_1	0.056	0.575	0.100	0.924				
γ_2	0.775	0.572	1.360	0.195	1.240	0.354	3.500	0.002
γ_3	0.157	0.534	0.290	0.773				
θ_c	−0.318	0.407	−0.780	0.446				
θ_w	0.466	0.170	2.750	0.015	0.334	0.097	3.450	0.002
θ_y	−0.427	0.310	−1.380	0.188	−0.517	0.155	−3.340	0.003
ϕ	3.042	1.319	2.310	0.036	1.949	0.641	3.040	0.006

Test on restrictions F(6,15)=1.30
Residual tests on restricted model
ARCH(1) $\chi^2(1)$=0.68
LM test for autocorrelation $\chi^2(1)$=0.01

Table 4.2a Influences on total consumption, 1981–2008

Number of obs	28	Number of obs	28
F (13, 14)	5.550	F (2, 25)	40.520
Prob > F	0.002	Prob > F	0.000
R-squared	0.837	R-squared	0.764
Adj R-squared	0.687	Adj R-squared	0.745
Root MSE	0.008	Root MSE	0.007

Table 4.2b

	Coef.	*Std. Err.*	*t*	*P>t*	*Coef.*	*Std. Err.*	*t*	*P>t*
α_1	0.184	0.264	0.700	0.497				
α_2	0.111	0.269	0.410	0.686				
α_3	0.343	0.276	1.240	0.234				
β_0	0.620	0.144	4.290	0.001	0.557	0.068	8.21	0.000
β_1	−0.113	0.227	−0.500	0.625				
β_2	−0.041	0.169	−0.240	0.810				
β_3	−0.121	0.162	−0.750	0.468				
γ_1	−0.046	0.076	−0.600	0.559				
γ_2	−0.098	0.074	−1.320	0.207				
γ_3	−0.066	0.070	−0.940	0.363				
θ_c	−0.579	0.300	−1.930	0.074	−0.332	0.091	3.65	0.001
θ_w	0.032	0.073	0.430	0.671				
θ_y	0.553	0.285	1.940	0.073	0.332	0.091	3.65	0.001
φ	−0.137	0.855	−0.160	0.875	−0.004	0.005	−0.79	0.436

Test on restrictions   F(11,14)=0.57
Residual tests on restricted model
ARCH(1) $\chi^2(1)$=0.004
LM test for autocorrelation $\chi^2(1)$=0.93

A framework to identify required saving

As noted, the discussion above has allowed us to project the UK's ratio of produced wealth to income without any framework for identifying what an appropriate ratio of produced wealth to income is. There have been a limited number of studies designed to assess required saving or required wealth. Perhaps the most prominent is that by Scholz *et al.* (2006). They looked at Americans aged 51–60 and explored how far the resources available to such people in 1992 might be adequate to pay for expected consumption needs over the remainder of their lives. In this study the available resources included physical and financial assets and expectations of future wage and benefit income. The study took due account of the fact that people's future incomes are uncertain and thus reflected the precautionary motives to which this gave rise.

The results suggested that, taking the benefit structure as given, the majority of Americans had accrued enough resources to pay for their retirement, and thus cast some doubt on the view that the USA suffered from low saving.

However, averaged over the period 1987–2007, the average net national savings rate in the USA has been only very marginally higher than that in the UK and it is quite possible that the situation has changed very sharply as compared with that shown for 51–60 year olds in 1992.

From a policy-maker's perspective, the study was incomplete in a number of respects. First of all, it did not address the question of whether it is 'fair' that the transfers between different generations that are implied by the pay as you go character of the USA's state pension system should in fact take place. Second, it did not consider whether the cohort considered was imposing a burden on younger generations in any other way. Finally, it was difficult to interpret because the calculations of consumption needs were based on the cross-section of mortality rates for the USA for 2002 rather than on any sort of projections of the mortality rates at the different ages of the members of the cohort in question.[5] What may have appeared to be adequate saving based on 2002 cross-section mortality rates may be much less adequate based on reasonable projections of mortality rates for people who were aged 69–78 in 2010. The difficulties that private-sector pension funds in the UK have faced as a result of making similar assumptions in the past are now very well known.

Barrell and Weale (2010) suggest that one can establish whether there are strong grounds for believing that there should be transfers between generations. As Dasgupta (2007) points out, the argument that future generations are likely to be richer than people currently alive is not, in itself, a good reason for making such a transfer; equally discounting of the future is not, in itself, enough to justify such an approach. The answer to the question also depends on the assumed inter-temporal elasticity of substitution and is best explored by examining the problem faced by a social planner.

Suppose that both the rate of interest, r, and the growth rate of output per person, g, are given exogenously and that the representative individual in generation t receives an endowment W_t. The life-time utility derived from this is $U(W_t)$ and there are no transfers between different generations except those resulting from the actions of the social planner. The social planner can determine the value of each generation's endowment by means of moving resources between generations. With a discount factor the planner does this to maximize

$$V = \sum_{t=1}^{\infty} \delta^{t-1} U(W_t) \tag{7}$$

As is well-known, in the absence of uncertainty the solution to this is to choose the W_t so that

$$\frac{U'(W_t)}{U'(W_{t-1})} = \frac{1}{\delta(1+r)} \tag{8}$$

If the utility function takes the standard constant elasticity of substitution form, so that

$$U(W_t) = \frac{W_t^{1-\alpha}}{1-\alpha} \tag{9}$$

Then

$$\frac{W_t}{W_{t-1}} = \{(1+r)\delta\}^{1/a} = 1 + g_s = G_s \tag{10}$$

defines the optimal rate of growth, g_s of the endowment of each generation. Alternatively, given the rate of growth (10) can be used to compute the optimum steady-state real interest rate, provided, of course, that the resulting solution $r^* > g$ (see note 5). If

$$\{(1+r)\delta\}^{1/\alpha} < 1 + g \tag{11}$$

then, after taking account of any transfers effected by legacies, the social planner should transfer resources from future generations to the current generation, while if the opposite is true the transfer should be in the opposite direction, a result also found by Romer (1988) despite his use of a rather different framework. Some combination of fiscal policy and pay as you go transfers can be used to have the required effect.

We note that the social planner has to observe the budget constraint. This implies that

$$\sum_{t=1}^{\infty} W_1 \left(\frac{G_S}{R^W}\right)^{t-1} = w_1 \left(\frac{G}{R^W}\right)^{t-1} \tag{12}$$

or

$$W_1 = \frac{W_1(R^W - G_s)}{R^W - G} \tag{13}$$

If $G_s < G$ the implication is that the life-time consumption of the initial generation should be raised above what would be affordable out of wage income, i.e. by reducing the nation's wealth. Barrell and Weale (2010) show that this can be done by some combination of national debt and transfer payments. However, it is important to note that, if transfers do take place, then consumption grows at a rate different from output. If $G_s < G$ the economy will begin with a national debt but the fiscal authority will reduce this over time, thereby ensuring that consumption grows more slowly than output with the opposite being true if $G_s > G$. Thus, starting from a *tabula rasa*, a policy of reducing the growth rate of consumption involves an initial budget deficit followed by a persistent surplus. This raises consumption in the short term but depresses it in the longer term. The appropriate budget deficit is nevertheless defined with reference to the required profile for generational consumption and thus with respect to required national saving and national wealth rather than with respect to any particular number for the budget deficit.

This framework implies that whether resources should be transferred from the present to future generations or in the opposite direction depends on the values of r, g, α and δ. Assumptions can be made about the values of r and g based on past experience. Khoman and Weale (2008) find, for the UK, that $r = 4.4\%$ per annum and g could be assumed to be 1.5% per annum per capita or perhaps some slightly higher value. Because r is substantially higher than g it is perfectly possible for discounting to take place ($\delta<1$) without there, nevertheless, being a case for transferring resources from the future to the present. There is no basis for being confident that appropriate parameter combinations justify a policy of burdening future generations, and it is probably therefore inappropriate to embark on such a policy. This argument becomes all the stronger once we make some allowance for the inherent uncertainty about the future, in terms of both the rate of return and the sustainable growth rate of the economy. Deaton (1992) shows that uncertainty inevitably implies a degree of precautionary saving and thus a steeper rate of growth of each generation's endowment. Inevitably, then, it makes transfers from future generations to the present less desirable.

Given this we may safely conclude that an inter-generational planning analysis does not in itself justify a transfer of resources from future generations to the present and, in particular, the argument that future generations are going to be richer than those currently alive is not itself strong enough to justify such a policy. A fiscal policy that implements inter-generational transfers could be justified only if one had good reason to believe either i) that the appropriate social rate of discount is clearly above zero and, to be safe, high relative to the growth rate, implying a value of δ well below one; and ii) that α is low so that the inter-temporal elasticity of substitution is high.

Moving on from this normative conclusion, we now turn to the practical question: how to establish what the implications of that are for sustainable consumption.

The appropriate framework for looking at this issue is provided by extending generational accounts (Auerbach and Kotlikoff 1999; Cardarelli *et al.* 2000). Generational accounts show the discounted value of the receipts expected by any cohort from the exchequer relative to the payments that the same cohort expects to make to the exchequer over its remaining life-span. Here receipts are broadly defined to include all public consumption made on the cohort's behalf, including both individual services provided by the government (such as health treatment) and collective services (such as defence) as well as payments of state benefits and other transfers. Given projections of likely receipts and payments as a function of age, it is straightforward to calculate the present discounted value of each of these. The excess of payments over receipts is the generational account of the cohort in question. If the fiscal structure is such that each cohort neither burdens others, nor supports them, the generational account at birth should be zero.

This framework invites extension to the private sector. For any cohort, how does the future income expected over the remaining lifetime compare with expected future expenditure? If income is defined to exclude income from property, the problem seems to resolve nicely into the inter-temporal budget constraint. In the absence of any transfers between generations beyond those implied by the workings of the public sector, the present discounted value of future non-property income plus the current value of wealth has to equal the present discounted value of future consumption plus taxes and other transfers to be paid to the government. A discounted value of consumption higher than this is unaffordable and, to the extent that people do have expectations of consumption higher than is consistent with the inter-temporal budget constraint, there are three possible outcomes. First of all, they may increase their income, perhaps by retiring later than the pattern suggested by past data. Second, they may simply accept disappointment and reduce their consumption level. Or third, they may devise some means of or exploit some opportunity for transferring the burden to future generations. The most obvious mechanism for doing this is by means of pressure for increased state pensions and other benefits. In fact, as we argue below, the argument that no one generation should consume more than its life-time resources requires that each generation should leave a legacy to its successor reflecting the point that some natural resources and, most notably, land are treated as private wealth.

Once the framework is extended to the private sector, we can put the two sectors together and add them up to establish the position for the nation as a whole. This provides a summary of the affordability of the nation's consumption plans, independently of whether the consumption is paid for by households or whether it is paid for by the government. We can consider a simple accounting table to show the relationships in which we are interested.

Table 4.3 A sectoral analysis of inter-temporal imbalances

Private sector	Public sector	Nation
Net assets	Net assets	Net assets
Discounted labour income	0	Discounted labour income
Discounted benefits	– Discounted benefits	0
– Discounted taxes	+ Discounted taxes	0
– Discounted consumption	– Discounted consumption	– Discounted consumption
= Inter-temporal budget imbalance	= Inter-temporal budget imbalance	= Inter-temporal budget imbalance

Here consumption is measured net of indirect taxes, which are instead included in the discounted value of tax payments. The table should be compiled for all people currently alive since the net assets belong to them, or perhaps more conveniently for all adults with the assumption that their children's consumption is treated as their own. Taxes and benefits net out, from the point of view of the nation, since they are, as in the standard national accounts, simply transfer payments.[6] A public sector that shows an inter-temporal budget deficit might be matched by a surplus in the private sector. In such a case, although the public sector needs to sort out its finances, it is not clear that the nation is living beyond its means. However, this table draws attention to the fact that the private sector may also have consumption patterns that are not affordable and, if this is the case, then so too does the nation. The process of adjustment is likely to be more difficult to manage than when it is simply a question of reallocating resources between public and private sectors.

In compiling a table of this type, generational accounts typically provide the information needed for the public-sector column. Discounted labour income can be computed from age profiles for labour income and the discounted consumption of the private sector can be computed by combining information from private-sector consumption profiles (after adjustment for indirect taxes) and the information on public provision of goods and services which is also required for the production of generational accounts. Khoman and Weale (2008) provide figures for the balance in the right-hand column, but further work is needed to present a fully articulated balance sheet showing the detailed picture.

This table could also be compiled for people starting their adult lives, on the assumption that their net assets are zero—but obviously also making the assumption that their consumption plans and prospects for labour income can be derived from the observed consumption and labour income of older people. It is perfectly possible that the inter-temporal budget balance condition is met for the population currently alive, but not for current young people, perhaps because young people are more affected by declining mortality than are the whole population currently alive.

The treatment of land and other natural resources

If the only resources of economic value to the economy were produced resources, then an absence of inter-generational transfers would imply that each generation consumed only the fruits of its own labour. However, economies also enjoy naturally occurring resources and the focus of much of the move towards green national accounting has been so as to ensure that proper account is taken of these. Since exhaustible resources were provided by nature, any generation that depletes the stock of these needs to leave something to replace them if it is not to consume at the expense of its successors. More generally, it is well understood that on the optimal consumption trajectory economies should replace natural resources consumed with produced capital, over and above any other capital accumulation that is needed (Hartwick 1990; Sefton and Weale 2006). This suggests that the analysis above should add on to the stock of produced capital that of natural resources, most notably North Sea oil and gas, and take account of these in looking at the way in which Britain has treated its wealth.[7] Such green national accounting is well understood at least with resources that are private goods and have clear market prices. The magnitude of the effect is obviously very sensitive to the price put on the resource. Without trying to quantify it, however, it is clear that the reduction in wealth relative to income has been larger than that shown in Figure 4.1. At the same time we note that the data in Figure 4.1 exclude intangible capital, and a case can be made that correct treatment of this has as offsetting effect.

The treatment of land is little discussed in the literature on green national accounting because green national accounts do not focus explicitly on generational effects. Nevertheless, it is arguably at least as important when discussing issues of generational transfers. Plainly, if one looks far enough back, land was not owned by anyone. The people who enclosed it transformed it from common into private property and accrued a resource which they were then able to sell to future generations. The implication of this is that their descendents had to pay for an asset that they had acquired for nothing. In effect, there was a transfer to the first generation in much the same way as arises from an issue of national debt or a pay as you go benefit system. To the extent that ownership of land offers a means of saving up for old age, it crowds out productive capital and thus depresses real income in much the same way as does national debt.

Of course, all this could be regarded as something that happened long ago, and put safely in the category of bygones, but many countries, and the UK in particular, have seen sharp increases in the price of land and, to the extent that this is not reversed subsequently, it has the same effect as the original enclosure. If land prices increase to a permanently higher level, then the cohort that happens to own the land at the time enjoys a windfall which it can realize by selling its land to younger cohorts, reducing the need to accumulate other forms of capital to fund retirement. Barrell and Weale (2010) present a formal analysis of the effects of a change to land prices in an overlapping generations model in which people save up for retirement. They draw attention to the similarity between this and an issue of national debt. Weale (2007) put the increase in the value of land in the UK between 1987 and 2006 as roughly equal to 100% of GDP; there has, of course, been some diminution since then.

People may, of course, leave the land that they own to their descendents, in which case they can enjoy the rent but not the capital value of the land during their retirement. If this were the case we would not expect to find much impact of changes in the value of land—or housing—on consumption. Micro-econometric studies present a mixed picture, with Campbell and Cocco (2007) arguing that consumption is affected by house values and Attanasio *et al.* (2009) arguing that it is not. Both studies suffer from the defect that the authors do not give precise definitions of the variables that they use, with the

authors of the second paper nevertheless suggesting that differences in definition may explain the different findings. Macro-econometric analyses find a
strong role for house prices as drivers of aggregate consumption, with the
implication that people do use capital gains on housing to finance their own
consumption, at least to some extent (Barrell and Davis 2007).

The implications of this for an analysis of the question of whether recent
consumption levels are consistent with the idea that each generation should
pay its own way are substantial. Scholz *et al.* (2006) looked at total household
wealth when they computed the budget constraints faced by the households
that they studied. They worked with 1992 data. Their results that 84% of households were well equipped to meet assumed consumption needs depended on
them being willing to realize their housing wealth to fund consumption. They
did, in an *ad hoc* way, investigate the possibility that people might be reluctant
to rely on housing wealth, by looking at the consequence of the assumption
that people were prepared to realize only one-half of their housing wealth to
fund their retirement. Even with this assumption they found that 61.2% of
households had resources at least adequate to pay for their retirement.

However, seen from the position that each cohort should pay its own way,
the question of whether people want to use their housing wealth to fund their
retirement is an irrelevance. One means of dealing with this issue would be to
assume that each cohort planned to leave a legacy equal to the value of the
land that it owns, to future generations. An alternative, which simplifies the calculations, is to assume that each generation enjoys the income from land but
does not expect to use the capital value of land to finance consumption. This
assumption was made by Khoman and Weale (2008) in their study on the
national balance between consumption and saving. Rent on land was assumed
to accrue evenly across the adult population, providing a means of paying for
consumption over and above that of labour income; however, only produced
assets were assumed to be available to finance the consumption of people
currently alive.

The UK's consumption imbalance

Khoman and Weale (2008) compiled estimates of the figures for the third
column of Table 4.3. In order to make these easily intelligible, they were con-
verted to show the level of consumption consistent with inter-temporal budget
balance, as a proportion of current consumption levels. This affordability
ratio was calculated as:

$$\text{Affordability ratio} = \frac{(\text{discounted consumption plus inter} - \text{temporal budget imbalance})}{\text{Discounted consumption}}$$

(14)

The calculations were performed for 2005.

Inevitably, the results are sensitive to the assumed real interest rate which is used to discount future receipts. This was set equal to 4.39% per annum, being the average real return on capital for the period 1989–2006, a period which included the recession of the early 1990s but not the more recent recession. The results are also sensitive to the assumed rate of growth of the economy since in the calculation of profiles for consumption and labour income Khoman and Weale worked from cross-section profiles taken from micro-economic data sources for 2005 (or for public consumption from the 2003 generational accounts) and tilted these to adjust for economic growth. Thus they assumed that consumption and labour by age grew at the rate of per capita economic growth and used this assumption to convert cross-section profiles[8] into profiles for people of any given age. At any given real interest the higher the rate of growth, the larger the budget imbalance, because although the tilt of both consumption and labour income is increased by a high growth rate, consumption levels in old age are higher than those for labour income and the impact on consumption therefore dominates.

Of course, one is interested not only in estimates of the actual position, but also factors that lie behind it and also how far an excess of consumption over available resources might be remedied not by reducing consumption but by raising income, for example by altering retirement patterns. We therefore show results assuming a growth rate of per capita consumption of 1.0% per annum for three assumptions. The first relate to working patterns as they were in the 2005 profiles, and with mortality rates derived from the cohort life expectancy figures published by the Government Actuary. The second set of results assumes that there is no further increase in mortality. Thus the difference between these and the earlier set indicates the extent to which declining mortality affects sustainable consumption.

The last set of results indicates affordable consumption on the assumption that working lives are extended by five years. Since the wage profile varies with age, we have implemented this by assuming that people aged between 55 and 60 earn the wages of those currently aged 55. Beyond this the wage profile is shifted five years to the right, so that the earnings figures for people aged 61 are computed from those for people currently aged 56.

It should be stressed that for the current adult population this is making an extreme example about what could be delivered by extending working lives. For this change to take place immediately, people who currently regard themselves as retired would have to go back to work. It would not be enough for people currently working to delay their retirement. If the change were generated simply by people currently working delaying retirement, then the extent to which the budget gap would be closed would be smaller.

The results suggest that in the period before the crisis consumption levels in the UK were substantially higher than those needed if each cohort were to finance its consumption without relying on the support of younger generations. Looking at the base case, taking mortality rates as projected by the Government Actuary and retirement patterns as observed in 2005, the results

Table 4.4 Estimates of sustainable to actual consumption in the UK for 2005

	Base case	No rise in longevity	Five years more work
Affordability for 20-year-olds	0.918	0.935	0.959
Affordability for current population	0.928	0.963	1.029

Source: Khoman and Weale 2008

suggest that consumption needed to be reduced by 7.1%. This would have had the effect of raising net saving from 4.5% of GDP in 2005 to 9.8%—a ratio similar to that achieved in the 1960s. Over-consumption by young people is more marked; their consumption would have needed to fall by 8.2%.

We can see that working five years more would raise income by more than enough to meet consumption plans for the current adult population; an increase of three and a half years would probably be adequate. However, for current young people the benefit is much smaller, because the extra income lies further in the future and therefore its current discounted value is lower.

Second, we can see that with retirement behaviour as it actually is, only about one-half of the savings shortfall of current adults is due to projected increases in longevity relative to what is currently observed. For young people the impact of rising longevity is less, even though the projected increase in longevity is greater. This discrepancy is again a consequence of discounting.

These calculations related, of course, to the state of the economy before the economic crisis of 2008/09. It is, at the moment, difficult to judge whether the situation has improved or worsened since then. On the one hand the government has announced cuts to public consumption relative to what would have been implied by a continuation of the pre-crisis path. At the same time household consumption is well below what the pre-crisis path implied. Offsetting this, however, output in mid-2011 was still about 4% below the level of GDP ahead of the crisis in the first quarter of 2008. Output per person employed was about 3% lower than it was ahead of the crisis. Whether the impact of the crisis has been to improve or to worsen the savings balance of the UK economy depends on how far productivity recovers towards its previous trend or, equivalently, on how large the permanent damage to the economy as a result of the crisis has been.

Conclusions

Inspection of consumption, saving and wealth data indicates that over the period since the early 1980s the saving rate in the UK has been too low to maintain the ratio of produced wealth to GDP. An econometric analysis suggests that the relationship between consumption, income and wealth was very different after 1980 from what it had been before, and that on the basis of post-1980 behavioural patterns the decline in the ratio of wealth to income had some way further to run.

One might regard it as odd that with rising longevity and an ageing population the UK should choose to manage with a ratio of produced wealth to GDP that is low compared to what was observed even after meeting the costs of the Second World War. While these data do indicate that the performance of the macro-economy from the mid-1980s until the crisis was not sustainable, they do not in themselves provide a normative analysis of desirable levels of produced wealth.

This can be done by looking at the problem from an inter-generational point of view. An analysis of the return on capital, the trend rate of growth and plausible assumptions about the discount rate and the inter-temporal elasticity of substitution suggests that one cannot argue strongly against the principle that each cohort should finance its consumption without transfers from other cohorts. An implication of this is that people currently alive should expect to finance their future consumption out of future labour income and the current stock of produced wealth (physical capital excluding land and net foreign assets).

Drawing on earlier work by Khoman and Weale (2008) we conclude that in 2005 the UK's rate of net saving as a share of GDP should have been 9.8% of GDP as compared to the actual figure of 4.5%, if the adult population alive then were to be able to afford future consumption given expectations of future income.

Uncertainty about the long-term effects of the crisis on the supply side of the economy mean that it is at present difficult to judge whether or how far the adjustments since the crisis have improved things. Nevertheless, these observations carry the implication that if the UK is to run on a sustainable basis in the future, economic recovery needs to be led by domestic investment and net exports. A revival of consumer confidence on its own, if it leads to higher consumer spending, will not be a solution to the economy's long-run problems.

Notes

1 However, the recent history of both Spain and the Republic of Ireland may be a warning that high borrowing from abroad may finance domestic investment that delivers very poor *ex post* returns. Ireland's construction boom was financed in part by borrowing from abroad and has resulted in a situation where up to 300,000 unwanted houses may be demolished.
2 If the condition holds for produced national wealth, it also holds for total national wealth including the value of land. The only circumstance in which this would not be true would be if the price of land were to rise at the rate of interest, but then the arbitrage condition implies that the rent on land would be zero and this is known not to be the case.
3 It might be objected that the equation was estimated by OLS (ordinary least squares) despite the fact that current income growth could be regarded as endogenous. However, estimation of the restricted equation using income growth lagged one and two periods as instruments for current income had very little effect on the results.
4 These estimates pay no attention to intangible produced wealth. Official estimates suggest that the stock of such capital has risen over the last 20 years or so, but

taking account of these would be unlikely to change the general impression of an economy that has steadily depleted its wealth.

5 Although the impact of this is unclear since the model was used to compare actual with required wealth in 1992.

6 Except insofar as they are levied on foreigners.

7 The economically coherent approach is to treat decumulation of natural resources as capital consumption but not to regard discovery of resources as saving. The former is the consequence of economic decisions while the latter is a capital gain and the result of good luck.

8 The use of cross-section profiles in this way is open to the criticism that it does not distinguish age, cohort and time effects. Deaton (1997) recommends use of a regression method to separate out these effects. However, when applied to UK consumption, the resulting parameters fail standard econometric tests for stability. We are currently working on models using time-varying coefficients.

References

Attanasio, O., L. Blow, R. Hamilton and A. Leicester (2009) 'Booms and Busts: Consumption, House Prices and Expectations', *Economica* Vol. 76: 20–50.

Auerbach, A.J. and L.K. Kotlikoff (1999) 'The Methodology of Generational Accounting', in A.J. Auerbach, L.J. Kotlikoff and W. Leibfritz (eds), *Generational Accounting around the World*, Chicago: Chicago University Press.

Barrell, R. and E.P. Davis (2007) 'Consumption liquidity constraints and housing wealth in eight major economies', *Scottish Journal of Political Economy* May.

Barrell, R. and M.R. Weale (2010) 'Fiscal Policy, Fairness between Generations and National Saving', *Oxford Review of Economic Policy* Vol. 26: 87–116.

Bohn, H. (1999) 'The Behaviour of US Public Debt and Deficits', *Quarterly Journal of Economics* Vol. 36: 949–63.

——(2007) 'Are Stationarity and Co-integration Restrictions Necessary for the Intertemporal Budget Constraint', *Journal of Monetary Economics* Vol. 56: 805–16.

Campbell, J.Y and J.F. Cocco (2007) 'How do House Prices Affect Consumption? Evidence from Micro Data', *Journal of Monetary Economics* Vol. 54: 591–621.

Cardarelli, R., J. Sefton and L.J. Kotlikoff (2000) 'Generational Accounting in the UK', *Economic Journal* Vol. 110, No. 467: 547–74.

Dasgupta, P. (2007) 'The Stern Review's Economics of Climate Change', *National Institute Economic Review* No. 199: 4–7.

——(2009) 'The Welfare Economic Theory of Green National Accounts', *Environmental and Resource Economics* Vol. 42: 3–38.

Deaton, A. (1992) *Understanding Consumption*, Oxford: Clarendon Press.

——(1997) *The Analysis of Household Surveys. A Micro-economic Approach to Development Policy*, Johns Hopkins University Press.

Feinstein, C.H. (1972) *National Income, Expenditure and Output of the United Kingdom, 1855–1865*, Cambridge: Cambridge University Press.

Hartwick, J. (1990) 'Natural Resources, National Accounting and Economic Depreciation', *Journal of Public Economics* Vol. 43: 291–304.

Johansen, S. (1988) 'Statistical Analysis of Co-integration Vectors', *Journal of Economic Dynamics and Control* Vol. 12: 231–54.

Khoman, E. and M.R. Weale (2008) 'Are we Living beyond our Means: a Comparison of France, Italy, Spain and the United Kingdom', *National Institute Discussion Paper* No. 311, www.niesr.ac.uk/pdf/100408_94720.pdf.

Romer, D. (1988) 'What are the Costs of Excessive Deficits?' *NBER Macroeconomics Annual*: 63–97.

Sargent, T.J. and N. Wallace (1981) 'Some Unpleasant Monetarist Arithmetic', *Federal Reserve Bank of Minneapolis Quarterly Review* Autumn, www.minneapolisfed.org/research/QR/QR531.pdf.

Scholz, J.K., A. Seshadri and S. Khitatrakun (2006) 'Are Americans Saving Optimally for Retirement', *Journal of Political Economy* Vol. 114: 607–43.

Sefton, J. and M.R. Weale (1995) *The Reconciliation of National Income and Expenditure: Balanced Estimates of United Kingdom National Accounts, 1920–1990*. Vol. 7 in *Studies in National Income and Expenditure of the United Kingdom*, Cambridge: Cambridge University Press.

——(2006) 'The Concept of Income in a General Equilibrium', *Review of Economic Studies* Vol. 73: 219–49.

Weale, M.R. (1990) 'Wealth Constraints and Consumer Behaviour', *Economic Modelling* Vol. 7: 165–78.

——(2007) 'House Price Worries', *National Institute Economic Review* No. 200: 4–6.

5 The UK's external position

Robert Kuenzel[1]

Introduction

Concerns about the United Kingdom's economic health have been fairly prevalent in the public debate over the course of the past decades, and have often been more openly voiced than in other European economies. Viewed with an economist's mindset, any such debate is an important input into economic policy-making. What is curious about the discussion surrounding the UK economy, though, is its distinctive concern with *external* aspects of the UK's economic performance. Be it the value of sterling, the spectre of outsourcing to emerging markets, eroding competitiveness, or the UK's balance of payments—in few advanced economies does the general thrust of the economic debate show such a clear recognition of the country's interdependence with the global economy as in the UK.

Should this kind of preoccupation come as a surprise? Probably not if one bears in mind two particularly traumatic episodes of the UK's post-war economic history, namely the £2.3 billion International Monetary Fund (IMF) bail-out requested in 1976, and the pound sterling's exit from the Exchange Rate Mechanism on 'Black Wednesday' in September 1992. What these events underline is that the fate of internationally integrated advanced economies is inextricably linked to the attitudes of foreign creditors, be they international organizations or financial market participants, and to a country's ability to convince these of its economic soundness. However, this chapter does not intend to offer any further investigation into the psychology underpinning the aforementioned type of economic debate. Instead, it aims to answer two central questions related to the UK's external position and its financial interlinkages, which once again rose to prominence during the global financial and economic crisis of 2007–09. These are, first, where the UK's long-standing current account deficit comes from, and second, how much of a problem (if any) it constitutes.

The UK's current account in a long-term perspective

For over 25 years the UK has been recording a deficit on its annual current account balance. The current account records economic transactions between residents of the UK and non-residents, linked to export and import activity, investment earnings and current transfers. As a current account deficit represents the excess of domestic demand over income—or, alternatively, the excess of investment over domestic saving—a current account deficit represents a commensurate transfer of ownership of UK resources to non-residents.[2] Depending on its magnitude and persistence, a current account deficit can mark a temporary period of large investment needs, for instance following a large-scale natural disaster or during a phase of 'catch-up' growth, but it may also be symptomatic of an economy that is persistently outspending its earning capacity.

It is therefore important to ascertain into which of these categories the UK falls, and this will be the subject of the present section. Normative implications of the analysis shall be addressed towards the end of this chapter. Beginning with a closer look at the evolution of the UK's current account deficit, the year of 1984 marks the beginning of the UK's unbroken succession of current account deficits up until 2010. Prior to 1984, the 1970s and the early 1980s saw a considerable fluctuation in the current account balance between a small surplus and a deficit of around 4% of gross domestic product (GDP). Much of this gyration was in one way or another due to oil, be it through the impact of the Organization of the Petroleum Exporting Countries (OPEC) oil crises of 1973 on oil import costs, or due to the discovery and subsequent production of significant volumes of UK North Sea oil. Between 1984 and 2010, however, the confluence of a number of developments in UK goods and services trade, as well as in investment income flows, has culminated in the UK's current account recording a deficit of around 2% of GDP on average.[3] One defining feature of this deficit pattern is its relative stability, as it consistently hovered between balance and –5% of GDP, and on average deviated only around 1 percentage point of GDP from its long-run average. Although the absolute magnitude of this string of deficits may not appear particularly noteworthy compared to the much-noted deficits in other major economies, for instance the USA, the various components underlying the UK's net balance show a number of more significant and interesting patterns. The following sections will examine the key trends in these items in turn, which are illustrated in Figure 5.1.

Trade balance deterioration driven by goods trade

Goods trade accounts for the largest individual part of the UK's current account, contributing between one-third and one-half of the overall flow of debits and credits recorded in the current account in any given year. Goods trade arguably attracts the most attention in the balance of payments, partly because of the traditional conception of trade as relating to tangible products, but also because its preponderance means that any adverse developments are comparatively difficult to be compensated for by other, smaller items of the balance of payments. The UK's goods trade balance has been marked by two

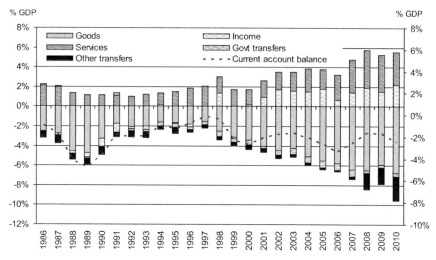

Figure 5.1 The UK's current account since 1986
Source: UK Office for National Statistics

dominant developments since the early 1980s, which are the emergence of a very large deficit in finished manufactured goods and the gradual erosion of its oil trade surplus.

The former is, in quantitative terms, the single most important driver of the UK's current account deterioration in recent decades, and is all the more significant in light of the fact that throughout the 1970s the UK was even a net exporter of finished manufactured goods, earning a surplus of around 3% of GDP each year. Through a continuous decline of this surplus over the following decades, driven by a process of domestic de-industrialization, increased globalization and the emergence of low-cost manufacturing economies in Asia, the UK became a net importer of such goods to the tune of 4% of GDP by 2010. Second, the UK's relatively brief period as a net oil exporter ended in the early 2000s after strong surpluses in the 1980s, the heyday of UK North Sea oil production. Since 2005 the UK now consumes slightly more oil (and non-oil fuels) than it produces, although the overall impact of the UK's marginal decline in oil self-sufficiency on the current account deficit has become less marked in recent years.[4]

By contrast, on the services side UK trade performed comparatively well in the 1990s and 2000s, with a particularly strong performance since 2007. Although the UK's industrial structure is more dominated by the services sector than in most other EU countries, its services trade intensity is only close to the EU-27 average, in contrast to the stereotypical impression of the UK being a hothouse of international services trade.[5] What is true, however, is that the UK has very successfully developed a specialization in *certain kinds* of traded services, with financial services standing among other services as earning the largest net annual surplus (2% of GDP on average) in the decade up to 2010, with other business services contributing roughly a further 1% of GDP surplus on average. Furthermore, the steady rise in the services trade balance since the early 1990s has been the principal reason why the stark deterioration in the UK's goods export performance over the period did not result in a significant deterioration of the overall current account deficit.

Investment income limits the rate of foreign debt accumulation

An additional reason for the relative stability of the current account deficit has been the emergence of a sizeable surplus in net foreign investment earnings, which have risen from a moderate deficit position in the early 1990s to an average surplus of around 1.5% of GDP between 2000 and 2010. This fortunate development owes much to the structure of the underlying UK net foreign asset position, also known as the international investment position (IIP), in particular the fact that the UK has large net asset holdings in foreign direct investment (FDI), which are worth around 27% of GDP.[6] Earnings on UK direct investment abroad have consistently exceeded earnings by foreigners from direct investment assets in the UK since 1985, due both to the volume effect of an excess of UK FDI assets over liabilities, and because UK FDI assets seem to generate a significantly greater rate of return than corresponding FDI liabilities.

The UK's role as a leading global financial centre is underscored by the fact that the UK's IIP shows large net foreign liabilities for loans and deposits (worth around 15% of GDP), which naturally results in the UK steadily paying out interest on a net basis to foreigners. While this net interest expenditure partially offsets the considerable direct investment earnings of the UK, it none the less leaves the current account with a sizeable—if somewhat volatile— boost from overall investment income. This creates a well-known paradox first observed for the USA: How can a net foreign debtor economy earn a positive income from its international investment position? The explanation for the USA of it benefiting from the 'extraordinary privilege' of issuing a reserve currency at benchmark rates and low risk premia does not hold for the UK as sterling is not a major global reserve currency. However, the UK's role as a financial centre may partly explain the UK balance sheet's skew towards net equity assets and quasi-debt liabilities, so that excess returns may represent compensation for bearing the greater risk of equity-type investments. Finally, measurement issues may also be an explanatory factor, and these are revisited in the next section.

This being said, the impact of the financial crisis on asset prices and write-downs has caused considerable oscillations in net direct investment earnings, which in the initial phase of the financial crisis (up until Q3 2008) benefited the UK, as foreign-owned monetary financial institutions in the UK incurred major losses from asset write-downs. This positive and somewhat paradoxical income blip benefited the UK external position in the sense that it was effectively 'exporting bank losses', although subsequently UK earnings on its FDI holdings also became more volatile. Ultimately, despite the UK's prominent position in the global financial marketplace, the financial crisis does not seem to have damaged the UK economy's ability to generate income from its international investment activities, as well as from financial services overall.

The steady trickle of external debt: assessing the UK's external credit risk

The above exposition of UK current account dynamics since the 1980s reveals a persistent current account deficit resulting from a number of divergent, and numerically larger, movements in net trade and income balances. Yet as pointed out above, the UK's current account deficit has been fairly stable at around 2%–3% of GDP for many years, a level not out of line with other major EU economies such as Italy and France, and even low in comparison to some other advanced economies' external deficits (e.g. the USA, Australia). It may therefore be tempting to conclude that, first, small but steady current account deficits have become a quasi-structural feature of the UK economy, and that, second, these do not carry further serious ramifications. After all, attempting to always target a zero current account balance would be both naïve and sub-optimal, given that current account deficits are perfectly legitimate equilibrium outcomes in much of the standard economic literature.[7] Furthermore, if a small current account *surplus* is no cause for concern, then how could a symmetrical deficit be judged any different, given that the two hypothetical economies in question might just be counterparties to precisely the same transactions?

This type of argument is not without its merit, particularly the former conclusion that the UK in fact has developed a structural current account deficit in recent decades. However, the conjecture that, given the apparent lack of UK balance of payments problems since 1992, this does not give cause for major concern is clearly invalid. The problem with accumulating debt is that, first, one has to pay it back one day, and second, one cannot exactly be sure when this day will be. This fairly obvious conclusion then forces a switch of perspective, away from the relatively small flow of new external debt represented by the current account deficit, towards the *stock* of (net) external debt the UK has accumulated over the previous decades as a result of the succession of current account deficits. The parentheses in the preceding sentence illustrate a crucial dichotomy in the analysis of UK external debt, as one's evaluation very much depends on whether one considers the *net* balance of UK foreign assets and liabilities, in other words the net IIP, or the gross stock of foreign assets and liabilities, which are considerably larger. These two competing perspectives will be examined in turn, and both provide important insights into overall UK external credit risk.

The UK's international investment position

The UK's IIP showed estimated net liabilities of around 15% of GDP in 2010, a level close to the euro area average.[8] Overall, the UK IIP has deteriorated considerably since its high point in 1986, when it showed net foreign assets worth 22% of GDP, but the deterioration has not been fully in line with the trajectory implied by a simple cumulation of the successive current account deficits: current account developments since 1986 would have implied much larger net liabilities of 26% of GDP. The reason why current account balances do not fully explain movements in the UK's net IIP as measured by official statistics can be in principle three-fold. First and foremost, the difference can reflect the net effect of valuation changes with respect to the UK's stock of gross external assets and liabilities. Second, the IIP can change due to reasons such as debt cancellations, write-offs or reclassifications. Third, net errors and omissions used as a balancing item to reconcile the IIP-relevant flows recorded under the current, capital and financial account may in principle be correcting a mismeasurement on the current account side, although errors are generally assumed to fall on the financial account.[9] However, in any given year the latter two effects are typically neither large nor of particular economic significance, which then leaves valuation effects as the second main determinant of a change in a country's net external wealth, in addition to current account flows. The following sections show that the UK has derived a net benefit from valuation gains over the past decades, although these are typically moderate in size and fairly volatile.

The UK's net foreign liabilities of around 15% of GDP are made up of much larger net positions for the three principal types of investment in the balance of payments (see Table 5.1).[10] As already outlined above, the UK holds a net asset position for direct investment (+27% of GDP), but shows net liabilities for portfolio investment (–38% of GDP) and 'other investment' (–19% of GDP), which mainly includes foreign loans and deposits. Furthermore, it holds smaller net asset positions in financial derivatives (6% of GDP) and foreign exchange reserves (3% of GDP). Overall, this picture is not untypical of an economy with a sizeable international financial centre: it attracts

Table 5.1 The UK's international investment position, 2009

Position	Gross assets	Gross liabilities	Net position
Direct investment	74%	−47%	+27%
Portfolio investment	134%	−172%	−38%
Other investment*	253%	−272%	−19%
Financial derivatives	158%	−152%	+6%
Reserve assets	3%	n/a	3%
Total	622%	−643%	−21%

Note: * Includes trade credits, loans and deposits, and selected public-sector assets.
Source: Office for National Statistics 2010

net investment from foreigners into UK bank deposits and loans, and into equity and debt securities issued by UK corporations, and some of these funds will be redirected into (direct) equity investments abroad. In other words, the UK's net IIP is effectively long in equity-type assets and short in debt-type assets.

The above net amounts arguably do not look particularly alarming, compared to the UK's gross general government debt, which stands at around 80% of GDP, most of which is held domestically. However, the gross stocks of foreign assets and liabilities that underpin this comparatively small net position are very large by most developed countries' standards. In 1980 gross assets and liabilities stood at around 100% of GDP, rising steadily throughout the 1980s and 1990s to levels around 250% of GDP in 1998. It is in the following decade up until 2008 that the UK's external balance sheet recorded a staggering expansion, with asset and liability holdings tripling in size to around 760% of GDP in 2008.[11] Although having shrunk somewhat in 2009 and 2010, the UK's external balance sheet remains large, at around 700% of GDP. This extraordinary increase has been primarily due to what has been termed 'financial globalization', i.e. an increasing global openness to international capital flows and a rise in cross-border financial investment positions. The size of the balance sheet is important in a number of respects, broadly divisible into valuation and risk issues, which are addressed below.

Valuation

The value of foreign assets and liabilities should be as closely aligned to current market prices as possible, to the extent that the items in question vary in price (loans and deposits, for instance, do not). Exchange rate movements can drive a wedge between the value of assets and liabilities, as these tend to be denominated in different currencies. Finally, FDI is typically recorded at book value, which will generally tend to underestimate the actual market value and, given the UK's net direct investment surplus, would tend to underestimate the strength of the UK's net foreign asset position and overestimate the UK's surprisingly high rate of return on its direct investment assets.[12]

The currency composition of UK foreign assets and liabilities in 2009 shows that the vast majority of UK foreign assets are denominated in foreign currency, whereas two-thirds of the UK's gross liabilities are in sterling.[13] The currency split varies considerably across the three main types of investment.[14] Broadly speaking, the UK's balance sheet for both direct and portfolio investment is denominated in foreign currency on the asset side, whereas UK liabilities are in sterling. On the other hand 'other investments' (loans and deposits) are overwhelmingly denominated in foreign currency, with a share of 94% for UK assets and around 80% for UK liabilities, owing again to the role of London as a global banking hub.

Overall, the currency structure of the UK's balance sheet entails that a major effective exchange rate depreciation of the kind observed for sterling between mid-2007 and the end of 2008 increases the value of UK assets by more than that of UK liabilities, resulting in a sizeable net IIP improvement. Modelling results by Whittard and Khan (2010) suggest that the currency-based IIP revaluations stemming from sterling's fall between the end of 2007 and the end of 2008 alone would have improved the UK's net IIP by a staggering 34% of GDP, even without taking into account any changes in asset prices. These gains were partly reversed throughout 2009 as sterling strengthened again on a nominal effective basis, but nevertheless by the end of 2010 some positive valuation effects remained.

A further source of valuation gains is asset price movements, notably those relating to shares, bonds and other traded financial instruments. Here, the UK's position as a net debtor in portfolio equity and debt instruments meant that in 2008 the sharp global asset price falls reduced UK portfolio liabilities by more (in absolute terms) than the loss in value of its portfolio assets, thus giving a further net boost to the UK's net IIP of around 6% of GDP in 2008 (Whittard and Khan 2010). However, asset price-related valuation gains were more than reversed in 2009, as the UK stock market rose faster than global share prices. Only partial balance of payments data are available for 2010, but preliminary data suggest that total valuation changes—both from asset prices and exchange rates—were again significant in this year, this time providing a positive lift to the UK's net IIP. So although the UK's balance sheet has been flattered by valuation changes in recent years, the volatility of such changes greatly limits their statistical significance.

Overall, the considerable size of these valuation effects underlines the extent to which high gross debt stocks amplify movements in exchange rates and asset prices, even to the extent that from one year to the next the entire net external debt of the UK can potentially be eliminated. Furthermore, the sheer size of the gross stocks means that even small measurement errors have a large impact on the estimated net external debt position of the UK. These two facts thus make it very difficult to make claims about the actual size of the UK's net foreign asset position with any degree of precision. Taking into account the likelihood that the fair value of UK direct investment assets may be up to three times as high as the recorded book value, as Senior and Westwood (2001) suggest, it would then not seem unreasonable to say that the UK probably does not have any significant net external debt stocks, despite two and a half decades of borrowing from abroad.[15]

Risks

Having examined the structure of UK external debt and its development over time, the initial question of whether the UK's external position constitutes a problem needs to be addressed, and here four main potential sources of risk can be identified. First, solvency risk increases with the size of net external debt. In principle, any large net debt position will eventually require future surpluses in order to pay it off, and the adjustment for the debtor economy will be more painful—and therefore less likely—the greater the required adjustment. This finding holds true when applied to a theoretical, finite time horizon, but an equally plausible but more pragmatic view has it that any debt (external) position can be sustained as long as the investors are willing to continue holding and rolling over the UK's net external debt. Given the probably small or even non-existent net external debt position of the UK, overall solvency risks seem negligible. However, a rise in future current account deficits would lead to a more rapid accumulation of net foreign debt, thus posing a 'flow' risk to the UK's external solvency.

Second, the higher the gross liabilities, the greater the liquidity risk, i.e. the risk of not being able to sell a given asset due to lack of market liquidity. Furthermore, liquidity risk may also include rollover risk, i.e. the propensity for liabilities not to be refinanceable, or only at prohibitive rates. As the UK external balance sheet shows a net asset position in (illiquid) direct investment but a net debt position for the more liquid portfolio and other investment categories, liquidity risk may be considered an issue in adverse scenarios of a major loss of confidence in the UK sovereign or the stability of the UK financial sector. The crisis of 2007–09 is instructive in this respect, as it saw a major withdrawal of foreign deposits in UK banks, worth around 40% of GDP in 2009 alone. While this should be viewed as a part of a crisis-induced deleveraging process, as both the UK's gross foreign assets and liabilities in loans and deposits shrank markedly over the course of 2009, one should not ignore a possible 'flight to safety' resulting from the deterioration in the UK banking sector and growing fiscal problems during the crisis. It is not clear how far this relatively orderly UK balance sheet shrinkage during the crisis can truly count as evidence for the UK's relative resilience to 'sudden stops', given that the crisis was global in nature and affected many countries in broadly symmetrical ways. However, there is some merit in the argument that if the UK's balance sheet could handle the stress test of the unprecedented falls in liquidity and prices on interbank and many securities markets, then the overall liquidity risk could not be all that significant.

Third, given London's role as a major financial centre, the large cross-border positions the UK banking sector and other financial institutions hold might pose a sectoral concentration risk. Over one-half of all UK foreign assets and liabilities at the end of 2009 were attributed to UK monetary financial institutions (MFIs), and the sector has consistently been in a net foreign debtor position since records began in 1987. In principle, an asymmetric shock to the UK banking sector such as a major housing market collapse might then affect the sector's ability to service what constitutes the majority of UK external debt. While this possibility should not be dismissed out of hand, it in fact forms part of wider UK financial stability risks that include also the domestic operations of UK MFIs. In this respect, capital adequacy and other determinants of the banking sector's strength are likely to be the overriding determinant of external banking sector risk.

Finally, currency and maturity mismatches between assets and liabilities could pose threats to a country's external balance sheet, even if this showed no significant net debtor position. As indicated above, all assets on the UK's balance sheet are denominated in foreign currency, while only one-third of its liabilities are. This sets the UK apart from the vulnerabilities posed by what has become known as 'original sin', i.e. the temptation for (emerging) economies to borrow externally in foreign currency so as to shield the lender from currency risk and thereby obtain cheaper funding, only to be caught out when the domestic currency depreciates and external debt service costs rise. Indeed, in the UK's case a sterling depreciation driven by, for instance, a sharp deterioration in the economic outlook, would tend to improve the UK's net foreign asset position and would be likely to improve the current account, both through a boost in the investment income account and a likely improvement in the trade balance.[16] Looking further at UK banks' foreign currency exposure, there appears to be practically zero currency mismatch between their liabilities and assets, both for the UK banking system as a whole as well as for their positions with non-residents.[17] Finally, the maturity profile of the UK balance sheet shows net liabilities for more short- to medium-term instruments, such as deposits and loans, which includes 'hot money', whereas its net equity holdings in direct investment and net debt position in portfolio equity do not have a maturity in any meaningful sense at all.[18] This mixed picture makes it difficult to judge how far the UK could be caught out by what has been described as a 'borrow short, invest long' strategy; suffice to say that again the absolute mismatch in terms of gross positions would seem comparatively small.

The UK's external outlook in an international perspective

The preceding analysis of risks surrounding the sustainability of the UK's external position can inevitably only offer a partial, static assessment of UK vulnerabilities, as possible external shocks to the economy would almost certainly be accompanied by considerable turbulence abroad as well. Furthermore, economic and financial developments in the rest of the world, especially the UK's trading and investment partners, will determine whether and to what extent possible negative shocks would be directed towards the UK economy at all. The sovereign debt crises in a number of euro-area Member States underline this point, as contagion effects and sudden changes in market participants' risk perception have accompanied—or even driven—the succession of sovereign funding squeezes in Greece, Ireland and Portugal. Such contagion effects can be direct and concrete, for instance through cross-border asset holdings, but may also be purely confidence-based, stemming from risk aversion towards countries showing the greatest *relative* vulnerabilities, however defined.

Against this background, it is instructive to put the UK's external situation in comparison with its European peers. Looking first at a comparison of external debt levels (defined as the net IIP), Figure 5.2 shows that in 2009 the UK was by no means excessively indebted to foreign creditors. With net foreign liabilities of around 20% of GDP, it ranked virtually on a par with the euro area (EA16 at that time) as a whole, and was placed slightly better than

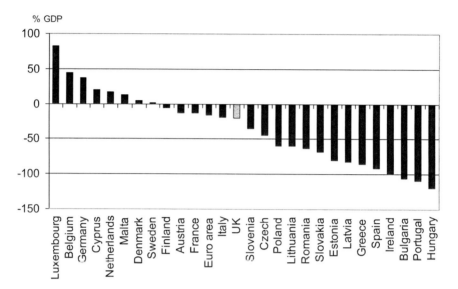

Figure 5.2 Net international investment position, 2009
Source: Eurostat

the median country, Slovenia. On the other hand, in terms of gross liabilities positions, the potential risk factors of which have been already discussed above, the UK does present itself as a comparatively highly leveraged economy. Although not nearly as saddled with gross liabilities as the financial centres that are Luxembourg (11,700% of GDP) or Ireland (1,600% of GDP), the UK follows in third position among EU countries (700% GDP).[19] While this undoubtedly still constitutes a high level of gross external debt, the UK's greater economic diversification puts it in a decidedly lower relative risk category than its two peers from a pure leverage perspective.

In terms of Member States' current account flows, for which the European Commission publishes regular economic forecasts, the UK is expected to achieve a considerable rebalancing of its current account position in 2011 and 2012, with the Commission's Spring 2011 forecast suggesting that the deficit will be entirely eliminated in 2012.[20] As domestic demand is expected to remain weak over the forecast horizon, import demand should also remain subdued, while a fairly robust recovery in the UK's main export markets should deliver an improvement in the UK's trade balance strong enough to balance the current account. The UK's historic over-reliance on domestic demand growth to drive economic activity is thereby expected to be corrected, at least for the medium term, as net exports become the strongest driver of growth in the comparatively lean years of public-sector consolidation and private-sector spending restraint that lie ahead for the UK.

Furthermore, this has further important implications for economy-wide sectoral net lending/borrowing. For much of the past decade, the UK has run a 'twin deficit' in the general government and external sector (via net borrowing from abroad). Up until the crisis, net lending from the UK's corporate sector more or less financed these two deficits, and with it moderate net borrowing by the household sector. Since the crisis, UK private-sector saving has risen, thus helping to finance the widening public deficit without forcing the UK into a greater net external borrowing. The Commission's spring 2011 forecast expects this comparatively orderly sectoral rebalancing to continue, as by 2012 the remaining UK government deficit of around 7% of GDP will be entirely domestically financed, thereby relieving potential external debt pressures emanating from the fiscal side. Crucially, a number of other EU member states are expected not to be in this comparatively fortunate position in the medium term: economies such as Greece, Spain, Cyprus, France, but also the USA are expected to still run large (i.e. greater than 5% of GDP) general government deficits in 2012, which are for the most part financed through considerable external borrowing.

Conclusion

The UK has been running persistent external deficits since the mid-1980s, principally due to a deterioration in its goods trade balance. This development occurred during a period where a marked shift in UK output composition towards services production took place. One arguably benign interpretation of this trend would identify the fall in UK goods supply relative to domestic absorption as the principal cause. The rising surplus in services trade that took place in the 1990s and 2000s would constitute *prima facie* evidence in support of this view. The UK further benefits from its uncanny ability to generate net investment earnings from what official balance of payments data suggests is a net foreign debtor position. Overall, this leaves the UK with a comparatively small and steady current account deficit, which thus more or less represents the annual excess of the UK's combined household, government and corporate sectors' spending over their joint income. The UK is, therefore, dependent on foreign investors' willingness to continue to accumulate net claims on the UK economy as long as there is no adjustment to the net saving behaviour of the UK's domestic sectors.

Turning to the reasons why investors may not want to continue doing this requires closer inspection of the UK's net and gross external balance sheet. It reveals that, for all the years of external deficits, the UK still has a relatively small external debt stock, and under different valuation approaches there may even be no net debt at all. While the sheer size of the UK's gross foreign assets and liabilities can cause considerable gyrations in its net IIP position, there seems to be little evidence that cyclical valuation effects from currency and asset price movements flatter the UK's net debt position in the long run. Overall, solvency risks are probably low in light of the small net foreign debt position, but the size of the gross stocks and the prevalence of MFIs' positions in the UK's external balance sheet carries some concentration risk and the possibility of maturity mismatches turning sour. However, the recent crisis has been a natural experiment to test the external resilience of the UK, and apart from the more widely observed process of cross-border financial retrenchment and balance sheet shrinkage, the UK has not displayed any major weaknesses that would be associated with a balance of payments crisis.

Looking ahead, one crucial determinant of the UK's external credit risk will be whether UK domestic sectors manage to reduce their reliance on net foreign lending. Available evidence currently points to this kind of rebalancing being likely to occur in 2011 and 2012, as the European Commission's and other institutions' recent forecasts show. The general shift towards greater saving in the UK economy constitutes a much-needed correction of a long-standing imbalance, as other chapters in this book also underline. While on the fiscal front the UK is still a considerable way from having achieved debt stabilization, at least the shift to greater saving in the UK's private sector should be sufficient to finance net government borrowing requirements by 2012, thereby taking further strain off the overall moderate external credit risk of the UK economy.

Notes

1 Disclaimer: The views expressed in this chapter are those of the author and do not necessarily reflect those of the European Commission. The author gratefully acknowledges valuable comments on earlier versions of this paper received from Gabriele Giudice and Reinhard Felke.
2 There are other useful ways to characterize the current account's economic significance over and above the statistical definition, but for the purpose of this chapter the above aspects are most useful.
3 All data taken from UK Office of National Statistics unless indicated otherwise. All UK balance of payments data up to and including 2009 based on 2010 *Pink Book* (June 2010), with subsequent (partial) data for 2010 based on Balance of Payments First Releases.
4 For an analysis of the impact of the UK's self-sufficiency in oil on public finances, see Scerri and Reut 2009.
5 Source: Eurostat; own calculations. Trade intensity = (services exports + services imports)/GDP (in volumes).
6 Valuation issues concerning the UK's international investment position are addressed later on in this chapter.
7 See, for instance, Obstfeld and Rogoff (1996). Strictly speaking, net external borrowing (or lending) would include net capital transactions with the rest of the world as well as the current account balance, but the former is comparatively small and stable at £3.5 billion a year.
8 Source: Eurostat. Throughout this chapter, a negative net IIP figure indicates a net foreign liabilities position, although on occasion the absolute value of either a net asset or liability position will be referred to, without sign.
9 Office for National Statistics 2010: 6.
10 The overall expansion is to a significant extent due to the inclusion of derivatives holdings in the 2010 Pink Book, data for which only reach back to 2006. Netting out derivatives positions still results in a doubling of the UK's balance sheet between 1998 and 2008.
11 See Whittard and Khan 2010.

12 In essence, this is similar to the 'dark matter' explanation for the USA's net income surplus. For an exposition of this theory, see e.g. Eichengreen 2006.

13 Source: Office for National Statistics data, authors' calculations.

14 The limited data available for derivatives complicates their analysis somewhat, and hence they are given comparatively little attention in this chapter. However, the estimated growth of cross-border derivatives positions may be of considerable importance for the UK's systemic risk, and further research is needed in this area.

15 Of course, the under-recording of direct investment through the book value approach is a general statistical problem in the balance of payments, which affects both UK assets and liabilities. However, given the UK's net direct investment surplus, a revaluation to fair value would be bound to be positive for the overall net IIP.

16 This chapter has not elaborated on the UK's weak net trade response to the sterling depreciation in 2008, due to space constraints and the difficulty in establishing a plausible counterfactual. However, the overall impression is that UK exporters have acted as price takers in the international marketplace and, by keeping their foreign currency prices fairly steady following the depreciation, have earned a greater sterling profit following the depreciation. The parallel rise in UK export and import price deflators in 2008 and 2009 underscores this. Other explanations for this pricing behaviour would be imperfect competition amongst UK exporters, high menu costs, the expectation of the depreciation being only temporary, or large pricing delays.

17 Source: Bank of England data, author's calculations. It should not be surprising that there is little aggregate currency mismatch in the UK banking system, as even naked overnight FX positions are severely restricted.

18 Bonds and notes, for which the UK is also a net debtor, are harder to classify by maturity using balance of payment data.

19 Author's calculation using Eurostat data for 2009.

20 European Commission 2011.

References

Astley, M., J. Giese, M. Hume and C. Kubelec (2009) 'Global imbalances and the financial crisis', *Bank of England Quarterly Bulletin*, Q3.

Astley, M. and J. Smith (2009) 'Interpreting recent movements in sterling', *Bank of England Quarterly Bulletin*, Q3.

Calvo, G., A. Izquierdo and L. Mejia (2008) 'Systemic sudden stops: The relevance of balance-sheet effects and financial integration', *NBER Working Paper* No. 14026, May.

Devereux, M. and A. Sutherland (2009) 'Valuation effects and the dynamics of net external assets', *NBER Working Paper* No. 14794, March.

Eichengreen, B. (2006) 'Global imbalances: the new economy, the dark matter, the savvy investor, and the standard analysis', *The Journal of Policy Modelling*, Vol. 28, Issue 6, September: 645–52.

European Commission (2011) 'European economic forecasts – Spring 2011', *European Economy* No. 2, May.

Nickell, S. (2006) 'The UK current account deficit and all that', Bank of England, speech given on 25 April.

Obstfeld, M. and K. Rogoff (1996) *Foundations of International Macroeconomics*, MIT Press.

Office of National Statistics (2010) *United Kingdom Balance of Payments – Pink Book 2010*, Palgrave Macmillan.

Scerri, K. and A. Reut (2009) 'UK public finances and oil prices: tax bonanza from black gold?', *ECFIN Country Focus*, Vol. VI, Issue 8, European Commission: Brussels, ec.europa.eu/economy_finance/publications/publication15853_en.pdf.

Senior, S. and R. Westwood (2001) 'The external balance sheet of the United Kingdom: implications for financial stability?' *Bank of England Quarterly Bulletin*, Winter.

Whittard, D. and J. Khan (2010) 'The UK's International Investment Position', *Economic & Labour Market Review*, UK Office of National Statistics, Vol. 4, No. 6, June.

6 Long-term effects of fiscal policy on the size and distribution of the pie in the UK

Xavi Ramos and Oriol Roca-Sagales

Introduction

Fiscal policy has traditionally been considered an effective instrument to smooth cyclical behaviour and to ameliorate inequality through redistribution. Yet, we know relatively little about the macroeconomic effects of distinct fiscal policies. Moreover, since the pro-growth effects resulting from a reduction in public expenditure found by Giavazzi and Pagano (1990, 1996), referred to in the literature as 'non-Keynesian effects', there is no consensus among economists as to the magnitude and even sign of these effects (Capet 2004; Perotti 2005).[1]

Little is also known about the distributional effects of overall government spending and taxation, with the notable exception of the redistributive effects of (direct) taxes and (monetary and in-kind) benefits, which do receive systematic attention, e.g. by the Office for National Statistics,[2] ever since the contributions by LeGrand (1982) and Goodin and LeGrand (1987), and have been underlined as one of the forces shaping the distribution of income over the 20th century (Atkinson 1999).

In this paper we present new evidence on the long-term effects of fiscal policy on gross domestic product (GDP) and inequality in the UK, the European country for which we have found the longest consistent time series on income inequality. Besides studying the effects of overall government spending and taxes, we also look at the effects of government spending components (i.e. current spending and public investment) and of the two types of tax: direct (on income) and indirect (on consumption). Thence, unlike previous studies, we are not only concerned about efficiency but also about equity, i.e. we study the effects of fiscal policy on the size and the distribution of the pie in the UK.

Recent contributions evaluate the macroeconomic effects of fiscal policy by means of vector autoregressive models (VAR), econometric techniques typically employed to assess the effects of monetary policy (Christiano *et al.* 1999, 2005). However, most of these studies refer to the USA and look at overall government spending and taxes (Perotti 2005 provides a survey of the literature). Moreover, none of the studies pays any attention to distributive issues. Yet, inclusion of income inequality is pertinent for at least two reasons. First, as stated in the opening sentence, fiscal policy is supposed to correct inequalities. Thus the inclusion of income inequality in the empirical model allows us to investigate whether fiscal policy is indeed achieving such a goal, or what fiscal policy instruments are contributing towards its achievement. Second, income inequality and economic growth determine each other. On the one hand, since the seminal contribution by Kuznets (1955) we have solid economic arguments to believe that growth shapes the distribution of income. On the other hand, a growing body of theoretical literature that originated in the early 1990s has suggested mechanisms through which income inequality may affect growth positively (see Bénabou 1996; Perotti 1996). However, empirical studies typically ignore such endogeneity and investigate only one side of the relationship.[3] Our empirical strategy is based on VARs, which permits investigation of the long-term relationship between income inequality and growth, allowing for feedback effects (i.e. where both variables are endogenous).

Our findings suggest that the long-term impact on GDP of increasing public spending and taxes is negative, and especially strong in the case of current expenditure. That is, tax cuts increase output, but increasing public spending harms output. We also find significant distributional effects associated with fiscal policies, indicating that an increase in public spending reduces inequality while a rise in indirect taxes increases income inequality. In short, our findings reflect the standard efficiency-equity trade-off: the smaller the size of the government the larger the size of the pie, but the less equally distributed. The only fiscal policy that may break this trade-off is indirect taxation, since a cut in indirect tax reduces inequality without a cost in terms of output.

The paper is organized as follows. Section 2 describes the data, while methodological issues, such as the identification strategy and model specification are explained in section 3. The estimated effects of government spending and taxes on output are presented in section 4. This section also includes the disaggregated analysis of the long-term effects of the two types of government spending and the two types of taxes. Distributional effects as well as the effects of inequality on growth are presented in section 5. Several robustness checks are presented in section 6, while section 7 provides a summary of findings and some concluding remarks.

Section 2: data

We use annual data for 1970–2007. The macroeconomic series are obtained from Eurostat (European Commission 2007) and expressed in real terms (millions of euros in 2000).[4] In addition to output (Y) we consider two public-spending categories covering about 89% of overall public expenditure (excluding interest payments) in the last decade, and two types of taxes covering about 91% of the total revenue. On the expenditure side, we consider current public expenditure (GC, expenditure on goods and services and current transfers) and public investment (GFBC), which represent about 32.8% and 1.6% of GDP, respectively, in the last decade. On the revenue side we distinguish between direct tax revenue (TD, from taxes on income and wealth, and payroll tax) and indirect tax revenues (TIND, from taxes on output and imports), which amount to 24% and 12.9% of GDP, respectively.

High-quality time-series on income inequality are not available for most European Union (EU) or Organisation for Economic Co-operation and Development (OECD) countries, the Institute for Fiscal Studies (IFS) series we use being a notable exception. Usually long time series face many problems, as there are many methodological issues one should resolve before arriving at an inequality estimate: definition of recipient unit, income concept, coverage, type of dataset, etc.[5] Also, and importantly, the inequality index reported is often not satisfactory (i.e. does not satisfy certain standard properties).[6] All these difficulties might have precluded studies on the effects of fiscal policy from taking due account of such relevant variables (see section 5).

Our measure of income inequality (I) is the Gini coefficient, obtained from the IFS files (Brewer *et al.* 2007).[7] Since inequality indices entail different value judgements on income differences at the tails of the distribution (Lambert 2001; Cowell 1995, 2000), which lead to different inequality orderings, we also employ another two inequality indices: the Mean Log Deviation (MLD) and the 90/10 percentile ratio—section 6 briefly presents the results. The income measure used to estimate inequality is the household disposable equivalent income, which derives from the Family Expenditure Survey for the period 1970–93 and from the Family Resources Survey for 1994–2007.[8]

Table 6.1 shows the evolution of relevant fiscal variables over the sample period. Current public expenditure represents the bulk of total expenditure and also tends to increase its relative weight, while public investment experiences a drastic reduction during the sample period. On the revenue side, the relative weight of both direct and indirect taxes is rather stable—see Clark and Dilnot (2002) for a complete description of the evolution of public spending and taxation in the UK.

Table 6.1 Fiscal data 1970–2007*

	1970	1980	1990	2000	2007	1998–2007 average
						Share
Public expenditure	31.1	35.5	33.9	32.4	36.0	34.4	100.0
Current expenditure	26.4	32.9	31.6	31.1	34.2	32.8	95.3
Public investment	4.7	2.6	2.3	1.3	1.8	1.6	4.7
Tax revenue	36.9	36.0	36.0	37.5	37.4	36.9	100.0
Direct taxes	22.7	23.1	24.1	24.2	24.9	24.0	65.0
Indirect taxes	14.2	12.9	11.9	13.3	12.5	12.9	35.0

Note: * Figures expressed as percentage of GDP.
Source: Eurostat

Income inequality increased substantially over the sample period, mostly due to the dramatic increase experienced in the 1980s—between 1977 and 1990 the Gini coefficient increased by 10 percentage points. Atkinson (1999) attributes this steep rise to the increase in earnings dispersion, the decline in the number of families with incomes from work—resulting from the rise in unemployment, ageing of the population and decline in labour force partici-pation—and to the reduced redistributional contribution of the government budget in the second half of the 1980s. Since the early 1990s, the changes in income inequality have been smoother, showing a timid increase over the second half of the 1990s, and a soft decrease since 2000 (see Figure 6.1).

Section 3: methodological issues

VAR models are particularly appropriate to estimate the medium- and long-term impact of public policy for at least three reasons. First, they take due account of the dynamic feedback between variables as well as their effect on other variables both in the short and long term. This is of primary impor-tance when the delay between the policy change (e.g. raising taxes or cutting public investment) and its implementation and posterior impact is not negli-gible, as is usually the case with fiscal policy. Moreover, the short- and long-term effects may differ in magnitude and sign. Second, VAR models are especially suitable when the variables of interest are endogenous, as is the case at hand, where output, public expenditure, tax revenue and inequality are inter-related. Finally, VAR models are not too demanding on the data, which has surely contributed to the recent proliferation of empirical research on the macro-economic effects of fiscal policy (Capet 2004; Kamps 2005; Marcellino 2006; Perotti 2004, 2005).

Previous studies have considered public expenditure and tax revenue as a whole, yet the distinct components of these two aggregates are likely to have different effects on output and inequality. For instance, public current spending might have large short-term effects while public investment may have a larger bearing in the longer run. Also, direct and indirect taxes influence inequality differently since they differ in terms of tax level and progressivity, which are the two elements that determine the redistributive effect (Lambert 2001). Unlike most previous studies, we employ data on the main two components of public spending and tax revenue, and thus are able to disentangle the effect of such components, which may operate in opposite directions. The inclusion of an inequality measure in the VAR specification allows the joint analysis of macroeconomic and distributive effects of fiscal policy, which constitutes a novel feature of our study.

Our estimates of the effects of fiscal policies are based on the impulse response functions, which result from the VAR estimates. We consider the effects on the growth rate of output and income inequality of a one-off 1-percentage-point shock in the growth rate of the fiscal policy variable. The impulse response functions converge rapidly—within the first five years, and therefore

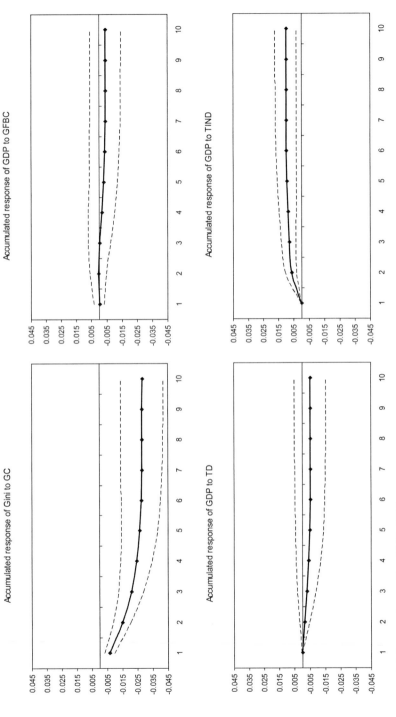

Figure 6.1 Income inequality, 1970–2007
Note: * Gini coefficient expressed in percentage.
Source: IFS files

the long-term effect of fiscal policy on output and income inequality growth is zero. In levels, however, such shocks bring about permanent effects on both output and inequality, since they cause permanent changes in the levels of the fiscal variables.

We start by determining the order of integration of the variables. The unit root results are based on the ADF (Augmented Dickey-Fuller) test, selecting the optimal number of lags according to the BIC (Bayesian Information Criterion) test and including deterministic components when statistically significant. Test results suggest that all of the series are non-stationary in log-levels and stationary in first differences of log-levels. We therefore proceed to estimate a VAR model in first differences of log-levels.

Our VAR specification results from a compromise between parsimony and avoiding omitted variable bias. On the one hand, we would like to include all relevant variables in a large unconstrained VAR, and report the implied system of dynamic response functions. The drawback of such a strategy is that it requires estimating a large number of parameters simultaneously. On the other hand, a specification with too few variables suffers from omitted variable bias. In the light of these considerations, we choose an intermediate strategy and consider four different models. The benchmark specification is the most parsimonious one and includes GDP (Y), overall government purchases (G = GC+GFBC), overall tax revenues (T = TD+TIND), and the Gini coefficient (I). The second model disaggregates revenue into direct and indirect taxes (G, Y, I, TD, TIND); the third model disaggregates public expenditure into current expenditure and public investment (GC, GFBC, Y, I, T); and finally, the last model includes both fiscal variables disaggregated (GC, GFBC, Y, I, TD, TIND).

In section 2, we point out that several factors may be responsible for the income inequality increase over the sample period. Since the effects of these determinants may confound the effects of fiscal policies, we have included them in the VAR models. However, they are found not statistically significant and their absence has no bearing on the results. Thus, they are finally omitted from the VAR models presented in section 4.

The baseline VAR specification in its reduced form can be written as

$$X_t = B(L)X_{t-1} + U_t \qquad (1)$$

where X_t is the vector of endogenous variables (GC$_t$, GFBC$_t$, Y$_t$, I$_t$, TD$_t$, TIND$_t$); B_i is the matrix of coefficients for the i-th lag; and U_t is the vector containing the reduced form residuals, which in general will have non-zero correlations. Equation (1) is estimated by ordinary least squares (OLS).

The reduced form residuals have little economic significance in that they are linear combinations of structural shocks. Thus, Var(U) is in general not diagonal and the identification of the structural components becomes necessary. The innovation model can be written as

$$A U t = V t \qquad (2)$$

where V_t is the vector of the structural orthogonal shocks and $E(V_t V'_t) = D$, D being diagonal. The system has been identified by using the Choleski decomposition with the ordering (GC, GFBC, Y, I, TD and TIND), as Equation (3) shows:

$$U_t^{GC} = V_t^{GC}$$
$$U_t^{GFBC} = a_{2,1} U_t^{GC} + V_t^{GFBC}$$
$$U_t^{Y} = a_{3,1} U_t^{GC} + a_{3,2} U_t^{GFBC} + V_t^{Y}$$
$$U_t^{I} = a_{4,1} U_t^{GC} + a_{4,2} U_t^{GFBC} + a_{4,3} U_t^{Y} + V_t^{I} \qquad (3)$$
$$U_t^{TD} = a_{5,1} U_t^{GC} + a_{5,2} U_t^{GFBC} + a_{5,3} U_t^{Y} + a_{5,4} U_t^{I} + V_t^{TD}$$
$$U_t^{TIND} = a_{6,1} U_t^{GC} + a_{6_2} U_t^{GFBC} + a_{6,3} U_t^{Y} + a_{6,4} U_t^{I} + a_{6,5} U_t^{TD}$$
$$\qquad + V_t^{TIND}$$

For the selection of the specifications of the VAR models, we use the AIC (Akaike Information Criterion), BIC and maximum likelihood ratio tests. The VAR specification has several dimensions: the order of the VAR specification, the specification of the deterministic components, and the consideration of possible structural breaks. Test results suggest a first order VAR model with a linear constant and no trend for the four specifications we consider. Furthermore, we find no evidence of structural breaks during the period analysed.[9] We also perform specification tests to check whether model residuals suffer from first-order autocorrelation, heteroscedasticity or non-normality. Test results, presented in Table 6.2, indicate that our models do not seem to have specification problems: at the 5% significance level there are no signs of residual autocorrelation, heteroscedasticity and non-normality.

In order to accommodate the contemporaneous correlations among shocks in the different variables we follow the standard procedure in the literature and consider the Cholesky decomposition of the variance-covariance matrix of the estimated residuals (see, for example, Kamps 2005; Fatás and Mihov 2001; Favero 2002). In order to determine the variable ordering used to identify our central case results, we turn to economic rationale and to previous evidence. However, as the ordering of the variables may affect the results, we also report the range of results for all alternative orderings.

In particular, for our benchmark model we assume that: (i) public spending does not react contemporaneously to shocks to the other variables in the system; (ii) output is affected contemporaneously by shocks to public spending, but does not react contemporaneously to shocks to inequality or taxation; (iii) inequality is affected contemporaneously by shocks to both public spending and output, but does not react contemporaneously to shocks to taxation; and finally (iv) tax revenue is affected contemporaneously by shocks to all other variables in the system.

Table 6.2 Specification tests (p-values)[1]

	Model 1 (G,Y,I,T)	Model 2 (GC,GFBC, Y,I,T)	Model 3 (G,Y,I,TD, TIND)	Model 4 (GC,GFBC,Y, I,TD,TIND)
Autocorrelation[2]	0.153	0.173	0.134	0.161
Heteroscedasticity[3]	0.304	0.587	0.863	0.722
Normality[4]	0.245	0.075	0.594	0.239

Notes:
1   Specification tests are based on the residuals from the estimation of unrestricted VAR (1).
2   Multivariate Box-Pierce/Ljung-Box Q-statistics for residual serial correlation (Lütkepohl 1991). Under the null of no serial correlation up to lag $h = 1$, the test statistics are approximately distributed χ^2 with $[k^2(h - p)]$ degrees of freedom, where p is the VAR order and k the number of parameters to estimate.
3   Multivariate extension of White's (1980) heteroscedasticity test (Doornik 1996). Under the null of homoscedastic residuals the test statistic is asymptotically distributed χ^2 with $[10(8p+2)]$ degrees of freedom.
4   Jarque-Bera normality test (Lütkepohl 1991). Under the null of normally distributed residuals the test statistic is asymptotically distributed χ^2 with two degrees of freedom.

This set of assumptions on the contemporaneous relationship between the variables presumes that demand effects dominate, which justifies the contemporary effect of public spending on output. However, the reverse is not plausible since, unlike tax revenue, government spending—and especially public investment—is largely unrelated to the business cycle. Because of the large decision and implementation lags caused by the budgetary process, decisions on public spending are undertaken before the public sector obtains information about the actual performance of the economy.

Changes in public spending may have an immediate impact on individuals' income, and thence on the distribution of income, even more so if such changes concern cash benefits. Arguably, income inequality changes may also have contemporaneous effects on public spending, if only because of means-tested benefits. However, income-conditioned programmes (or social expenditure) account only for a rather limited portion of overall spending.[10]

As suggested above, we also presume a contemporaneous impact of output on tax revenue, which operates through the tax base: in the very short term, changes in tax revenue are due exclusively to changes in the tax base—i.e. output. However, the opposite effect (of revenue on output) occurs only in the longer term: changes in tax revenues do not have contemporaneous effects on output because the former come only through changes in tax rates, and the political process implies substantial delays between consideration and implementation.

Output changes are not usually distributionally neutral, thus affecting income inequality. On the other hand, output is most likely to respond to changes in inequality only in the longer term, since the (relevant) transmission mechanisms identified in the literature—e.g. human capital accumulation with imperfect financial markets, endogenous fiscal policy or the joint education-fertility decision—need their time to operate (Bénabou 1996; Perotti 1996).[11]

As argued above, in the very short term changes in the tax base are the only likely source of changing tax revenue, and the tax base is only likely to change as a result of output or distributional changes. Thus it seems plausible to assume that tax revenue reacts contemporaneously to inequality and output shocks.[12]

The ordering that results from these assumptions, for the central case of the benchmark specification is: public spending, output, inequality and tax revenue. It is worth noting that alternative orderings do not have a major bearing on our results, as the range of results reported in parentheses show—see Table 6.3 and Table 6.6.

As to the ordering of the variables in the disaggregated models 2 to 4, we force the two components of public spending (GC, GFBC) as well as the two types of taxes (TD, TIND) to enter the specification one after the other (i.e. allowing no other variable in between the two). Further to the assumptions made for the benchmark model, we identify the central case of the disaggregated models by means of the following assumptions. On the revenue side, we assume that direct tax revenue does affect contemporaneously indirect tax revenue, but does not react contemporaneously to shocks to the latter. Shocks to direct tax alters disposable income, which in turn may lead to consumption changes, and thus to changes in the revenue from indirect taxation. Hence, the ordering of the tax variables in the central case of models 2 and 4 is (TD, TIND). On the expenditure side we assume that current spending precedes public investment. This assumption reflects the standard view that budgetary decisions on public investment are conditioned by decisions on current spending, while the reverse is not true. As a result, the ordering of the expenditure variables in the central case of models 3 and 4 is (GC, GFBC). Models 2 (G, Y, I, TD, TIND) and 3 (GC, GFBC, Y, I, T) include five variables and allow for (4! × 2 =) 48 possible orderings,[13] which yield the range of results reported in Table 6.3 and Table 6.6. For the central case results of

Table 6.3 GDP long-term elasticities

	Model 1 (G,Y,I,T)	*Model 2* (GC,GFBC,Y, I,T)	*Model 3* (G,Y,I,TD, TIND)	*Model 4* (GC,GFBC,Y, I,TD,TIND)
Public spending	−0.620*		−0.639*	
Current spending		−0.592*		−0.592*
Public investment		−0.009		−0.010
Overall tax revenue	−0.236*	−0.233*		
Direct tax revenue			−0.156	−0.168
Indirect tax revenue			−0.096	−0.080

Note:
* Indicates that 0 is outside the region between the two one-standard-error bands at 10 years horizon.

the most disaggregated model 4 the order of the variables is (GC, GFBC, Y, I, TD, TIND), and the range of results is obtained from (4! $\times$ 2 $\times$ 2 =) 96 alternative ordinations.

Section 4: output effects of fiscal policy

This section presents estimated output elasticities derived from the accumulated impulse response functions that obtains from the Choleski decomposition. These elasticities measure the long-term accumulated effect on output of a 1-percentage-point initial shock on the fiscal variable under consideration. To assess the comparative effects of different fiscal shocks we also report marginal products.

A priori, the effect on output of a public spending shock is uncertain since distinct theoretical models provide arguments that go in either direction. Standard neoclassical models with non-distortionary lump-sum taxation (Baxter and King 1993), as well as neoKeynesian models (Linnemann and Schabert 2003), predict a positive effect of government spending. However, the neoclassical model predicts a fall in output with sufficient tax distortions. Precisely because of such a distortionary effect of taxes, output is expected to fall as a result of a tax increase.

As is common practice in the empirical VAR literature, throughout the paper, we consider as 'statistically significant' the estimates for which an error band of one standard deviation—identified by the 16th and the 84th percentiles—does not include zero. As pointed out by Sims and Zha (1999), 68% confidence intervals are often more useful than 95% ones, since they provide a more precise estimate of the true coverage probability.

The elasticities reported in Table 6.3 suggest that expansionary fiscal policy has a negative long-term effect on output. Note also that estimated elasticities are very robust across orthogonalization strategies. Our estimates are consistent with previous UK evidence given in Perotti (2005). Tax elasticities are also in line with previous evidence for the largest euro area countries (Marcellino 2006) and the USA (Blanchard and Perotti 2002). However, our negative public spending elasticity estimates for the UK are in contrast with the positive elasticities reported in these two studies for Germany, France, Italy, Spain and the USA.

The disaggregated analysis by components reveals the differential response of output to shocks to the different expenditure components and types of taxes. On the expenditure side, the public investment elasticity of output is much smaller than the current public spending elasticity and not statistically significant, as shown in Table 6.3 and the accumulated response functions of Figure 6.2. Notice that the effect of public capital on GDP is usually found to be not significant (Perotti 2004; Kamps 2005).

The figure displays the accumulated response to one SD (standard deviation) innovation and one SE (standard error) band on the two sides of the response.

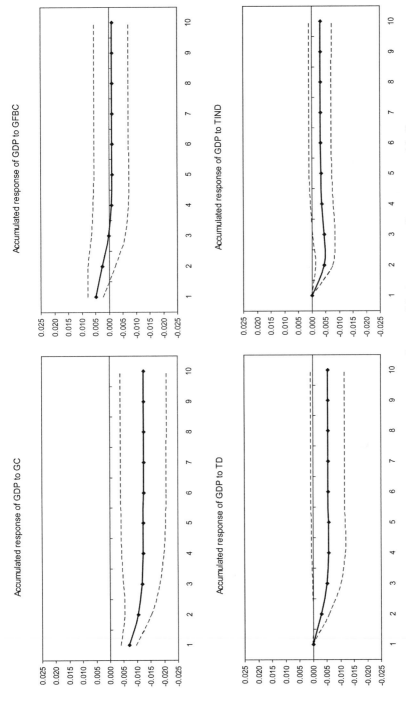

Accumulated response of GDP to GC

Accumulated response of GDP to GFBC

Accumulated response of GDP to TD

Accumulated response of GDP to TIND

Figure 6.2 Accumulated GDP responses to shocks to current expenditure, public investment, direct taxes and indirect taxes

On the revenue side, the effect of shocks to direct and indirect taxes cannot be estimated with precision, as the standard deviation bands of Figure 6.2 show. Notwithstanding this, it is worth noting that the estimated negative direct tax elasticities are statistically significant at the 40% level—instead of the 32% level that corresponds to one standard deviation band. Accordingly, shocks to indirect taxation seem to involve no effects on economic activity, while shocks to direct taxation may be contractionary in the long term, although estimates are rather imprecise.

Despite the poor precision of the estimate of some disaggregated variables, it is worth noting that point estimates are robust to model specification. Overall, our findings suggest that output effects of fiscal policies are consistent with a neoclassical model with distorting taxes.

Marginal products

Table 6.4 presents marginal products, calculated in the conventional manner from the elasticities and the ratios of the fiscal variables to GDP. We use average ratios for the last 10 years of the sample period, which allows us to interpret the marginal products as the accumulated long-term effects of policies implemented at the end of the sample period, and avoids contamination by business cycle effects. The marginal products are calculated considering the accumulated response of output to an initial shock in the fiscal variables, as in Blanchard and Perotti (2002) and Mountford and Uhlig (2005).

Marginal products clearly illustrate the significant contractionary effects resulting from an increase in public expenditure: a shock in expenditure of €1 reduces output in the long term by nearly €2. These effects dominate in the case of an increase in taxation, indicating that output decreases significantly as a result of increases in tax revenue.

Marginal products allow us to identify the impact of budget-neutral fiscal policies, i.e. simultaneous increases in expenditure and tax revenue. According

Table 6.4 GDP marginal products

	Model 1 (G,Y,I,T)	Model 2 (GC,GFBC, Y,I,T)	Model 3 (G,Y,I,TD, TIND)	Model 4 (GC,GFBC,Y, I,TD,TIND)
Public spending	−1.80*	−1.86*		
Current spending			−1.80*	−1.80*
Public investment			−0.56	−0.63
Overall tax revenue	−0.64*		−0.63*	
Direct tax revenue		−0.65		−0.74
Indirect tax revenue		−0.70		−0.62

Note:
* Indicates that the underlying elasticity is statistically significant using one standard error bands.

to the estimates of the more aggregated model 1, the effect on output of such policies is always negative irrespective of the type of policy implemented, but especially so when current expenditure is used (see model 3). Thus, the results presented in this section provide new empirical evidence for the UK that suggest negative impacts of increasing the size of the public budget.

It is worth noting the consistency of the estimates obtained in the four models. Marginal products are robust across models, but also the effects of overall expenditure and tax obtained with more aggregated models 1 to 3 are very close to those that would obtain by adding the marginal products of their components in the most disaggregated model 4.

Weighted marginal products

Marginal products of the spending and revenue components presented in Table 6.4 do not take due account of the relative importance of each component within overall spending or tax revenue. Table 6.5 reports the impact (in euros) on output of a €1 shock to fiscal revenue or spending, distributed according to the relative shares of spending and revenue components.[14] The weighted marginal product of current spending accounts for nearly the entire impact of a €1 shock to overall public spending on output. Such a large contribution of current spending results from its larger weight in overall spending as well as its much larger (unweighted) impact. As regards tax revenue, the weighted impact of direct tax revenue accounts for most (two-thirds) of the impact of a €1 shock to overall tax revenue on output. Now the larger share of direct tax revenue is mostly responsible for the larger weighted effect of this type of tax.

The contribution of direct tax revenue to overall tax revenue should be taken with caution since the underlying elasticity is only statistically significant with 0.85 standard error bands. However, notice that estimated impacts are consistent, since weighted marginal products of overall public spending and overall tax

Table 6.5 Weighted GDP marginal products

	Model 1 (G,Y,I,T)	Model 2 (GC,GFBC, Y,I,T)	Model 3 (G,Y,I,TD, TIND)	Model 4 (GC,GFBC,Y, I,TD,TIND)
Public spending	−1.80*	−1.86*	−1.75	−1.75
Current spending			−1.72*	−1.72*
Public investment			−0.03	−0.03
Overall tax revenue	−0.64*	−0.68	−0.63*	−0.67
Direct tax revenue		−0.42		−0.46
Indirect tax revenue		−0.26		−0.22

Note:
* Indicates that the underlying elasticity is statistically significant using one standard error bands. Figures in *italics* are not directly estimated but a mere addition of the two components. Therefore, the statistical significance of these coefficients cannot be assessed.

revenue (in bold in Table 6.5) do not differ much across models, i.e. effects on aggregate variables do not change when computed using their components.

Section 5: distributional effects of fiscal policy

As pointed out in the introduction, our analysis goes beyond mean output effects and also looks at distributive effects, which is one of our contributions. The inclusion of income inequality in our VAR models allows us to estimate the long-term distributional effects of fiscal policy—together with the output effects. As Table 6.6 shows, public expenditure has a sizeable negative and significant effect on income inequality, i.e. it reduces inequality. However, the effect of public investment is small in size and not statistically significant.

The inequality effect of taxes is much smaller and positive—i.e. the elasticity of inequality with respect to tax revenue is positive. As expected, point estimates of direct and indirect taxation yield opposite effects on inequality—see Figure 6.3. However, the effect of direct taxation is not statistically significant, which may reflect the rather flat structure that results from rather proportional social security contributions and more progressive income tax. With a progressive tax, increases in direct tax revenue—be it through increases in the tax base, in the overall average tax rate, or in the progression of the tax structure—would yield a larger redistributive effect, and thus lower inequality (Lambert 2001).

Notwithstanding this, the positive effect of indirect tax revenues cannot be attributed to the direct impact of a regressive tax on income since value-added tax (VAT), the largest component of indirect tax revenue, does not directly alter disposable income, which is the income definition we use to measure inequality (see section 2).[15] The positive long-term elasticity is consistent with a situation where the elasticity of savings with respect to indirect taxation is larger for poorer than for richer individuals.[16] In a world where individuals either consume or save, when as a result of a tax increase consumption becomes more expensive relative to savings, people tend to save more, as long as both

Table 6.6 Inequality elasticities

	Model 1 (G,Y,I,T)	Model 2 (GC,GFBC, Y,I,T)	Model 3 (G,Y,I,TD, TIND)	Model 4 (GC,GFBC,Y, I,TD,TIND)
Public spending	−1.190*		−1.188*	
Current spending		−1.349*		−1.335*
Public investment		−0.047		−0.041
Overall tax revenue	0.210	0.136		
Direct tax revenue			−0.091	−0.162
Indirect tax revenue			0.258*	0.237*

Note:
* Indicates that 0 is outside the region between the two one-standard error bands at 10 year horizon.

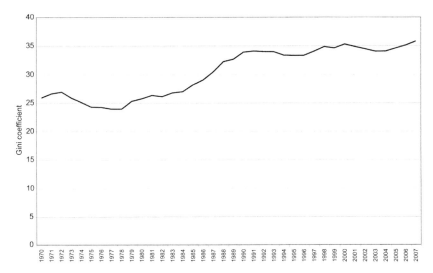

Figure 6.3 Accumulated inequality responses to shocks to current expenditure, public investment, direct taxes and indirect taxes

options are normal goods. Now, assuming that the elasticity of savings with respect to indirect taxation is larger for poorer than for richer individuals, a positive shock to indirect taxation implies a larger savings increase for the rich relative to the poor, which in turn and in the longer term results in a larger income inequality—that is, provided there is a positive relationship between current savings and future income.

In sum, our findings are consistent with previous evidence, which focuses on the effects of public spending or taxes and benefits on household incomes (Wolff and Zacharias 2007; Office for National Statistics 2007). Notwithstanding this, one should bear in mind that these studies differ not only in important methodological aspects, such as the income definition or the unit of analysis, but also in their scope—covering only some taxes and cash and in-kind benefits. Finally, note that estimated elasticities are robust to the orthogonalization strategy and across model specification.

Figure 6.3 displays the accumulated response to one S.D. innovation and one S.E. band on the two sides of the response.

The inclusion of income inequality in our VAR models also allows us to investigate the relationship between income inequality and output. Over the last two decades a number of influential studies have argued rather convincingly about the importance of considering the impact that rising inequality may have on output, suggesting that inequality may have detrimental effects on output due to, for instance, financial market imperfections hindering human capital accumulation or more redistributive policies that result from inequality increases. Our findings do not provide empirical support to such hypotheses. Although point estimates of the output elasticity with respect to inequality and the inequality elasticity with respect to output have the expected (negative and positive) sign, they are statistically insignificant. Thus, shocks to output do not affect inequality in the long term and, vice versa, shocks to inequality have no long-term bearing on output.

Section 6: sensitivity analyses

This section reports the results from three sensitivity analyses performed to check the robustness of our main results. First, we exclude inequality from the analysis. Second, we employ different inequality indices, and third, we change the definitions of the income variable over which inequality is measured to adjust for housing costs. Recall that in addition to these three robustness checks, in previous sections we have also checked that our main results are robust to changes in the ordering of the variables in the VAR models, and to introducing a structural break in 1980, as is done in related literature.

Sensitivity to excluding inequality in the central case

Previous studies do not take into account inequality when computing the long-term effect of fiscal policy on output. As argued above, since long-term elasticities incorporate feedback effects, inequality may magnify or mitigate some of the effects of other variables that accumulate into the estimated overall long-term impact on output.

Thus, we would expect estimated long-term impacts on output to differ, depending on the inclusion or exclusion of inequality from the analysis. However, it is difficult to predict ex-ante the direction of change. Notwithstanding that, Table 6.7 shows that long-term elasticities are rather insensitive to the inclusion of inequality.

Sensitivity to using other income-inequality indices rather than the Gini coefficient

Throughout the paper we use the Gini coefficient to measure income inequality. Since inequality indices entail different value judgements on income differences at the tails of the distribution (Lambert 2001; Cowell 1995, 2000), which in turn may lead to different inequality orderings, next we check if estimated long-term effects on output are robust to different inequality indices: the MLD and the 90/10 percentile ratio, which do not satisfy the most basic properties that good measures are supposed to fulfil (Amiel and Cowell 1992), but are often used in macro empirical research.

As the estimated long-term elasticities reported in Table 6.8 show, output effects are robust to different inequality measures. Estimates using different inequality indices have the same sign and very similar size, and their statistical significance does not change either.

Table 6.7 GDP long-term elasticities, without (above) and with (below) the inequality variable

	Model 1 (G,Y,I,T)	Model 2 (GC,GFBC, Y,I,T)	Model 3 (G,Y,I,TD, TIND)	Model 4 (GC,GFBC,Y, I,TD,TIND)
Public spending	−0.681* −0.620*		−0.693* −0.639*	
Current spending		−0.636* −0.592*		−0.636* −0.592*
Public investment		−0.010 −0.009		−0.009 −0.010
Overall tax revenue	−0.216* −0.236*	−0.222* −0.233*		
Direct tax revenue			−0.159 −0.156	−0.170 −0.168
Indirect tax revenue			−0.075 −0.096	−0.069 −0.080

Note:
* Indicates that 0 is outside the region between the two one-standard error bands at 10 year horizon.

Sensitivity to income inequality when income is measured after housing costs

Since the share of the family budget that goes to pay for housing-related expenditures (rent, bills, etc.) is substantial and not the same across the income distribution, studies typically report main results before and after housing costs have been deducted (Brewer *et al.* 2007, and references cited therein). We have also used income definitions with and without housing costs and have found robust output and inequality effects, as Table 6.9 and Table 6.10 show. All estimated elasticities have the same sign and very similar size, and their statistical significance does not change either.

Section 7: conclusions

Distributional aspects of economic policies have traditionally been assessed through their impact on economic growth. However, it is widely accepted by now that economic growth alone does not shape the income distribution, and that qualitative aspects of economic growth are probably more important than economic growth *per se*. Similarly, when it comes to fiscal policy, composition—as well as size—matters for economic growth and income inequality. That is, the composition of public expenditure between, say, public investment and current consumption, as well as the mix of direct and indirect taxes used to raise revenue, are central to determining the impact of public policy on growth and income distribution.

Notwithstanding this, most macroeconomic studies of fiscal (and monetary) policy constantly overlook the distributional effects, and do not offer a

Table 6.8 Robustness of GDP long-term elasticities to different inequality indices (Gini, MLD, 90/10 ratio)

	Model 1 (G,Y,I,T)	Model 2 (GC,GFBC, Y,I,T)	Model 3 (G,Y,I,TD, TIND)	Model 4 (GC,GFBC,Y, I,TD,TIND)
Public spending				
Gini coefficient	−0.620*		−0.639*	
MLD	−0.656*		−0.669*	
90/10 ratio	−0.641*		−0.653*	
Current spending				
Gini coefficient		−0.592*		−0.592*
MLD		−0.621*		−0.621*
90/10 ratio		−0.612*		−0.612*
Public investment				
Gini coefficient		−0.009		−0.010
MLD		−0.010		−0.009
90/10 ratio		−0.011		−0.011
Overall tax revenue				
Gini coefficient	−0.236*	−0.233*		
MLD	−0.233*	−0.228*		
90/10 ratio	−0.250*	−0.235*		
Direct tax revenue				
Gini coefficient			−0.156	−0.168
MLD			−0.161	−0.170
90/10 ratio			−0.165	−0.171
Indirect tax revenue				
Gini coefficient			−0.096	−0.080
MLD			−0.090	−0.075
90/10 ratio			−0.100	−0.078

Note:
* Indicates that 0 is outside the region between the two one-standard error bands at 10 year horizon.

disaggregated analysis of expenditure and revenue. In contrast to previous work, this chapter provides a joint analysis of the output and distributional long-term effects of fiscal policy in the UK. Moreover, our study explicitly looks at the differential incidence of the various components of fiscal policy, both from the expenditure and the revenue side. Our empirical strategy is based on VAR models, which permit investigating the long-term effects allowing for feedback effects.

Our findings suggest that tax cuts increase output, but increasing public spending harms output. We also find significant distributional effects associated to fiscal policies, indicating that an increase in public spending reduces inequality while an increase in indirect taxes increases income inequality. In short, our findings reflect the standard efficiency-equity trade-off: the smaller the size of the government the larger the size of the pie, but the less equally distributed. The only fiscal policy that may break this trade-off is indirect taxation, since a cut in indirect taxes reduces inequality without harming

Table 6.9 Robustness of GDP long-term elasticities to different definitions of income, income inequality after housing costs

	Model 1 (G,Y,I,T)	Model 2 (GC,GFBC, Y,I,T)	Model 3 (G,Y,I,TD, TIND)	Model 4 (GC,GFBC,Y, I,TD,TIND)
Public spending	−0.652* −0.620*		−0.669* −0.639*	
Current spending		−0.617* −0.592*		−0.615* −0.592*
Public investment		−0.010 −0.009		−0.011 −0.010
Overall tax revenue	−0.223* −0.236*	−0.223* −0.233*		
Direct tax revenue			−0.155 −0.156	−0.166 −0.168
Indirect tax revenue			−0.084 −0.096	−0.072 −0.080

Note:
* Indicates that 0 is outside the region between the two one-standard error bands at 10 year horizon.

Table 6.10 Robustness of inequality long-term elasticities to different definitions of income, income inequality before housing costs

	Model 1 (G,Y,I,T)	Model 2 (GC,GFBC, Y,I,T)	Model 3 (G,Y,I,TD, TIND)	Model 4 (GC,GFBC,Y, I,TD,TIND)
Public spending	−0.997* −1.190*		−0.960* −1.188*	
Current spending		−1.308* −1.349*		−1.261* −1.335*
Public investment		−0.007 −0.047		−0.008 −0.041
Overall tax revenue	0.186 0.210	0.063 0.136		
Direct tax revenue			−0.139 −0.091	−0.235 −0.162
Indirect tax revenue			0.267* 0.258*	0.226* 0.237*

Note:
* Indicates that 0 is outside the region between the two one-standard error bands at 10 year horizon.

output. Our findings on output effects are, broadly speaking, consistent with previous empirical evidence (Perotti 2005; Kamps 2005), while, to the best of our knowledge, the estimated effects on inequality are new.

Sensitivity analyses indicate that our macroeconomic results are robust to the inclusion of income inequality, while both output and inequality effects appear robust to different identifying assumptions on the contemporaneous effects between variables, and to changes in the inequality measure and the definition of income.

From a policy perspective our results have clear implications. According to our estimates, increasing the size of the public sector (i.e. a larger budget) improves the distribution of income at the expense of economic growth. This said, the long-term effects of public investment and direct tax on both output and inequality are found to be statistically insignificant.

Despite and maybe because of the practical relevance of our results it is prudent to conclude with several cautionary notes. First, in this paper we consider only the effects of non-systematic fiscal policies, i.e. policy shocks. The effects of systematic policies could be rather different. Second, we are considering exclusively the effects on output and inequality. It would be important also to consider the effects on other macroeconomic indicators, such as inflation or interest rates. Third, we are implicitly assuming that fiscal policy shocks do not have effects before they are implemented. Finally, we also suppose that non-linear effects of fiscal policies are not relevant. However, this would be problematic in the context of credibility or solvency issues.

Notes

1 Conversely, estimates of the macroeconomic effects of monetary policy have received greater attention in the literature, surely due to the greater availability of high-frequency statistical data, and in this case there exists agreement with respect to the resulting economic impact (Bernanke and Mihov 1998).
2 The Office for National Statistics publishes an annual report on 'The effects of taxes and benefits on household income'. Such analysis was previously part of the economic report 'Economic Trends'. See www.statistics.gov.uk/StatBase/Product. asp?vlnk=10336 for more information.
3 See Acemoglu and Robinson 2002, Galor and Tsiddon 1996, Jha 1996 for studies on the Kuznets hypothesis, and Perotti 1996, Tanninen 1999, Castelló-Climent 2001 for studies on the influence of income distribution on economic growth.
4 The data is available at ec.europa.eu/economy_finance/publications/european_economy/ 2007/statannex0107_en.pdf.
5 Time series on income inequality use various recipient units: households, individuals, income recipients or economically active persons; are based on different income definitions which may include different income sources; are measured before or after tax (and then, what taxes), before or after housing costs; take account of differing needs by using some equivalent scale (and then, what scale), etc. Coverage can be nation-wide, limited to urban or rural areas, or to specific types of agents (e.g. employees, taxpayers), and data may come from surveys or from administrative records, such as social security records or tax files.
6 It is not Lorenz-consistent or, at least, consistent with the Pigou-Dalton principle of transfers.
7 The data is available at www.ifs.org.uk/bns/bn19figs.zip. The coverage of our income inequality series is not uniform over the whole period. Up to 2001 inequality applies only to Great Britain, while after that year inequality is

measured for the whole UK. However, as Table 6.11 below shows, the few income inequality estimates available for Northern Ireland suggest that inequality does not differ much between Britain and Northern Ireland. Moreover, population in Northern Ireland accounts for a very small proportion of the UK population—less than 3%.

Table 6.11 Income inequality in Great Britain and Northern Ireland

	1985	1998/99	1999/00	2000/01
Great Britain	0.30	0.39	0.38	0.39
Northern Ireland	0.32	0.38	0.36	0.39

Source: Data for Great Britain come from the IFS files. 1985 data for Northern Ireland come from Borooah and McGregor 1990, while the other three years come from Hillyard *et al.* 2003. Income inequality measured after housing costs.

8 Household income is rescaled or equivalized to take due account of the different needs of households with different size and composition. The scale factor employed is the 'modified OECD equivalent scale', which assigns weights of 1, 0.5 and 0.3 to the first, remaining adults and children of the household, respectively. Disposable income is measured *after* income tax, employee and self-employed National Insurance contributions, and council tax, and *before* housing costs—taking housing costs into account does not have any bearing on the estimates (see section 6).

9 Introducing a structural break in 1980, as suggested in Perotti (2005), does not alter our main findings.

10 In 2005 income-related benefits amounted to 10.7% of total government expenditure, according to the information provided by the Department for Work and Pensions and the Pre Budget Report.

11 Since our analysis refers to a democratic country, the channel based on the relationship between income distribution and socio-political instability is not considered relevant.

12 Arguably, other assumptions on the contemporaneous effects of the variables are tenable. For instance, it would be reasonable to presume that (direct) taxes contemporaneously affect inequality. However, it is important to underline that alternative orderings—and thus assumptions—do not have a major bearing on our results.

13 The number of alternative orderings is not (5! =) 120 because no variable can be placed between TD and TIND for model 2, or between GC and GFBC for model 3.

14 We use average relative shares over the last 10 years of the sample period, reported in Table 6.1.

15 Our finding of an overall nil effect of the tax system on inequality contradicts at face value the findings systematically reported by analyses of the impact of the tax benefit system on household disposable income performed annually by the Office for National Statistics. The differences, however, are surely due to the different definition of income—we employ income net of direct taxes, while other studies base their conclusions on an income definition that is net of direct *and* indirect taxes—and the time span over which effects are considered—while our concern is on long-run effects, other studies analyse only very short-term (one-year) effects.

16 To the best of our knowledge there is no direct empirical evidence on these elasticities. However, our conjecture is that poorer people's savings are more sensitive to indirect tax increases since they spend a larger share of their budget in basic consumption, whose demand is rather inelastic. Thus, increases in the final price of such goods do not modify consumption but (reduce) savings.

References

Acemoglu, D. and J.A. Robinson (2002) 'The Political Economy of the Kuznets Curve', *Review of Development Economics* 6(2): 183–203.

Amiel, Y. and F.A. Cowell (1992) 'Measurement of Income Inequality: Experimental Test by Questionnaire', *Journal of Public Economics* 47: 3–26.

Atkinson, A.B. (1999) 'The Distribution of Income in the UK and OECD Countries in the Twentieth Century', *Oxford Review of Economic Policy* 15 (4): 56–75.

Baxter, M. and R.G. King (1993) 'Fiscal Policy in General Equilibrium', *American Economic Review* 83(3): 315–34.

Bénabou, R. (1996) 'Inequality and Growth', Working Paper 5658, National Bureau of Economic Reserch.

Bernanke, B. and I. Mihov (1998) 'Measuring Monetary Policy', *Quarterly Journal of Economics* 113: 869–902.

Blanchard, O.J. and R. Perotti (2002) 'An Empirical Characterization of the Dynamic Effects of Changes in Government Spending and Taxes on Output', *Quarterly Journal of Economics* 117: 1329–68.

Borooah, V.K. and P. McGregor (1990) 'The Decomposition of Income Inequality: An Analysis based on the Northern Ireland Family Expenditure Survey for 1985', *Bulletin of Economic Research* 42(4): 265–83.

Brewer, M., A. Goodman, A. Muriel and L. Sibieta (2007) 'Poverty and Inequality in the UK: 2007', IFS Briefing Note No. 73, London: Institute for Fiscal Studies.

Capet, S. (2004) 'The Efficiency of Fiscal Policies: a Survey of the Literature', CEPII, Working Paper No. 2004 – 11.

Castelló-Climent, A. (2001) 'Desigualdad en la distribución de la renta, políticas impositivas y crecimiento económico en los países de la OCDE', *Investigaciones Económicas* XXV(3): 473–514.

Christiano, L., M. Eichenbaum and C. Evans (1999) 'Monetary Policy Shocks: What Have We Learned and to What End?', in John B. Taylor and Michael Woodford (eds), *Handbook of Macroeconomics*, Vol. 1A., Elsevier Science, North Holland, pp. 65–148.

——(2005) 'Nominal Rigidities and the Dynamic Effects of a Shock to Monetary Policy', *Journal of Political Economy* 113: 1–45.

Clark, T. and A.W. Dilnot (2002) 'Long-term Trends in British Taxation and Spending', Briefing Notes 25, June, Institute for Fiscal Studies.

Cowell, F.A. (1995) *Measuring Inequality*, Hemel Hempstead: Harvester Wheatsheaf, 2nd edn.

——(2000) 'Measurement of Inequality', in A.B. Atkinson and F. Bourguignon (eds), *Handbook of Income Distribution*, Amsterdam: Elsevier.

Doornik, J.A. (1996) *Testing for Vector Error Autocorrelation and Heteroscedasticity*, Oxford: Nuffield College, www.doornik.com/research/vectest.pdf.

European Commission (2007) 'Statistical Annex of European Economy, Spring 2007', European Economy 2007, Directorate General for Economic and Financial Affairs, ec.europa.eu/economy_finance/publications/european_economy/2007/statannex0107_en.pdf.

Fatás, A. and I. Mihov (2001) 'The Effects of Fiscal Policy on Consumption and Employment: Theory and Evidence', unpublished manuscript, INSEAD.

Favero, C. (2002) 'How Do European Monetary and Fiscal Authorities Behave?', CEPR Discussion paper, No. 3426, June.

Galor, O. and D. Tsiddon (1996) 'Income Distribution and Growth: The Kuznets Hypothesis Revisited', *Economica* 63: S103–17.

Giavazzi, F. and M. Pagano (1990) 'Can Severe Fiscal Contractions Be Expansionary? Tales of Two Small European Countries', *NBER Macroeconomics Annual* 5: 75–111.

——(1996) 'Non-Keynesian Effects of Fiscal Policy Changes: International Evidence and the Swedish experience', *Swedish Economic Policy Review* 3(1): 67–103.

Goodin, R. and J. LeGrand (1987) *Not Only the Poor: The Middle Classes and the Welfare State*, London: Allen & Unwin.

Hillyard, P., G. Kelly, E. McLaughlin, D. Patsios and M. Tomlinson (2003) *Bare Necessities: Poverty and Social Exclusion in Northern Ireland*, Democratic Dialogue Report 16, Belfast.

Jha, S.K. (1996) 'The Kuznets Curve: A Reassessment', *World Economics* 24(4): 773–80.

Kamps, C. (2005) 'The Dynamic Effects of Public Capital: VAR Evidence for 22 OECD Countries', *International Tax and Public Finance* 12(4): 533–58.

Kuznets, S. (1955) 'Economic Growth and Income Inequality', *American Economic Review* 45(1): 1–28.

Lambert, P.J. (2001) *The Distribution and Redistribution of Income*, 3rd edn, Manchester University Press.

LeGrand, J. (1982) *The Strategy of Equality. Redistribution and the Social Services*, London: Allen & Unwin.

Linnemann, L. and A. Schabert (2003) 'Fiscal Policy in the New Neoclassical Synthesis', *Journal of Money, Credit and Banking* 35(6): 911–29.

Lütkepohl, H. (1991) *Introduction to Multiple Time Series Analysis*, Berlin: Springer.

Marcellino, M. (2006) 'Some Stylized Facts on Non-systematic Fiscal Policy in the Euro Area', *Journal of Macroeconomics* 28: 461–79.

Mountford, A. and H. Uhlig (2005) 'What are the Effects of Fiscal Policy Shocks?', SFB 649 Discussion Papers, Humboldt University, Berlin, Germany.

Office for National Statistics (2007) *Effects of Taxes and Benefits on Household Income, 2005/06*, www.statistics.gov.uk/downloads/theme_social/Taxes_Benefits_2005-6/Taxes_Benefits_2005-06.pdf.

Perotti, R. (1996) 'Growth, Income Distribution, and Democracy: What the Data Say', *Journal of Economic Growth*, 1: 149–87.

——(2004) 'Public investment: Another (different) look', WP 277, IGIER – Universita' Bocconi, www.igier.uni-bocconi.it/perotti.

——(2005) 'Estimating the Effects of Fiscal Policy in OECD Countries', CEPR Discussion Paper No. 4842.

Sims, C.A. and T. Zha (1999) 'Error bands for impulse responses', *Econometrica* 67: 1113–55.

Tanninen, H. (1999) 'Income Inequality, Government Expenditures and Growth', *Applied Economics* 31: 1109–17.

White. H. (1980) 'A Heteroskedasticity Consistent Covariance Matrix Estimation and a Direct Test for Heteroskedasticity', *Econometrica* 48: 817–38.

Wolff, E.N. and A. Zacharias (2007) 'The Distributional Consequences of Government Spending and Taxation in the US, 1989 and 2000', *Review of Income and Wealth* 53(4): 697–715.

7 The changing relationship between the UK economy and its banking sector

Tom Springbett

The UK economy's relationship with its banking sector has often been mutually beneficial, but has occasionally been tempestuous. In the decade to 2007, the banking sector expanded rapidly, building on the many natural advantages of the City of London, including its time zone (which allowed traders to wake up with Asia and go to bed with America), the availability of skilled staff and its regulatory framework which, although recent events have demonstrated the need for substantial reform, was for a long time seen as a world leader. Survey measures of financial centre attractiveness consistently put London around joint top with New York.[1] At the same time as UK banks were conquering world markets—in 2007, the then big four UK banks made 44% of their profits overseas—the banks were also financing a major leveraging of consumer balance sheets. Between December 2000 and December 2007, median leverage of British banks rose from 21 to 35. Between 1960 and 1999 it had averaged 19, peaking at 25 in 1984.[2]

The 10 years up to 2007 were, by contemporary standards at least, good ones for the UK banking sector as well as for its contribution to the economy. It made large profits, paid large amounts of tax and (in combination with the rest of the financial sector) was the largest single contributor to UK net exports. The banking sector is important to the UK economy for three main reasons:

- as a generator of value added;
- as an intermediary between borrowers and lenders; and
- as a cornerstone of the monetary system.

After the financial crisis took hold, the time seemed right for the UK fundamentally to reconsider the role of its banking sector in view of the possible risks associated with its large share of output and high degree of leverage. How much has really changed, though, and how much needs to change in the future? This paper examines each of the three planks of the relationship between the UK banking sector and the broader economy both before and after the financial crisis.

The banking sector as a generator of value added

Even at its peak, the UK financial sector, while very large, was not enormous. Popular perception has been of an economy dominated by the City, but at approximately 8% of gross domestic product (GDP) in 2007 the UK's financial services sector was of similar relative size to that of the USA (7.5%) and Japan (6.7%).[3] The UK did, however, stand out among big European Union (EU) economies, with financial services accounting for 4.6% and 3.8% of GDP in France and Germany, respectively. Since the crisis, the share of the financial sector may in fact have increased, as it contracted less severely than the economy as a whole, although definitive statistics are not yet available. In 2009 financial intermediation accounted for 10% of UK gross value added (GVA).

Financial services seem also to have been a significant but not dominant contributor to the recession. Quarterly GVA from financial intermediation followed a similar pattern to total GVA. The peak to trough fall for quarterly GVA was larger for financial intermediation than for total GVA,[4] but this was largely because the financial sector appears to have kept growing in mid-2008, while the rest of the economy was contracting, before falling back more sharply afterwards. Turning to annual comparisons, 2009 total GVA was 5% lower than 2007, while 2009 financial intermediation GVA was approximately equal to its level in 2007, explaining the increase in financial intermediation's share in the total.[5]

As a caveat to these figures, measuring the output of the financial sector is notoriously difficult. The thorniest issue is measuring earnings from the spread between banks' cost of capital and interest earned on their lending. Financial intermediation services indirectly measured (FISIM), introduced into the United Nations System of National Accounts in 1993, aims to capture the added value represented by this margin. The estimate is based on the difference between the interest earned by the bank and the risk-free rate. However, as Haldane *et al.* (2010) discuss, FISIM calculated on this basis may overstate financial sector GVA since banks' lending margins include compensation for the bearing of risk. It is doubtful whether this risk bearing is in fact value-creating since the risk is not reduced by the banks' bearing of it. If a business were financed entirely by its owners instead of partially by bank credit, there would be no contribution to FISIM even though the quantum of risk borne is the same. National accounting experts are working to refine the FISIM methodology in order to include some risk adjustment.

A further caveat is that the financial sector's broader importance to the economy goes beyond what is captured by the sectoral shares. First, one should consider professional services like legal and accounting, the success of which in London is closely linked to the presence of the financial sector. It is important also to recall the influence that the health of the financial sector can have on the economy—if banks ceased operating the payments system or providing intermediation between borrowers and lenders, the economic impact would be far greater than the direct impact on financial sector GVA. These other aspects of the sector's importance are covered later in the chapter.

An area where the economic contribution of the financial sector does stand out is in the share of tax it pays. The financial sector share of corporation tax (CT) receipts peaked at 27%[6] in 2006–07 before falling back. Lower revenues from the financial sector have been highlighted as a key driver of the radical worsening of the fiscal position over the course of the financial crisis. Financial sector CT receipts fell 55% in cash terms from their 2007–08 peak to 2009–10, equivalent to 65% of the overall fall in CT receipts over the same period. However, because corporation tax itself accounts for only a small share of total receipts (8% in 2010–11 according to the government's June 2010 emergency budget), and around 17% of taxes borne and collected by financial-sector companies,[7] the total revenue impact of this fall was not enormous. The general government deficit in 2009–10 would have been only around 0.5 percentage points of GDP smaller had financial sector CT receipts been at their 2007–08 level.

Looking at a broader measure of all taxes borne and collected by the financial sector (including employee income tax and national insurance contributions and tax deducted at source on interest payments), PWC (2010) estimate that the financial sector accounted for £53.4 billion or 11.2% of total government receipts in 2010. This was £14.4 billion lower than in 2007 or £12.9 billion (1% of GDP) lower than it would have been had total taxes from the financial sector moved in line with the total tax take. This constitutes a substantial fall and shows that the deterioration of the UK's general government deficit was appreciably aggravated by the UK's reliance on financial services receipts. However, it appears that financial services will remain a large (and disproportionate) contributor to overall revenues.

Indeed, the financial sector's contribution is likely to increase following recent measures. The government has introduced a tax on bank balance sheets aimed at discouraging excessive bank risk-taking and recouping some of the implicit subsidy that banks receive from taxpayers. Following a decision in February 2011 to reverse plans to phase the tax in over two years, the tax will be levied at its full rate 0.075% of adjusted liabilities as from 2011. The government estimates that this will raise £2.5 billion or 0.2% of GDP annually in its early years. This new tax is relatively small in comparison to Bank of England estimates of the effective subsidy that UK-based banks received from the implicit state guarantee of their debt. The Bank of England (2010a) estimated that UK-based banks saved £11 billion in 2007, £56 billion in 2008 and £104 billion in 2009 through lower borrowing costs. However, it would be a leap to argue that the bank levy would have to be set at these levels in order to offset the effective public subsidy. First, the 2008 and 2009 figures were distorted by the huge increase in risk premia seen in those years. Second, tougher bank regulation at the UK and international level, as discussed in Chapter 8, should reduce this effective subsidy by reducing the probability of bank failure and therefore the size of the implicit subsidy. Indeed, if living wills and other arrangements to manage the impact of future bank insolvencies prove effective enough to allow governments to let banks fail without providing support, the implicit subsidy should disappear. However, it seems unlikely that any bank failure regime could be so effective that governments could be sure of never needing to step in to support their banking sector whatever the circumstances.

A final measure of the financial sector's importance in terms of value added is its contribution to net exports. As set out in Chapter 5, the UK economy has a substantial surplus in services with a larger deficit in goods, leading to a small but persistent current account deficit. The financial services sector accounts for around two-thirds of that services surplus with net exports of £33 billion in 2009. The UK's financial services surplus could be viewed as a legitimate exploitation of comparative advantage or as a potentially dangerous over-reliance on a volatile sector. Recent data tend to support the former interpretation. In 2009, arguably the worst year in living memory for the financial sector, financial services gross exports did fall 17%, but this undid only a fraction of the 347% increase that took place during the decade to 2008. Despite this sizeable fall, 2009 financial services exports were only 3% below their 2007 level. Goods exports fell 10% in 2009, remaining 3% above their 2007 level. So crisis experience does not provide strong support for the hypothesis that relying on financial services rather than goods exports is a risky strategy for the UK.

The question of whether financial services exports are more volatile than other sectors deserves further attention. A more complete examination can be made by comparing the volatility of volume growth across different export sectors. Other things equal, the larger the share of volatile sectors in a country's exports, the more volatile its current account balance will be. Figure 7.1 compares the variances of de-meaned growth rates of export volumes for each of the sectors covered in the Office for National Statistics (ONS) *Pink Book* over the period 1992 to 2009, the longest for which data for all sectors are available. As shown in the figure, insurance stands out as clearly the most volatile sector, but financial services excluding insurance is only the ninth most volatile of the 26 sectors covered. While the volatility of insurance may be undesirable, given that it accounted for only 1.4% of exports over the period (compared to 7.9% for the rest of financial services), its macro consequences look unlikely to be significant.

Overall, based on past growth rates it is difficult to find support for the hypothesis that relying on financial services exports is a dangerous strategy. This does not rule out the possibility of a more sustained decline in global demand for financial services or, perhaps more likely, the emergence of strong, low-cost competition from emerging financial centres in the Middle and Far East. However, these risks would seem just as present in any export sector with little reason to suppose financial services is especially at risk.

The banking sector as an intermediary

Perhaps the most important role of the UK banking sector is as an intermediary between savers and borrowers. As banks became more leveraged,

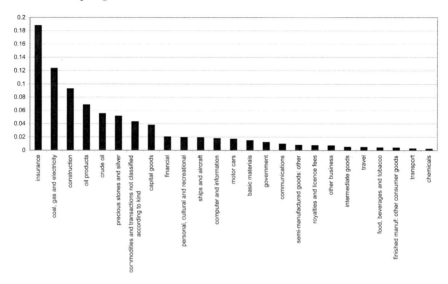

Figure 7.1 Volatility of UK gross exports across sectors from 1992 to 2009
Source: Office for National Statistics Pink Book 2010 and author's calculations

other things equal, they were able to offer more loans for every pound of their equity capital. However, as ever with leverage, this ratchet effect operates in both directions—higher leverage meant that for every pound of losses banks made on their asset bases during the crisis they had to shrink their balance sheet by a greater amount if they were to maintain a given leverage ratio.

To give an extremely stylized example, assume a bank the only assets of which are loans, and which has to make write-downs of 2.3% of those loans. This is the level of loan write-downs that the Bank of England estimates UK banks made in 2009. Assume the bank is leveraged 35 times, as the UK banking sector was in 2007. The losses will cause the bank's leverage ratio to rise to 173, as most of its equity is wiped out. If it were to seek to restore its original leverage ratio of 35 purely by shrinking its loan book, it would have to reduce the size of this loan book by 80% relative to its pre-losses level. If instead the bank had been leveraged only 19 times, the UK average between 1960 and 1999, the picture changes dramatically. The bank would have to shrink its loan book by only 44% to return to a leverage ratio of 19 times. Of course this is a gross simplification. In reality the bank's asset base would have included other assets than just loans, potentially diluting the overall percentage loss. It would also have the option of reducing its leverage by increasing equity capital, either through retained earnings or issuing new shares, as UK banks did during the crisis. Finally, banks may be prepared to allow their leverage ratios to vary over time, within reasonable bounds. However, even if in practice the volatility of bank lending in response to unexpected losses is likely to be smaller, crisis experience suggests it was significant. It therefore seems very likely that the severity of the reduction in credit availability which

the real economy suffers following a banking crisis will be positively correlated with the banking sector's pre-crisis leverage.

In this crisis, bank deleveraging had real consequences for credit availability. Growth in the stock of bank loans to UK non-financial corporations
was negative for 21 of the 24 months of 2009 and 2010. It is impossible to
assess precisely what share of this stock reduction is down to banks' reduced
willingness to lend and how much is explained by lower overall credit demand
and greater reliance on public debt issuance by large corporates. Corporate
bonds were in net issuance for 2009 and 2010. The UK corporate sector's
significant net saving also suggests that investment intentions have been
reined in. However, as the Bank of England (2010b) points out, the fact that
spreads on corporate lending widened during the crisis suggests that reduced
credit supply was a dominating factor; assuming a straight-line positive correlation between credit supply and the spread, and a straight-line negative
correlation between credit demand and the spread, a negative demand shock
would result in a higher market-clearing spread while a negative supply
shock would result in a higher market-clearing spread.

The extent to which volatility in bank credit availability matters for the
economy depends significantly on the extent to which non-financial corporations rely on it for funding. HM Treasury (2010) presents a cross-country
comparison showing that UK firms in 2007 got 32% of their financing from
bank loans, compared to 26% in the USA, 23% in France and 39% in Germany. The UK has a lower share of equity financing than its European peers
and lower corporate bond financing than the USA. Thus, while not exceptional, UK corporates' reliance on bank financing appears slightly above
average. This in turn may partially explain the enormous drop in corporate
investment during the crisis. Private sector gross fixed capital formation at
current prices fell 34% in the UK between 2007 and 2009, compared to 22%
in the EU as a whole. Of course, investment would have been lower regardless
of credit availability, but the scale of the drop suggests credit must have
played a significant role.

Policy initiatives underway should go some way to addressing this vulnerability. Stricter bank capital solvency standards should reduce both gross and
risk-adjusted leverage. The introduction of counter-cyclical aspects to bank
solvency regulation should help further.[8] Reducing UK corporations' overall
reliance on bank financing, as discussed in HM Treasury (2010), could also
be a significant step forward.

The banking sector as a cornerstone of the monetary system

A third role of the UK banking sector is as a transmitter of monetary policy
to the real economy. For much of the first decade of Bank of England independence, the UK banking sector acted as such a reliable component of the
monetary transmission mechanism that it risked being taken for granted. The
central cog in this mechanism was the relationship between three-month

LIBOR and the Bank of England policy rate. Between 1997 and 2007 the average absolute margin between base rate and LIBOR was 17 basis points, with a peak of 85 basis points. As LIBOR is the principal base for the pricing of corporate loans, base rate had a direct and accurate impact on private sector borrowing costs. With this predictable and effective transmission mechanism, the Bank of England succeeded in keeping inflation within 1 percentage point either side of the official target continuously for almost 10 years after gaining full independence, before consumer price index (CPI) inflation hit 3.1% in March 2007.

During 2008 and 2009 that transmission mechanism became much less reliable. The average absolute margin between base rate and LIBOR was 72 basis points, peaking at 168 basis points. Inflation simultaneously became much more volatile, hitting 5.2% in September 2008 and falling back to 1.1% in September 2009. At the same time as the transmission mechanism was breaking down, the Bank had to deal for the first time in its history with the challenge of hitting the lower bound[9] for interest rates.[10]

During 2010 a degree of normality returned to the monetary transmission mechanism. The margin between base rate and LIBOR remained between 10 and 28 basis points throughout the year. The speed of this return to normal is perhaps surprising given the degree of upheaval during 2008 and 2009. However, one lasting effect of the crisis has been to highlight the importance of the transmission mechanism and the consequences of its breaking down.

More recently, a new set of monetary policy challenges—with inflation consistently high in spite of an apparently large negative output gap—has emerged, leading the policy debate to focus on different aspects of the monetary transmission mechanism. As set out, for example, in Sentance (2007), monetary policy can work through three main channels: domestic demand, the exchange rate and inflation expectations. The operation of the domestic demand channel remains subject to broad uncertainty linked to the differing pictures of spare capacity presented by macro-level estimates showing a large output gap and survey evidence of firms running close to capacity. The likely unreliability of this channel has led to increased consideration of the other two. Some commentators have argued for a tightening of monetary policy almost purely on the basis of expectations arguments; that a signal from the Bank of England that it was prepared to tighten policy would recalibrate inflation expectations and thus rein-in wage increases.

Also of increased importance is the exchange rate channel. Given that the positive differential between UK interest rates and those in the euro area, the USA and Japan appears to have been the main driver of sterling's long period of strength and stability in the pre-crisis period, it seems reasonable to assume that a market expectation that UK interest rates would increase more rapidly than in those other economies in the near future would help drive some sterling appreciation. This seems to have been borne out by recent market experience, where changing market expectations of future rate rises have been closely correlated with sterling's strength against the US dollar and the euro.

Given that sterling's almost unprecedented depreciation in 2008 and 2009[11] has been one of the most significant contributors to recent UK inflation overshoots, it also seems very likely that such an appreciation would pull down UK inflation, although the typically long lags between import prices and headline inflation suggest that this process would take time.

As such, another side effect of the crisis has been to drag the centre of monetary policy debate away from consideration of how to keep the economy in the zone between overheating and deflation and towards consideration of the expectations and exchange rate channels. However, this development is unlikely to reduce substantially the importance of the financial sector in the monetary transmission mechanism as a whole. Although the operation of the expectations channel does not strictly require a *contemporaneous* link between policy and market interest rates in order to operate, it does require a public expectation that interest rate-based transmission mechanisms will operate effectively in the future. The exchange rate channel clearly requires the banking sector to help translate changes in policy rates into market interest rates.

Conclusions and implications for the future

A definitive assessment of the crisis' impact cannot yet be made. However, evidence so far suggests that the relationship between the UK economy and its banking and financial sector has not changed fundamentally. Its share in overall UK output may even have risen since 2007. While the financial sector's tax contribution did fall sharply during the recession, it looks likely to rebound as banks return to profit and the new bank balance sheet tax kicks in. On the exports side, the financial sector remains an important net exporter, making a significant contribution to the UK current account balance. There is no strong evidence from historical volatility to suggest that such reliance on financial sector exports is a particularly risky strategy.

On the intermediation side, more has changed. Credit availability has become an issue with a high public profile. Lower credit availability must have played a role in the rapid falls in corporate investment that occurred during the crisis, and which are still a long way from being reversed. This experience has reinforced two lessons. The first is that ready credit availability built on high bank leverage is more quickly withdrawn in a crisis than it would be if banks had drawn more of their funding from shareholders. The second is that higher reliance on bank intermediated lending implies a greater intertwining of the fortunes of the banking sector and the real economy.

Turning finally to the monetary transmission mechanism, the crisis clearly showed some of the limits on the effectiveness of monetary policy. While a degree of normality has returned to money markets, the UK economy is far from returning to a typical Taylor rule-type scenario with inflation well above target in spite of a large negative output gap. Perhaps the most important lesson of the crisis on this front is that good monetary policy is a necessary but not sufficient condition for financial and economic stability.

While the crisis has not necessarily caused a fundamental change in the relationship between the UK economy and its financial sector, there are clearly lessons to draw. The fact that pre-crisis regulation and supervision focused on the solvency and stability of individual institutions rather than on risks to the financial system as a whole has been well documented. This coincided with a gap in the incentives to banks' senior managers. While they had a clear incentive to protect their banks against individual failure (albeit that this incentive was sometimes diluted by sub-optimal bonus schemes), their incentive to consider the impact of aggregate financial sector behaviour on overall market stability was much less evident. All of this demonstrated a clear need for a new top level of financial surveillance, responsible for monitoring and mitigating these system-wide risks.

The UK has already begun responding to this challenge with a radical programme of reform centred around the creation of a new Financial Policy Committee (FPC), which will have responsibility for defending financial stability. While the details of the FPC's powers are still being determined, the government has indicated that they are likely to include: making public pronouncements and warnings; influencing international macroprudential policy; making recommendations to the Treasury on changes to regulatory perimeter or to other parts of the Bank; and making directions to the Prudential Regulatory Authority or the Financial Conduct Authority, the two new bodies to be set up to take over solvency and conduct of business regulation, respectively. These recommendations and directions could cover a broad range of issues including solvency and liquidity standards, collateral requirements and capital weights for particular asset classes. In all, the FPC is likely to possess a powerful and wide-ranging toolkit.

The solutions to some of the other problems highlighted by the crisis are perhaps less easy to identify. The impact of the negative credit shock on corporate investment and on the economy more broadly has been clear to see, but the way to stop it happening again is less obvious. While the FPC architecture should certainly reduce the risk of the financial sector ever coming so close to the brink of collapse as it did in 2008 and 2009, it would be too much to expect it to prevent any future disturbance in the banking sector. As explained earlier in the chapter, mandating lower overall levels of leverage should help to reduce the scale of future credit shocks. Greater competition would also help if it reduced the concentration in the market for lending to corporates, since it would reduce the probability of all participants in a market suffering the same negative shock. It is therefore encouraging that competition is one of the main issues being considered by the Independent Commission on Banking.

In sum, while the banking and financial sectors remain very important to the UK economy also after the crisis, it is evident that the risks they bring with them will also persist, while new instruments seem necessary to manage them. As the complete elimination of systemic risk will remain impossible, steps must be taken in good times to contain the vulnerability to and impact of future shocks. Though in many areas the best way to deal with the challenges still needs to be identified, most lessons of the crisis have already been reflected in policy since and the new innovations are likely to represent an important step forward. The details of the new regulatory approach are discussed further in the next chapter.

Notes

1 See, for example, City of London Corporation (2008).
2 Source: Bank of England 2010a and Commission calculations.
3 Source: International Financial Services London.
4 Financial intermediation GVA fell 9% between Q3 2008 and Q4 2009. Total GVA fell 7% from Q1 2008 to Q3 2009.
5 Chained volume gross value added is used as the principal measure here because of the availability of contemporary data. Results do vary slightly according to different measures and deflators used. Weale (2009) provides a good comparison.
6 Source: HMRC and Commission calculations. Financial sector including life insurance as a share of total corporation tax receipts including from North Sea oil.
7 See PWC (2010).
8 These points are discussed in more detail in Chapter 8.
9 The previous recorded low point for base rate was 2% between 1939 and 1950.
10 The Bank's response to these challenges is discussed in more depth in Chapter 8.
11 Sentance (2011) finds that this depreciation was probably the largest the UK has experienced in such a short period over the past two centuries, excluding the departure from the Gold Standard in the 1930s.

References

Bank of England (2010a) *Financial Stability Report*, December, Issue No. 28, www. bankofengland.co.uk.
——(2010b) 'Understanding the Weakness of Bank Lending', *Quarterly Bulletin* Q4, www.bankofengland.co.uk/publications/quarterlybulletin/qb100406.pdf.
City of London Corporation (2008) *The Global Financial Centres Index 3*, www. cityoflondon.gov.uk.
Haldane, A., Brennan, S. and Madouros, V. (2010) 'What is the contribution of the financial sector: Miracle or mirage?' in *The Future of Finance*, London School of Economics.
HM Treasury (2010) *Discussion Paper on Non-Bank Lending*, www.nationalarchives. gov.uk.
PWC (2010) *The Total Tax Contribution of UK Financial Services*, www.cityoflondon. gov.uk.
Sentance, A. (2007) *The Global Economy and UK Inflation*, speech at Bentley Jennison in association with the Leeds Financial Services Initiative, www.bankofengland.co.uk.
——(2011) *The UK's inflation problem: selling England by the pound?* speech to the Institute of Economic Affairs 2011 State of the Economy Conference, www. bankofengland.co.uk.
Weale, M. (2009) 'Commentary: Growth Prospects and Financial Services', *National Institute Economic Review* No. 207, January: 4–9.

8 Policy efficacy in the crisis, exit strategies and the return of growth

E. Philip Davis and Dilruba Karim

Introduction

The UK has had a turbulent recession, emerging at the time of writing with a very large fiscal deficit and major loss of output relative to trend, as well as quite high headline inflation and slow credit growth. There has been widespread discussion of the role of discretionary policy in overall developments and this is the focus of this chapter. We mainly analyse central-bank monetary, macroprudential and banking policies, although we also comment on certain structural and regulatory policies, and on macro/financial linkages in the UK. The paper is in four sections: first we comment on certain issues in the run-up to the crisis; second we assess policy efficacy in the crisis itself; third we discuss exit strategies; and fourth we consider the scope for a return to growth, focusing on the housing market and the banking sector.

Section one: policy in the run up to the crisis

Monetary policy

The role of banks in the prolonged credit and asset–price cycle that turned so dramatically raises the question of whether monetary policy should have been used to 'lean against the wind' during the upswing. Experience of conducting such policies is limited internationally, although Wadhwani (2008) argues that the Swedish authorities were able to undertake them, raising rates more than appeared warranted by the inflation target to allow for the potential impact of the credit and asset price boom.

According to National Institute of Economic and Social Research (NIESR) estimates, for example, in the UK house prices rose by 30% over equilibrium levels during the boom. Accordingly, the question arises as to whether monetary policy contributed to the subsequent crash in house prices by being too loose. The counterargument is that the bubble was a consequence of misguided expectations of growing prosperity in the wider population, rather than the level of interest rates. It was possibly also linked to loose fiscal policy (Davis 2011) in the sense that a structural deficit over the early 2000s may have itself generated unrealistic growth expectations in the household (and banking) sectors, thus giving rise to false expectations about the sustainability of attained levels of leverage and of asset prices.

Macroprudential policy

Beyond the macroeconomic impact of monetary policy on the cycle, one can consider system-wide macroprudential concerns about banking system stability that go beyond the institution-specific concerns that have been the focus of microprudential regulation. We would argue that the major difficulty for the UK was in such macroprudential policy, with macroprudential surveillance not fully predicting the crisis per se, policy not acting on crisis risks up to August/September 2007, and to some extent also underestimating them right up to Lehman Brothers' failure, as discussed further below. From a Bank of England perspective, Tucker (2008: 329) notes, 'perhaps with hindsight, it is baffling that the authorities internationally contented themselves with issuing warnings'.

For example, as regards performance of macroprudential surveillance before the crisis, the last Bank of England *Financial Stability Report* before the crisis began in August 2007 concluded that the 'UK financial system remains highly resilient' (Bank of England 2007: 5), while noting that macroeconomic stability and competition in the financial sector have 'encouraged a further increase in risk taking' (ibid.: 6) and that this 'increased the vulnerability of the system as a whole to an abrupt change in conditions' (ibid.: 5). Risks were considered to arise from credit markets, and these risks weakened credit risk assessment, impaired risk monitoring and made financial institutions more dependent on market liquidity leading to 'warehousing risk' if institutions piled up loans they were unable to securitize. These were held to compound pre-existing risks arising from high asset prices and vulnerabilities in risk premia, high levels of corporate and household debt, dependence on market infrastructure, large financial imbalances among the major economies, as well as from rising systemic importance of large complex financial institutions. There was seen to be a risk of unwinding of low-risk premia, triggering a pick-up in corporate defaults, an unwinding of leveraged positions in corporate credit markets and consequently lower market liquidity and further falls in asset prices with a generalized retreat from risk-taking and a rise in correlation across markets reducing the scope for diversification against shocks. Such a scenario was seen as calling the 'originate and distribute' business model into question.

Meanwhile, the Financial Services Authority (FSA 2007) in its Financial Risk Outlook (FRO), highlighted as 'priority risks' that firms should evaluate their responses to extreme situations (stress tests) despite current low volatility; they should be aware of valuation problems with illiquid instruments (albeit in the context of conflicts of interest); and they should consider operational and legal risks with derivatives. They were also urged to bear in mind dangers arising from terrorism, crime and, interestingly, the volume of regulatory reform. The FRO also noted that some consumers were at risk from high debt levels. However, the authors felt that 'it is highly unlikely that consumer indebtedness problems could lead to a financial stability problem'.

As detailed further in Davis and Karim (2008), while highlighting a number of risks and capturing a number of the mechanisms by which these materialized, the Bank of England and the FSA, in common with other macroprudential analysts, did not foresee the full extent of the crisis. In particular, they failed to highlight the risk of contagion from the US housing and securitization markets, the danger of seizure of wholesale markets, including the interbank markets and the extent of risky disintermediation via conduits and Special Investment Vehicles (SIVs). Indeed, as noted in Davis (2009a), 'although aware of the exposure of individual UK banks, the FSA was surprised by the scope and size of the overall market for SIVs when the crisis began'.

We would contend that it was possible to estimate equations that would have highlighted the UK economy's vulnerability to a financial crisis. Underlying research is presented in Barrell, Davis, Liadze and Karim (2010a, 2010b), which provide estimates of models for predicting banking crises in Organisation for Economic Co-operation and Development (OECD) countries, looking at determinants of banking crises in 14 countries using the multivariate logit estimation methodology. They used a range of 'traditional' macroeconomic indicators, as used for global crisis samples in Demirgüç-Kunt and Detragiache (2005) (such as gross domestic product (GDP) growth and credit growth), but also rises in house prices, bank capital and liquidity measures, adding the current account/GDP ratio in Barrell, Davis, Liadze and Karim (2010b). The latter variables had not been tried previously in crisis models owing to lack of data for most non-OECD countries.

In Barrell, Davis, Liadze and Karim (2010a) following a general-to-specific modelling eliminating insignificant variables, we arrived at the model as depicted in Table 8.1, which relates crisis risk in OECD countries to the lag of banks' unweighted capital adequacy ratio (LEV), the lag of liquidity of banks relative to total assets (LIQ), and the third lag of real house price growth (RHPG). The version the performance of which is shown in Table 8.2 was estimated over 1980–2006 and it is remarkably accurate, picking up 67% of crises in-sample. The UK authorities could have estimated this equation and then used it to forecast using actual right-hand side variables. It forecasts the sub-prime crisis well, signalling a crisis in the UK in 2007 and 2008, in common with a number of other countries hit by banking problems. Inclusion of the current account in Barrell, Davis, Liadze and Karim (2010b) also allows the crisis in the USA to be predicted.

In making the suggestion that the UK could have predicted the crisis and reacted appropriately, we note that taking the model at face value, it is not clear that monetary policy alone could have offset the risk, except by acting aggressively on house prices well ahead of time, or reducing demand sufficiently to improve the current account. Indeed, perhaps based on the FSA's view of the remoteness of risks from household debt, no specific action at the

Table 8.1 Logit equations for OECD banking crises estimated over 1980–2006

Variable	Coefficient	Std error	z-statistic
LIQ(−1)	−0.118143	0.033321	−3.545622
LEV(−1)	−0.333534	0.116794	−2.855739
RHPG(−3)	0.113078	0.040419	2.797660

Source: Barrell, Davis, Liadze and Karim 2010a

Table 8.2 In-sample model performance based on correct calls

	Estimated equation		
	Dep=0	Dep=1	Total
P(Dep=1)<=C	214	4	218
P(Dep=1)>C	110	8	118
Total	324	12	336
Correct	214	8	222
% Correct	66.05	66.67	66.07
% Incorrect	33.95	33.33	33.93

Source: Barrell, Davis, Liadze and Karim 2010a

Table 8.3 Forecast predictions of banking crises based on the 1980–2006 model

	2007	2008	Definition 1	Definition 2
BG	X	X	X	X
CN	–	–		
DK	–	–		
FN	–	X		
FR	X	X	X	X
GE	–	–	–	–
IT	X	–		X
JP	–	–		
NL	X	–	X	X
NW	X	X		
SD	–	–		–
SP	X	X		X
UK	X	X	X	X
US	–	–	–	–

Source: Barrell, Davis, Liadze and Karim (2010a)

level of bank regulation was taken to limit household debt, such as tightening regulations relating to mortgages or increasing capital requirements.

Such measures were used to a modest extent, by contrast, in countries such as Estonia and Ireland which faced similar housing booms. Hence the result also highlights the need for complementary countercyclical macroprudential policy operating on capital and liquidity, as discussed further below. The system of countercyclical provisioning in Spain may also have helped its institutions (although it did little to restrain a credit boom), as might setting capital requirements as a function of interest rates as is done in Argentina. Such levers were not available in the UK in the run-up to the sub-prime crisis but are being discussed intensively at the time of writing in UK and international forums (see Basel Committee 2010, for example). In section four we discuss their potential impact on the UK banking system.

Section two: easing policies during the crisis

Interest rate policy

We now examine policies adopted during the crisis itself, i.e. from August 2007 onwards. As shown in Table 8.4, the UK authorities followed a cautious policy in terms of interest rates, with rates only falling decisively in the wake of Lehman Brothers' failure in autumn 2008. The high rates earlier in 2007–08 were felt to be justified by inflation risks at the time.

Martin and Milas (2010) estimated Taylor Rule equations for the UK, relating interest rates to inflation and the output gap. They found that, according to their estimates, the UK 'abandoned' inflation targeting during the crisis, with interest rates not responding to inflation after 2007/4, although another structural break was found in 2008/10.[1]

We would argue that, owing to the impact of the crisis on credit rationing, with an impact on inflation and output which is not captured in the Taylor Rule, it was appropriate for the UK authorities to abandon a simple Taylor Rule (bearing in mind the Taylor Rule itself is only an approximation for the sophisticated policy of inflation targeting). Indeed, the authors acknowledge that a policy of 'ensuring deviations from the target are not too large and prolonged' was maintained. However, the timing of the breaks could be significant. Whereas 2007/4 suggests remarkable foresight, Martin and Milas

Table 8.4 Official UK bank rate (quarterly average)

Q1 2007	5.22
Q2 2007	5.4
Q3 2007	5.74
Q4 2007	5.69
Q1 2008	5.35
Q2 2008	5.03
Q3 2008	5
Q4 2008	3.37
Q1 2009	1.07
Q2 2009	0.5
Q3 2009	0.5
Q4 2009	0.5
Q1 2010	0.5

Source: Bank of England

suggest (see note 1) that this was partly an artefact of the data period and statistical conventions.

If the second break in 2008/10 is the true one, then one might suggest that the realization of the risk of crisis-driven recession and banking system collapse came possibly too late, with high interest rates in early 2008 to combat inflation deepening the recession. This may in turn link to underestimation of the probability and impact of severe financial tensions on the economy, even in advance of the Lehman Brothers bankruptcy, as implied in the section above. Since then, the policy of low interest rates has, of course, been appropriate given the size of the output gap and continuing financial tensions.

Liquidity policy

Turning to liquidity policy, a key manifestation of the crisis in the UK, as in the USA and the euro area, was a large premium of LIBOR over the central bank rate, reflecting risk aversion among banks in the interbank market, as well as credit rationing *per se*, especially at maturities in excess of one week. This pattern was unprecedented, with the relation of LIBOR to central bank rates having been very close up to mid-2007. Accompanying the widening LIBOR spread was closure of securitization markets and of the asset-backed commercial paper (ABCP) market, which had been used to finance off-balance sheet vehicles such as SIVs and conduits. In effect, obtaining wholesale funding became very difficult for a number of UK banks, and sterling interbank market lending was down to one-third of its previous levels (Table 8.5). Together these created a challenge to the authorities in the UK, as elsewhere, to provide liquidity to banks and attempt to restart the money markets.

Table 8.5 Bank of England assets (end quarter) in £ million

	Total assets	*Issue department*	*Banking department*
Q1 2007	79,633	38,661	41,020
Q2 2007	79,737	39,787	40,005
Q3 2007	98,081	40,425	57,723
Q4 2007	102,241	45,022	61,013
Q1 2008	98,805	42,951	67,713
Q2 2008	91,837	42,180	56,326
Q3 2008	137,685	42,769	94,975
Q4 2008	238,490	46,886	204,255
Q1 2009	181,515	45,571	162,139
Q2 2009	220,105	46,143	204,549
Q3 2009	226,407	47,040	200,397
Q4 2009	237,694	52,866	212,969
Q1 2010	252,336	51,249	226,703
Q2 2010	250,671	51,412	230,296

Source: Bank of England

As background, note that the Bank of England's objectives in its normal money market operations are to assist monetary policy by keeping overnight rates in line with the Bank Rate, and reducing the cost of disruptions to the liquidity and payments services supplied by the commercial banks (Bank of England 2008a). The traditional operating procedure provides liquidity insurance to banks by various means, namely: (i) a reserves-averaging scheme, whereby eligible UK banks and building societies undertake to hold target balances (reserves) at the Bank on average over maintenance periods running from one Monetary Policy Committee (MPC) decision date until the next. If an average balance is within a range around the target, the balance is remunerated at the Bank Rate. This enables banks to vary reserve holdings from day to day to absorb payment shocks without being penalized as long as the average is maintained; (ii) a standing facility, like a bank account, which provides standing deposit and (collateralized) lending facilities to eligible UK banks and building societies with the Bank of England, which may be used on demand. In normal circumstances they carried a penalty, relative to the official Bank Rate, of +/–25 basis points on the final day of the monthly reserves maintenance period, and of +/–100 basis points on all other days. Standing facilities provide a buffer against day-to-day payments shocks; and (iii) open market operations (OMOs) to provide short- and longer-term liquidity directly. Technically, these are used to provide to the banking system the amount of central bank money needed to enable reserve-scheme members, in aggregate, to achieve their reserves targets. OMOs in normal times comprise short-term repos at Bank Rates, long-term repos at market rates determined in variable-rate tenders and outright purchases of high-quality bonds.

There was an initial period in August and early September 2007 when the Bank of England was more restrained than other central banks, owing to fear of moral hazard, leading to low provision of emergency liquidity. Accordingly, it maintained the normal criteria for money market assistance using the instruments highlighted above. This attitude, in turn, was possibly linked to underestimation of macroprudential risk as noted in section one above, as well as poor information flows from the FSA to the Bank about the risks of failure in institutions such as Northern Rock. It could have contributed to the eventual failure of Northern Rock by this approach, although inability to securitize played a role in the failure as well as shortages of liquidity. By contrast, after the crisis of Northern Rock in September 2007, the Bank of England provided regular large quantities of liquidity to the markets from early in the crisis by a number of means.

First, whereas the regular operations are weekly repos and monthly operations at maturities of 3–12 months, the authorities increased the volume of liquidity available at the three-month maturity so as to compensate for the closure of the interbank market. Weekly auctions of dollars were also a feature. More collateral was made eligible; for the weekly operations it was to include UK government bonds, supranationals above AA3 and European government bonds. In the monthly operation it included also AAA tranches of mortgage-backed securities from the UK and European Economic Area (EEA), covered bonds, US and euro credit card bonds and a wider range of sovereign debt. After the Lehman Brothers failure, it also included any debt guaranteed by the government under the October 2008 financial support package, discussed below.

Supplementing regular Bank of England liquidity operations is the Special Liquidity Scheme, which was introduced in January 2008. The Bank of England set up a system of long-term swaps between mortgages and asset-backed securities (ABS) on the one hand and government bonds on the other. The system was designed to avoid the stigma of borrowing from the central bank via the bank's emergency overnight lending facility, as discussed below. Such stigma seems to be a consequence of the occasional use of the instrument at times of stress rather than regular use as for the European Central Bank (ECB).

The Special Liquidity Scheme uses swaps rather than being on the central bank's balance sheet and hence is not reflected in the latter. Furthermore, stigma is reduced by all banks having agreed to say they are using the scheme. The scheme is only for assets already held on the banks' balance sheets in December 2007. Haircuts are imposed on the assets in order to protect the Bank from risk of loss due to credit risk.[2] The value was initially thought likely to total around £50 billion, but the Treasury later acknowledged that funding in excess of £100 billion was available for the Special Liquidity Scheme. In the package of banking support measures announced in October 2008, the ceiling was raised to £200 billion.

There were initial concerns that the Special Liquidity Scheme may have created an end date problem. The end date was aimed to prevent counter-parties relying on the scheme in an unlimited way but it may have intensified concern over liquidity of some banks in the crisis of September–October 2008. The end date was later extended to January 2009 and then to January 2012, by which time the scheme should be wound up successfully, as discussed in section three. Another issue was that banks had the incentive to hoard top-quality collateral because the Special Liquidity Scheme was willing to absorb the lower-quality paper, while high-quality paper can be reserved for private-sector transactions. The Bank of England risked becoming lender of first resort, facing adverse selection as banks had an incentive to offer the worst-quality assets as collateral. However, as the liquidity crisis worsened, such concerns became less pressing, and haircuts were used for low-quality assets.

In October 2008 three further initiatives were announced by the Bank to aid banks in managing liquidity (Bank of England 2008a). First there was a replacement of Standing Facilities by so-called Operational Standing Facilities with the sole aim of dealing with money market imbalances and not giving support to firms in distress, with penalty rates of 25 basis points at all times. This responds to a perception of stigma in the use of Standing Facilities (Tucker 2008). Second is a Discount Window, allowing banks to get liquidity at times of stress in the form of government bonds or cash for up to 30 days against a range of collateral. Third is a permanent long-term repo open market operation against classes of collateral, where counterparts bid separately and against different types of collateral. The new regime is more in line with those already adopted in the USA and eurozone.

Following these policies, as shown in Table 8.6, the Bank of England's balance sheet grew markedly in the second half of 2007 before falling back in the first half of 2008 when the Special Liquidity Scheme was introduced, then growing markedly again in the third quarter of 2008 as the crisis deepened. On balance, asset swaps via the Special Liquidity Scheme and acceptability of a widening range of collateral via long-term repos contained financial system stress by providing financing against illiquid securities (Tucker 2009) and prevented fire sale of illiquid ABS. Accordingly, liquidity policy, after a hesitant start, made a strong positive contribution to financial stability.

Lender of last resort

Northern Rock, a large and rapidly growing mortgage bank with assets of £101 billion at the end of December 2006, suffered a loss of wholesale funding and of scope for securitization, on which it was heavily dependent, at the beginning of the crisis in August 2007 (Treasury Committee 2008). Lender of last resort support was offered to the solvent bank in September 2007, because its failure was considered to pose a major risk of contagion and systemic risk. This support was planned to be announced by the Bank of England, unlike its past behaviour to keep such interventions secret. It has been reported that the Treasury Solicitor gave advice that secrecy was illegal under European Union (EU) financial regulations[3]—but equally, the judgement was made that a large intervention could not readily be kept secret in modern market conditions. There were also believed to be provisions in company reporting that require lender of last resort borrowing to be declared to the market by the recipient. However, the announcement was pre-empted by a leak to the British Broadcasting Corporation (BBC) on the previous day.

This is in stark contrast to earlier episodes such as in 1973 and 1991 when Bank of England emergency liquidity support was covert and successfully so (George 1994).[4] There followed a retail run which was only stopped by a government guarantee—the bank was ultimately nationalized.[5] The internet facilitated the retail run in a manner that would not have been feasible in the past, both via direct withdrawals and panic when the bank's website crashed. An important role was played by a sudden realization on the part of the public of the partial nature of UK deposit insurance, as well as the likely long delay in the payment of compensation.

Particularly in the wake of this, banks were unwilling to access central bank lending facilities, for fear of similar reputation risk—so-called stigma. Even before Northern Rock, a 'witch hunt' in August–September 2007 had forced Barclays PLC to deny having liquidity problems after using central bank facilities. Rather, banks increased market demands for liquidity, for example, via back-up facilities that may have worsened the tight liquidity situation

Table 8.6 UK banks' sterling interbank lending and balance sheet totals (£ million)

	Interbank lending	Total assets	Interbank as a % of total	% growth of interbank	% growth of total
31-Jan-07	620,195	2,999,890	20.7		
28-Feb-07	656,025	3,109,881	21.1	5.8	3.7
31-Mar-07	621,247	3,123,141	19.9	−5.3	0.4
30-Apr-07	622,072	3,190,463	19.5	0.1	2.2
31-May-07	622,935	3,240,600	19.2	0.1	1.6
30-Jun-07	614,141	3,158,944	19.4	−1.4	−2.5
31-Jul-07	635,217	3,231,092	19.7	3.4	2.3
31-Aug-07	639,637	3,244,613	19.7	0.7	0.4
30-Sep-07	248,618	2,876,462	8.6	−61.1	−11.3
31-Oct-07	186,038	2,821,493	6.6	−25.2	−1.9
30-Nov-07	191,554	2,861,268	6.7	3.0	1.4
31-Dec-07	185,633	2,851,472	6.5	−3.1	−0.3
31-Jan-08	197,557	2,944,251	6.7	6.4	3.3
29-Feb-08	197,382	2,996,993	6.6	−0.1	1.8
31-Mar-08	192,843	2,950,156	6.5	−2.3	−1.6
30-Apr-08	209,210	2,987,472	7.0	8.5	1.3
31-May-08	203,417	2,921,192	7.0	−2.8	−2.2
30-Jun-08	194,283	2,930,383	6.6	−4.5	0.3
31-Jul-08	203,120	2,963,150	6.9	4.5	1.1
31-Aug-08	202,201	2,983,077	6.8	−0.5	0.7
30-Sep-08	208,070	3,094,834	6.7	2.9	3.7
31-Oct-08	167,571	3,058,390	5.5	−19.5	−1.2
30-Nov-08	174,476	3,123,689	5.6	4.1	2.1
31-Dec-08	174,033	3,085,474	5.6	−0.3	−1.2
31-Jan-09	180,215	3,156,744	5.7	3.6	2.3
28-Feb-09	200,895	3,201,577	6.3	11.5	1.4
31-Mar-09	191,825	3,205,456	6.0	−4.5	0.1
30-Apr-09	206,900	3,218,786	6.4	7.9	0.4
31-May-09	185,518	3,218,291	5.8	−10.3	0.0
30-Jun-09	196,603	3,210,569	6.1	6.0	−0.2
31-Jul-09	191,894	3,224,205	6.0	−2.4	0.4
31-Aug-09	208,038	3,265,742	6.4	8.4	1.3
30-Sep-09	238,549	3,337,926	7.1	14.7	2.2
31-Oct-09	240,054	3,371,076	7.1	0.6	1.0
30-Nov-09	335,259	3,462,340	9.7	39.7	2.7
31-Dec-09	424,088	3,508,092	12.1	26.5	1.3
31-Jan-10	438,469	4,060,315	10.8	3.4	15.7
28-Feb-10	437,245	4,032,935	10.8	−0.3	−0.7
31-Mar-10	414,459	4,014,081	10.3	−5.2	−0.5
30-Apr-10	396,130	3,967,082	10.0	−4.4	−1.2
31-May-10	249,130	3,801,479	6.6	−37.1	−4.2

Note: There is a change in definition at the beginning of 2010 from 'other UK banks' to 'UK Monetary Financial Institutions excluding the central bank'.
Source: Bank of England

(IMF 2008). The responses to such reputational issues after Northern Rock included the Special Liquidity Scheme and operational standing facilities as discussed above.

The Northern Rock run was partly due to leaks of information, but would arguably have happened in any case after the official announcement. Under the Banking Reform Act of 2009, more scope was introduced for delayed disclosure, with a possible exemption of charges from Companies Act registration for banks in receipt of lender of last resort. The Bank of England's weekly return, which shows inflows and outflows to the accounts including lender of last resort, could be stopped under the Act.

Following these changes, emergency lending in October 2008 to HBOS and RBS was very substantial—around £62 billion—but it was kept confidential for over a year. It benefited from a fiscal backup, with the Treasury offering a fiscal indemnity of £18 billion (NAO 2009), as well as the Bank taking £100 billion of collateral. Justifying confidentiality, it was feared, in the wake of Northern Rock, that formal disclosure implying that financial institutions were calling in their loans to HBOS and RBS on such a colossal scale would have heightened panic. Because of the considerable sensitivity of the support operation at the time, the Treasury judged that it was not in the public interest to follow procedures that allow for confidential notification to the chairs of the Committee of Public Accounts and the relevant departmental select committee.[6] In our view this approach was justified, given the circumstances.

Further issues that arose are that Lehman Brothers' failure exposed the problem of global pools of liquidity for Large Complex Financial Institutions. All of the liquidity was supplied from New York as a matter of ongoing policy, meaning that the London operation was totally illiquid on the day of failure.

As was the case for liquidity policy, there is evidence that the authorities' approach developed so as to become more effective as a lender of last resort by the time of the Lehman Brothers failure. There remain some challenges. Longer-term and lower-quality collateral in liquidity policy as well as the risks of stigma from the lender of last resort pose challenges to the traditional Bagehot doctrine where in crises the central bank will lend freely against 'good' collateral at a 'high' rate. The UK may need to move closer to the euro area model which accepts a much wider range of collateral from a wider range of banks at all times.

Bank recapitalizations

In the crisis of early October, the UK authorities acted decisively to address banks' balance sheet weaknesses at a system-wide level. It was realized that liquidity assistance was not sufficient and the crisis concerned solvency and the unsustainability of the banks' funding model (King 2008). The response entailed a voluntary recapitalization valued at £50 billion for major banks, in the form of preference shares or ordinary shares. The government aims to be a temporary investor, with the preference shares, in particular, repaid over a short period of time. This was implemented in October 2008, and was aimed to cut default risk and hence stem not only funding pressures but also markets' tendencies to value banks by market and not economic intrinsic value.

The complementary policies aimed to address funding problems were to offer guarantees of liabilities up to three years' maturity (financed by fees), amounting to £250 billion for banks seen as adequately capitalized. By November 2009 the Treasury was thought to have disbursed about £117 billion (NAO 2009). There was also an extension of the Bank of England's Special Liquidity Scheme, as discussed above. In order to participate, banks taking on capital assistance were required to maintain lending to households and small businesses at 2007 levels—a promise that was not fulfilled, as discussed further below. Meanwhile, controls were also to be exerted by the government on dividends and remuneration policies of banks taking capital injections.

Controversially, financial stability was added to the criteria in the Enterprise Act under which mergers can be referred to the Secretary of State for Business, Enterprise and Regulatory Reform to consider whether it is in the overall public interest for the normal competition approval process to apply, although mergers remain subject to the EU rules. In effect, the minister can take a rapid decision, advised by the tripartite committee and the Office of Fair Trading. This change allowed the merger of HBOS and Lloyds TSB to be approved speedily. In this case, however, the merger created a bank with almost one-third of the UK market in retail products, which may affect competition in the sector and has created an institution that is likely to have extreme systemic implications if it were to fail.

A number of countries undertook similar policies of recapitalization and guarantees following the UK initiative (Bank of England 2008b). Existing shareholders are concerned about dilution following the government recapitalization (which could give it majority stakes in several major banks), but this could be offset by beneficial falls in funding costs.

Overall, the policy can be judged a success in that there have been no disorderly failures of UK banks, and no retail depositor in a bank operating in the UK has lost money. There remain substantial costs—in the April 2009 Budget the Treasury estimated that the final net cost to the taxpayer might lie within a range from £20 billion to £50 billion, depending on the length and depth of the economic recession and the strength of any recovery. The major determinant will be the prices obtained for the taxpayers' current holdings in the various banks. This, in turn, means the authorities have had to restrain themselves from politically attractive moves to, for example, limit bonuses in the nationalized banks, because consequent loss of key staff would reduce the banks' resale value.

While the recapitalization policy was clearly appropriate, the requirement to maintain lending may be unrealistic, given the need for deleveraging, balance sheet contraction and widening of margins to retain solvency, as well as likely deterioration in credit quality of those seeking credit and indeed lower demand for credit by the private sector. It is noteworthy that the Bank of

England (2008b) estimated that UK banks' balance sheets needed to contract by one-sixth even after capital injections, to return leverage to 2003 levels. Indeed, forcing the banks to lend as in 2007 was feared to be a recipe for major losses and need for further recapitalization. In practice, it has not been achieved, as discussed further below. The mix of preference and ordinary shares may need more justification. Whereas the use of preference shares demanding high interest rates gives an incentive to repay early, ordinary shares give greater control over the institution, as well as a lesser pressure on net income. The latter are arguably preferable during a banking crisis.

Quantitative easing

Following Lehman Brothers' failure, there was seen to be a need for further monetary easing to boost the economy, initially by cutting rates close to zero. In such cases, there are four options to further increase monetary stimulus, as noted by the IMF (Klyuev *et al.* 2009). These are as follows:

- Commitment to maintaining low short rates, to prevent deflation and encourage recovery. As long as the central bank is credible, there should not be risks of inflation or deflation from this action.
- Enhancing liquidity provision beyond traditional liquidity and lender of last resort functions as set out above, sterilized, which may ease risks of credit rationing to the private sector.
- Buying long-term government bonds (unsterilized) to affect the long rate and hence private borrowing rates, albeit not spreads (where the key problem is market risk).
- Buying private-sector assets with a view to directly improving credit market conditions, sterilized or unsterilized (where the key problem is credit risk).

The adoption in early 2009 of the policy of quantitative easing (QE) led the Bank of England, via an off-balance sheet vehicle, to purchase assets from non-banks as well as banks, equivalent to 14% of GDP. This meant that by late 2009, the Bank of England held a significant proportion of UK government bonds, complemented by bank deposits on the liability side. The Bank claims that the QE policy restrained long-term interest rates by around 100 basis points (Dale 2010). This claim is backed by event studies of the impact of QE announcements on gilt yields (Joyce *et al.* 2010), and this seems reasonable. Whereas it was more adventurous than the ECB, which expanded its balance sheet via somewhat longer-term, bank-based instruments, the policy chosen contrasts with the USA where more private assets were purchased. This despite the UK Treasury guarantee which meant that the Bank of England was not vulnerable to credit risk.

In November 2008 the Federal Reserve announced purchases of housing agency debt and agency mortgage-backed securities (MBS) of up to US $600 billion. In March 2009 the Federal Open Market Committee (FOMC) decided to substantially expand its purchases of agency-related securities and to purchase longer-term Treasury securities as well, with total asset purchases of up to $1.75 trillion, an amount twice the magnitude of total Federal Reserve assets prior to 2008. The FOMC stated that the increased purchases of agency-related securities should 'provide greater support to mortgage lending and housing markets' and that purchases of longer-term Treasury securities should 'help improve conditions in private credit markets' (Federal Open Market Committee 2009). However, BIS (2008) note that the policy also was necessitated by the introduction of guarantees for bank debt as noted above, which widened the spreads on unguaranteed agency debt. Volumes of total QE, at 12% of GDP, were similar to the Bank of England (Gagnon *et al.* 2010).

Besides purchasing Treasuries and Agency securities, the Fed adopted a number of programmes with the effect of assisting particular markets (Davis 2009b). The Commercial Paper Funding Facility (CPFF) provided a liquidity backstop to US issuers of commercial paper through a special purpose vehicle that purchased three-month unsecured and asset-backed commercial paper directly from eligible issuers. There was also the creation of the Term Asset-Backed Securities Loan Facility (TALF), a facility that aimed to help market participants meet the credit needs of households and small businesses by supporting the issuance of ABS collateralized by student loans, auto loans, credit card loans, and loans guaranteed by the Small Business Administration (SBA).

The Bank of England claims that although the Bank did not buy private assets in significant quantities, there would be an indirect stimulus to asset demand as non-banks bought equities and private bonds instead of gilts bought by the Bank (Miles 2010). In the eurozone (Lenza *et al.* 2010) QE was considered to have operated through its effect on money market spreads, with a small total effect. Meanwhile, in the USA Gagnon *et al.* (2010) estimate that the overall reduction in the 10-year term premium on US Treasuries in response to the Fed's purchase programme was between 30 and 100 basis points. In addition to this effect, however, they find an even more powerful effect on yields on agency debt and agency mortgage-backed securities 'by improving market liquidity and by removing assets with high prepayment risk from private portfolios' (Gagnon *et al.* 2010: 57).

Meier (2009) of the International Monetary Fund (IMF) suggests reasons why the Bank focused almost entirely on government bonds in its QE policy. One is a concern to avoid propping up markets that may not be viable in the long run, another is to avoid replacing private investors, i.e. in markets where liquidity is already adequate. More generally, it is argued that the Bank of England has signalled a preference for restraint toward operations in private credit markets, citing the fundamental need to avoid reputational risks and keep monetary and fiscal policy apart.

Tucker (2009: 16), for instance, argues that 'not only does exposure to reputational risk matter. Central banks should not be involved in providing facilities which [...] would be likely to result in a transfer of resources to the private sector. That is the realm of fiscal policy. Central banks should stick to central banking'. King (2009: 1) insists that 'the Bank must not become the arbiter of the allocation of public credit to individual companies or sectors— such decisions are rightly and necessarily the province of government. So there is a limit to the scale of the Bank's activities in this area'. Klyuev *et al.* (2009: 11) acknowledge that 'such interventions could distort relative prices, potentially hurt commercial bank profitability, and favour some segments of the credit markets while damaging others'. As Meier (2009) notes, these concerns did not extend to the substantial market risk of the UK's QE, nor the potential scope for fiscal dominance from Bank gilt purchases. They also do not reflect potential concerns about monetization of government debt.

The differing strategies pose the question whether the UK missed the opportunity to influence spreads and credit availability to the private sector more strongly, in other words 'directly improving market liquidity and lowering spreads' (Meier 2009: 44). Certainly, there is little evidence that banks on-lent the reserves that had been created, which would have been another possible benefit of QE. This is despite the focus put on this reserves channel by the Bank where operations have been geared to increasing broad money through transactions that increase bank reserves; '(t)he instrument of monetary policy shifted towards the quantity of money provided rather than its price (Bank Rate)' (Bank of England 2009a). Goodhart (2010) notes that the instability of the 'money multiplier' meant that it was unrealistic to expect the rise in so-called 'high-powered money' (i.e. reserves) to generate any predictable rise in broad money, and indeed the financial stress and volatility in the UK economy plus reserve remuneration made it predictable in current circumstances that banks would just sit on their reserve holdings, while receiving interest on them from the Bank of England. He also notes that the quantity approach is generally misconceived and a price-based approach is correct, 'whereby the Central Bank and the commercial bank set the interest rates at which they will operate, and then the various agents in the private sector and amongst the banks determine monetary quantities endogenously' (Goodhart 2010: F82).

Barrell and Holland (2010) suggest that the impact of QE on GDP could have been 1% instead of 0.5% in 2009 if a quarter of the QE policy had been devoted to 'credit easing', as permitted. As relevant background to this suggestion, they highlighted the greater spread narrowing for BAA bonds over Treasuries in the USA than the UK and attributed this to the above-mentioned credit-easing policies in the USA (although the change in the UK was greater than in the eurozone, suggesting that there were beneficial results to buying from non-banks).

The counter argument to Barrell and Holland (Miles 2010; Dale 2010) is that UK corporate spreads did narrow, yields were lower, bond issuance was higher and LIBOR spreads were lower in the first half of 2010 than hitherto. Whereas this is incontestable, set against it is the fact that this was a global trend. On the one hand, the Bank contributed to this by its policy, but on the other, the benefit could have been greater according to Barrell and Holland.

Section three: exit strategies

Interest rate policy

We now turn to considering exit strategies from the current extraordinary policies set out above. Concerning monetary policy, current market expectations are for a gradual renormalization of short rates, with rises over the medium term from the current level of 0.5%. Whereas current inflationary pressures are partly temporary, e.g. due to the past and future rises in value-added tax (VAT), underlying inflationary pressures seem likely to intensify in the medium term, especially if fiscal policy is not tightened sufficiently or the output gap is overestimated. (The new government forecasting group, the Office of Budgetary Responsibility's June 2010 forecast suggests this could be so.) Of course, there is a need for balance between aggression in monetary tightening and the risk of a double dip recession.

The Bank for International Settlements (BIS 2010a) raises a number of concerns about sustained low short-term interest rates, which are relevant for countries such as the UK. For example, there may be undue rises in asset prices and compression of risk premia. Also, because long-term rates are considerably higher, there may be increased exposure to interest-rate risk and delays in restructuring private- and public-sector balance sheets. Furthermore, it is argued that the low short rates in themselves have contributed to a lasting decline in money market activity. All of these suggest that there will be additional benefits from renormalization of short rates beyond their normal macroeconomic effect, but it needs to be well signalled and cautious to avoid causing losses and credit rationing to the banking system.

Applying these points to the UK, it seems unlikely that there will be a renewed housing boom owing to the ongoing burden of debt, as discussed below. Rather, the low short rates are benefiting the housing market by preventing a sharp rise in arrears and repossessions that would have occurred with higher mortgage interest rates. This is due to the predominance of flexible-rate mortgages in the UK which give rise to low repayments in such a situation. It is hoped that by the time short rates do rise, household income and balance sheet positions will be strong enough to withstand the rise in payments. As regards commercial property, the UK is still suffering from the after effects of the previous boom, as discussed in section four. Hence, the issue of rises in asset prices and compression of risk premia does not seem to be acute in the UK at present. If lending rates are sticky, it may be that the future rise in short rates above 0.5% will itself compress risk premia, rather than the current low level of rates *per se*.

Concerning exposure to interest rate risk, this is again limited in the UK, since banks tend to hold floating rate assets and liabilities (most loans to households and companies are floating rate). On the other hand, the new FSA liquidity regulations (FSA 2008) will require banks to hold more government bonds, which will imply greater interest rate risk. As regards money market activity, it is clear that, as is the case elsewhere, money market activity in the UK remains much lower than in the years up to 2007 (see Table 8.5), but dividing the causes of this between risk perceptions and interest rate levels is not easy. To the extent that there is an additional reduction in interbank lending from the low level of short rates, their renormalization in the future will benefit the UK money markets.

Liquidity policy

In terms of liquidity policy, it is useful to compare prior concerns with reality. As noted above, there was concern regarding the Special Liquidity Scheme with the end date, which was aimed to prevent counterparties relying on the scheme in an unlimited way, but which may have intensified concern over liquidity of some banks in the crisis of September–October 2008. It was announced that although the drawdown window to access the Special Liquidity Scheme closed as planned in January 2009, the Scheme will remain in place for three years, thereby providing participating institutions with continuing liquidity support and certainty. In fact, the successful winding down of the Special Liquidity Scheme to date, in advance of its eventual closure in January 2012, shows that there can be a natural wind-down of short-term operations as interbank markets revive. On the other hand, the Greek crisis led to knock-on effects in the availability of money market funding, also in the UK, showing that the overall situation remains quite fragile, with a 37% fall in interbank assets in May 2010 alone (see Table 8.5).

In the long term, it is doubtful that the Bank can return to the tradition of requiring high-quality collateral at short maturities from sound institutions. Hence there may be a need to consider pricing the 'liquidity insurance' that the central bank provides. Note in this context that the EU Commission wants a new European law in 2011 that would require governments to set up national resolution funds to cover future bail-out costs. These national funds would be financed by an obligatory levy on financial institutions. The UK has expressed interest in imposing a levy, but not necessarily for use in financing a rescue fund. Nevertheless, the level of fees could have a macroprudential effect by being related to the 'liquidity insurance' banks receive and their contribution to systemic risk.

Further issues needing resolution in respect of liquidity policy relate first to the use of wholesale funding, which central bank liquidity replaced—are the banks' strategies sufficiently adjusted to survive without central bank support? This issue is discussed further in section four.

Second, can securitization recover, or are further reforms needed? UK banks were heavily dependent on securitization to sustain the flow of lending that was being made through their operations: securitization amounted to 25% of new mortgages in 2007. This meant that they were hit particularly hard by the onset of the sub-prime crisis.[7] The UK authorities passed legislation early in 2008 enabling the issuance of regulated covered bonds compliant with the UCITS Directive,[8] thereby putting the UK at par with some of its European counterparts. This was hoped to be a vehicle for recovery of securitization in the UK, but the issuance collapsed at the time of Lehman Brothers.

Third, can banks be obliged to hold pools of liquidity in every host jurisdiction, which would offset the Lehman Brothers problem that the UK authorities faced?[9]

Fourth, there is already a major tightening of FSA prudential liquidity regulation underway. The current proposal[10] includes a significant increase in banks' buffers of liquid assets. The FSA would require banks to hold 6%–10% of assets in government bonds compared with an average of 5% for the 10 largest banks at present. The FSA calculates that this implies that banks could switch £87 billion to £350 billion of their assets into government bonds. The question arises whether the policy can successfully oblige banks both to rebuild liquidity and reduce reliance on wholesale funding.

Lender of last resort and bank rescues

Lender of last resort and bank rescues also raise important issues. On the one hand, it seems clear that the net loss the government is likely to make is much less than the gross expenditure. In due course, the stakes in the major banks will be sold on the market, while losses on guaranteed assets will be realized. Current estimates (e.g. by NAO 2009) suggest eventual losses of around £20 billion.

However, more important than the winding down of support is expectations and incentives—whether current regulatory plans are sufficient to prevent a recurrence of bank support, given the expectations and incentives generated by the rescue. Haldane (2010) points to the difference between support credit ratings and standalone credit ratings of banks, where the former reflect expectations of government support. Anticipated government support was shown to give a huge benefit in terms of a lower cost of funds. The differential has widened for all banks during the crisis as their underlying fragility has increased (reducing the standalone rating), while the clarity of government support has also increased (underpinning the support rating). The rating differential widened by three notches during the crisis on average.

Haldane (2010) also notes a bias in this shift to large banks. The average rating difference is up to five notches for large banks and only up to three notches for small ones. In effect, large banks are benefiting hugely from expected public support in terms of their cost of funds, in return for lesser systemic risk due to public support. Some 90% of UK support goes to the largest institutions. Not only did larger banks get more support but they also imposed greater risk on the economy than small ones, since they all exposed themselves to similar systematic risks as well as holding higher-volatility assets, perhaps due to 'too big to fail' perceptions.

This pattern is consistent with results of earlier work by Davis and Zhu (2009), who found commercial property price movements (a form of systematic risk) to have a smaller effect on the loan quality and provisions for small banks than for large banks. Also small banks' profits were less geared to commercial property prices than are those of large banks. They argued that this is consistent with large banks being more willing to take risk, perhaps as a consequence of enjoying higher protection by the safety net with consequent moral hazard.

Haldane sees this pattern as an externality which he calls 'banking pollution'. How can it be reduced in an appropriate exit strategy? There are two ways to deal with an externality, taxing it and putting direct controls on the adverse activity, what he calls 'prohibition'.

We can see tighter banking regulation as a 'taxation' approach to the externality. In this context, the FSA (Turner 2009), for example, has proposed inter alia new capital and liquidity requirements to constrain commercial banks' role in risky proprietary trading activities; the quality and quantity of overall capital should be increased; capital required against trading book activities should be increased significantly; a counter-cyclical capital adequacy regime should be introduced, with capital buffers that increase in economic upswings and decrease in recessions; and a maximum gross leverage ratio should be introduced as a backstop discipline against excessive growth in absolute balance sheet size. Many of these are being currently pursued in international arenas, for example see section four. It is important that improvements in the UK regulatory regime are not delayed by the consequences of the shift of bank regulatory responsibility to the Bank of England.

A further form of taxation will be the new bank rescue fund being set up in the UK in line with the rest of the EU. The fee structure will have to be designed carefully to ensure that it does not generate moral hazard.

However, Haldane (2010) questions whether taxation will ever be enough. Banks can always increase risk-taking to offset any feasible increase in capital, and return the level of risk to one that threatens the system. Accordingly, there may be a need for 'prohibition'. Banks of over $100 billion in size, for example, appear to generate major systemic risks but apparently do not offer any economic benefits in terms of economies of scale or scope. Should they be broken up? Or could there be a benefit from reducing banks' exposure to proprietary trading, as is planned in the USA? The UK sees a need for structural measures to resolve the banking structure, as it has set up a Banking Commission to consider structural policy as discussed below.

A further issue in exit strategies is the 'reward of failure' for Lloyds in allowing it to take over HBOS and gaining a dominant position in the banking market, with the government over-ruling competition authorities. This is again an area where there is a need for further investigation by the competition authorities, with a break-up of the large institution being desirable once the situation becomes calm again.

Quantitative easing

Regarding exit from quantitative easing, a pause took place in early 2011, although scope remained for a second round if conditions recommend it; in

2011 there was no sign of the Bank seeking to tighten interest rate policy, given ongoing weakness in economic data. Meanwhile, the above-mentioned new FSA liquidity policy will make banks the natural 'home' for excess gilts, meaning again that any impact on yields may be attenuated, depending on the timing of these respective policies. In this context, access to credit for small firms and households remains constrained, despite ongoing QE, raising the question of whether its conclusion may aggravate the situation. Finally, some have suggested that the Bank of England may possibly hold some 'excess' securities to maturity to avoid market risk and a boost to yields.

Timing of exit strategies

There is a form of endogeneity in the timing of exit strategies; once crisis containment policies are implemented they, along with the crisis itself, influence subsequent short-term economic and financial stability, and these in turn dictate when monetary and fiscal support can be withdrawn. Consequently, the IMF (2010a) observes that since the timing and extent of economic recovery will vary across countries, domestic exit strategies need to be flexible.

For the UK, getting the timing right requires the monitoring of certain macroeconomic and financial trends: both direct leading indicators of financial instability such as property prices (Barrell, Davis, Liadze and Karim 2010a) and factors that indirectly influence financial instability by affecting leading indicators, such as investment.

For this reason, as well as its direct relevance to the future of the UK economy, we will therefore in the next section give an overview of the current state of the UK economy's macrofinancial linkages which are likely to be important for recovery, notably the housing market, investment and financial market conditions. We will then consider the macroeconomic impact of any new macroprudential regulations in the UK and what these imply for UK financial service provision.

Section four: scope for return to growth

The UK housing market

The UK housing market has become of major importance as a repository of household wealth which is relevant for consumption, and also as collateral for the large volume of mortgage debt outstanding. Between the first quarter of 1998 and the third quarter of 2007, UK house prices increased by 179% on average, whereas between the third quarter of 2007 and the first quarter of 2009, prices fell by 17% (ONS 2009a).[11]

Although the ONS (2009b) suggests house price declines may have stabilized recently, residential properties still appear to be overvalued. They suggest that prices of assets in (relatively) fixed supply should grow at the rate of the economy as a whole in the long run, hence the pattern of the house price to income ratio can be used to draw general conclusions about housing market overheating: ONS (2009a) suggests the long-term average house price to income ratio was 4.02 (Q1 1998–Q1 2009). In contrast, for Q1 2009 the ratio stood at 4.35, implying that house prices were overvalued,[12] and that more correction will be observed.

Figure 8.1 shows that house price falls in response to the crisis have improved housing affordability for existing home owners (Halifax index) and first-time buyers (Nationwide index) recently. Mortgage payments as a proportion of income capture the impact of interest changes on housing affordability. In this context, the timing of any exit strategies will influence future afford-ability since if interest rates are to increase in line with inflation during a recessionary period when incomes are lower, housing could become much less affordable.

Reflecting the crisis, the number of mortgage approvals in 2008 was one-half that of 2007 and one-third of the 2006 peak value (ONS 2009a). Overall credit growth to households in early 2010 was close to zero. However, mortgage debt remains very high as a proportion of GDP, at around 80%, and total household debt/GDP is around 107% with little decline since the crisis (partly, of course, reflecting changes in the denominator). Lower interest rates have reduced household income gearing (interest payments as a proportion of income) from 11% in 2008 to around 7%. As noted above, this has restrained arrears and repossessions. However, a renormalization of short rates to 5% could raise income gearing to levels as high as the early 1990s crisis (13%), if spreads remain wide (Bank of England 2010b). This could expose banks to major default risks, not least if negative equity starts to grow further due to falling house prices.

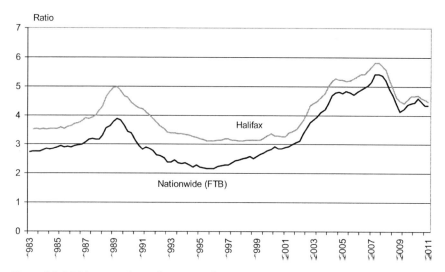

Figure 8.1 UK house price to income ratios
Source: Adapted from ONS 2009a; sources Halifax and Nationwide

Changes in house prices generate a collateral effect and a wealth effect which influence consumption behaviour. Falling house prices reduce scope for equity withdrawals (negative wealth effect), thereby restricting the funds available for consumption. Simultaneously, lower house prices reduce collateral values, limiting households' access to cheaper forms of secured borrowing (negative collateral effect) (ONS 2009b). There is also direct credit rationing in the wake of the banking crisis, with mortgage spreads having widened from 1.5%–2.0% in 2008 to 3.0–4.0% in May 2010 on comparable loan-to-value mortgages (Bank of England 2010b). In combination, these effects have reduced households' propensity to consume and the amount of credit available for consumption, as can be seen in Figure 8.2.

Moreover, the probable further reductions in consumer confidence likely after the government's proposed spending cuts mean that positive collateral and wealth effects from house price increases are unlikely to be significant in the near future. Signs that these negative trends have already started to materialize are apparent from the Bank of England's (2010a) latest Agent's

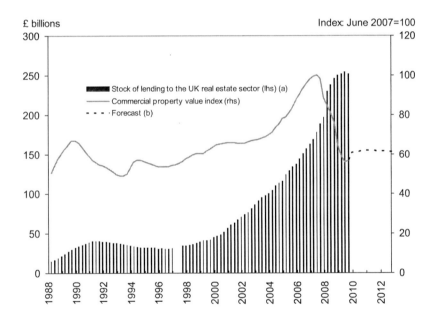

Figure 8.2 Stock of lending by UK resident banks and building societies to the UK real estate sector and UK commercial property capital values

Notes: (a) Data cover lending in both sterling and foreign currency, expressed in sterling terms; (b) dotted line is implied property price forecast calculated by adjusting the value of total-return derivatives contracts for income returns, which are assumed to revert to their long-run average by the end of 2010.

Source: Reproduced from Bank of England 2009b.

Original sources: Bank of England, IPD, Morgan Stanley Research, Thomson Datastream and Bank calculations.

Summary of Business Conditions for August 2010. According to this, the supply of housing on the market has increased but demand has been limited due to households' concerns about government cuts and their future job security.

In comparison to Spain, where a housing bubble and concurrent construction boom unravelled around the sub-prime crisis, the UK has experienced a smaller increase in unemployment. Nevertheless, unemployment in the UK has increased somewhat, with a further impact on consumer confidence. More job losses are likely from fiscal consolidation. Interviews with private-sector firms indicate that they have been reluctant to make new hires, preferring to use temporary staff or overtime where possible. They do not expect this position to change in the near future and, moreover, they suggest that any contribution they do make towards employment will be outweighed by the coalition government's cuts to public-sector jobs. At the same time, construction firms report that growth in new residential builds is slow, as is the pace of commercial property construction. Many public-sector contracts for building work have been put on hold or cancelled and these trends are likely to continue over the coming year.

There is a wider impact of employment trends on economic performance. Associated declines in productivity are greater than in past downturns. To an extent, this may be due to labour hoarding in the UK, which restricts the reallocation of labour during a recovery process. However a considerable part of the decline in per capita output will be due to the downsizing of the financial sector (IMF 2009). We now turn to wider investment and financial conditions in more detail.

Investment and financial conditions

Banking-sector problems are likely to transmit to other real activities in the economy. Falling household income hits demand for products while credit rationing makes it harder for businesses to secure credit. Indeed, the stock of bank lending to companies has been falling since early 2009, albeit reflecting demand as well as supply conditions in the credit market. Spreads on lending to small firms in mid-2010 were close to levels seen at the end of 2009, and almost 1 percentage point above their levels at the end of 2008, although spreads for larger firms have narrowed (Bank of England 2010b). Between 2008 and 2009 corporate bankruptcies increased by 50% and despite the Bank of England maintaining historically low interest rates and using moral suasion upon the banking system, firms have seen a drop in the availability of investment financing. Consequently, there is potentially a slow recovery ahead during which output expectations and investment are likely to fall further.

In recognition of the impact of reduced credit availability, HM Treasury has pressed for improved access to non-bank credit for firms. In 2007 UK corporate borrowing via bond issuance stood at 9% of their total financing compared to 32% via loans. This contrasts with US firms, which obtain 14% of their financing from bond issuance and only 26% in loans (HM Treasury

2010). However, the asymmetric information that surrounds small and medium-sized enterprises (SMEs), which are not publicly listed, means non-bank financing is likely to be costly and thus considered unaffordable when borrowers expect future demand for their output will be low. The inability to substitute bank credit with alternative non-bank credit is thus likely to negatively impact future investment further.

UK banks also face significant potential losses from their exposures to commercial property markets where prices had risen continuously over the past decade (see Figure 8.2). By Q3 2009 the UK financial system held £250 billion in outstanding commercial property loans, a 10-fold increase over the previous decade. The Bank of England (2009b) notes that between 2007 and 2009 the IPD All Property Index,[13] which tracks commercial property prices, had declined by nearly 45%.[14] Although there was an increase of 10% over the first half of 2010, prices remain well below their peak levels, and recovery is slow: IPD (2010) notes that during May 2010 the IPD index grew by only 0.5%. Concurrently, as can be seen in Figure 8.3, rents have fallen by 10.7%,[15] which has reduced yields on commercial leases. Average loan to value ratios on recent commercial property loans are over 100% and more recent data suggest that these ratios are set to worsen, as discussed below.

The Bank of England suggests that these property market trends reflect an increase in demand for prime properties which is counteracted by decreases in demand for non-prime properties, and that prices of the latter will continue to fall. Moreover, as Figure 8.4 shows, the declines in commercial property

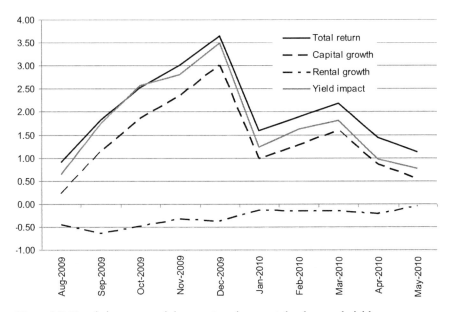

Figure 8.3 Trends in commercial property prices, rental values and yields
Source: Investment Property Databank

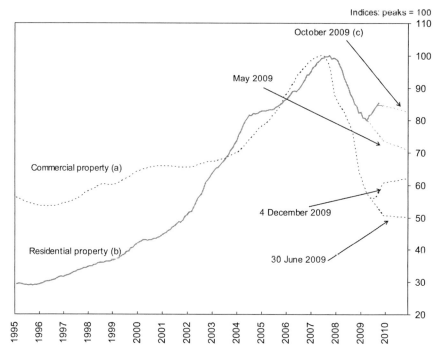

Figure 8.4 UK property price forecasts
Note: (a) Commercial property price projections are calculated by adjusting total return derivatives for income returns, which are assumed to revert to their long-run averages by the end of 2010; (b) house price projections are based on a range of external forecasts from forecasts for the UK economy: a comparison of independent forecasts, May 2009 and October 2009, as compiled by HM Treasury; (c) sample of external forecasts too small in November for the results to be representative. Source: Reproduced from Bank of England 2009b. Original sources: Halifax, HM Treasury, IPD, Morgan Stanley Research, Nationwide, Thomson Datastream and Bank calculations

prices are much deeper than those of residential properties, with correspondingly negative implications for banks with property portfolios concentrated in the commercial sector.

The repercussion for borrowers is that they will continue to violate their loan-to-value (LTV) covenants, with the Property Industry Alliance predicting that LTVs on recent loans will reach 114% on average by the end of 2010 (Bank of England 2009b). As collateral values decline, real estate firms will continue to face borrowing difficulties. Nevertheless, Bank of England (2009b) suggests the impact on bank balance sheets may be mitigated due to some banks' willingness to show forbearance towards LTV covenant breaches and, in some cases, their decisions not to revalue underlying properties where loans continue to perform. They have also helped to restructure debt taken out by borrowers experiencing cash-flow pressures. However, Bank of England (2010b) notes a risk that should banks become less willing or able to forbear

on breaches of covenants, this could prompt an increase in corporate liquidations and a greater supply of foreclosed property. That could in turn trigger
a renewed fall in prices and a rise in losses in the event of default on banks'
commercial exposures, with a renewed downward spiral.

Aside from the ongoing corrections to property prices, Bank of England
(2009b) notes that deteriorating macroeconomic conditions will exert additional negative effects on bank balance sheets via significant increases in the
probabilities of default by real estate firms. There are two channels by which
this could occur: income risk and scheduled re-financing.

Borrowers will face income risk from the reductions in rental demand
during the recession. As Figure 8.3 shows, yields on commercial property
have fallen significantly and if this continues as is expected, larger numbers of
real estate firms will face debt servicing problems. Consequently, banks will
see a rise in non-performing loans and subsequent loan impairment charges;
these scenarios appear to be corroborated by more recent commercial property
market trends (Bank of England 2010b).

Commercial property loans are usually non-amortizing, so that on maturity
the borrower must pay back the outstanding principal amount which is close to
the initial amount borrowed. Thus on maturity, borrowers must either sell the
property or refinance. Banks are increasingly reluctant to accommodate the
latter; Bank of England (2009b) cites research by De Montfort University which
suggests that banks have constrained LTVs on new lending to between 60%
and 65%. Borrowers facing negative equity will find it challenging to raise the
necessary capital for refinancing. This will affect smaller companies more
since, as discussed above, unlike larger firms they are constrained in non-bank
funding sources such as rights issues. The ECB (2010) comments on the potential losses that UK banks face and their negative implications for domestic
and global financial stability.

Performance of the UK financial services sector

The performance of the financial sector is relevant both in itself for its impact
on the wider economy, via availability of credit, and also its direct contribution to GDP. Recent data (Bank of England 2010b) suggest that the operating
environment for the UK banking system has deteriorated for several reasons:

First, there is exposure to sovereign risk; the distribution of sovereign risk
exposures of individual international banks is largely unknown to investors.[16]
In spring 2010 this asymmetric information caused investors to substitute
away from what they perceive as potentially risky lending to banks towards
safer assets such as US treasury bills, in the wake of the Greek crisis. Given
that public deficit reductions in several economies will be a protracted process
with substantial public opposition, confidence in banks with sovereign exposures may not recover for some time. Consequently, banks' access to funds in
future will become increasingly restricted and may manifest as higher borrowing rates for consumers of bank credit. Although the UK banking system

has limited exposure to sovereign risk, balance sheets of UK banks contain large amounts of counterparty exposures from European banks which do hold substantial sovereign risk. These indirect exposures may therefore raise the risk profile of UK banks. The Bank of England (2010b) notes how uncertainty regarding European banks' counterparty exposures to sovereign risks has already led to drastic increases in credit default swap premia for large banks,[17] although 'stress tests' published in summer 2010 were expected to be helpful in reducing tensions.

Second, there is the problem of endogeneity, which could put pressure on the UK banking system via indirect means. As global investors substitute away from lending to international banks in general, wholesale funding will be harder to obtain. This is likely to raise the cost of borrowing for firms and households and consequently these borrowers will find it increasingly difficult to refinance debt on favourable terms. The knock-on effect will be an increase in loan impairments, non-performing loans and defaults on UK bank balance sheets.

Third, many UK banks have shown forbearance towards distressed borrowers during the post-crisis period, which has mitigated the recessionary impact on systemic stability. The strategy of forbearance by banks has been largely possible due to historically low interest rates set by the Bank of England; this has meant that the debt-servicing capacity of household and corporate borrowers has been upheld. Moreover, public support of the UK banking system has put moral pressure on banks to restructure loans rather than record actual defaults. However, Bank of England (2010b) notes that this leniency may come to an end if interest rates are forced to rise in response to above-target inflation or, alternatively, if economic growth does not prove to be sustainable. Such conditions are likely to increase the volume of non-performing loans on banks' balance sheets, further raise banks' aversion to risky lending and thus reduce the amount of forbearance they are willing to show towards distressed borrowers, as noted above.

If UK banks do become unwilling to show leniency towards borrowers whose repayment characteristics worsen (e.g. increases in loan-to-value ratios due to falling asset prices), there are likely to be negative implications for corporate sectors with high exposures to commercial property. As discussed in the previous section, prospects for UK commercial property are far from buoyant (IPD 2010) and an inability to restructure or refinance loans could result in corporate liquidations. Given the level of exposure of the UK banking system to commercial property price risk, a decline in economic activity or an increase in interest rates would reduce the net worth of the UK banking system. The impact of these two transmission mechanisms may have been muted so far. The Bank of England (2010b) has empirically modelled the growth of corporate liquidation rates as a function of GDP growth rates, commercial property price growth, the growth rate of corporate lending and the average borrowing rate faced by corporate firms in an attempt to explain why corporate liquidation rates associated with the recent recession are lower than those associated with previous recessions. They conclude that the historically low interest rates surrounding this recession have limited liquidations. In addition, recessions of the 1980s and 1990s show that there is a lag before reductions in GDP growth translate into corporate insolvencies, because firms can run down their liquid assets before entering liquidation.[18]

Fourth, there are also structural reasons for the decline in prospects for the UK financial system. Banks will face considerable challenges of their own as public support is withdrawn, because the largest UK banks will need to secure funds to replace taxpayer bailouts to the tune of £750 billion–£800 billion by the end of 2012. This refinancing burden will be exacerbated by the need to restructure existing sources of wholesale funding, 60% of which are due to mature within a year. Banks had been relying on short-term debt funding, preferring to substitute historically costly longer-maturity debt with cheaper central bank funding. Given the ambiguous outlook for the UK economy, negotiating extensions to maturity may not be straightforward. Indeed, IMF (2010b) suggests that funding spreads in the UK and USA have become negative since the end of 2009 so that funds have already become more costly for banks in these regions. Looking ahead, considerable short-term debt is due to mature over the next five years and refinancing will be costlier.

The Bischoff Report (HM Treasury 2009) argues for measures to protect the competitiveness of the UK financial services sector on the basis of its contribution to the UK economy; it generates 8% of GDP and almost 14% of government tax receipts, boosting public spending. As well as the UK being endowed with a comparative advantage in services as a consequence of the success of financial services, the financial sector arranges financing for leading industries which also hold comparative advantages such as IT, pharmaceuticals and aerospace engineering. The Bischoff Report argues that despite the importance of the financial services sector, the UK economy has not become unbalanced; over the last decade UK financial services have contributed between 5% and 8% towards UK output, but this is in line with other market-based economies such as the USA, Singapore and Hong Kong. The accumulation of skills and experience within the sector has allowed financial institutions to branch into new revenue-generating areas: carbon trading, Islamic finance, sovereign wealth funds and financing emerging market growth. Moreover, financial services do not appear to have crowded out other important sectors: manufacturing continues to account for 14% of UK output.

The gains from financial services in the UK are much higher than in other sectors: productivity per capita in the financial service sector is well above the economy average[19] and the industry employs over 1 million workers who contribute to four main areas of service: banking, insurance, investments (e.g. institutional investors) and financial infrastructure (e.g. payments systems). The IMF (2009) observes that the losses to this productive sector, which are still to fully materialize, will cause a considerable decline in UK potential output in the medium term. Furthermore, the predominance of financial services suggests a need for caution in public finances, since the collapse in fiscal revenue from financial services was a key reason for the UK's worse fiscal position than other OECD countries.

Reform of financial services

While future regulatory reforms to financial markets are being widely debated, it is hard to predict the precise structure that the UK financial services sector will take. Proposals for regulatory reform are coloured by domestic and international agendas. Moreover, the domestic debate is in flux due to the changeover of the UK government and their plans for revised regulatory structures; it had been announced at the time of writing that the FSA was to be dissolved and its prudential-supervisory duties were to be taken over by the Bank of England.

What is clear is that returns on equity in finance may decline owing to new regulatory rules on capital adequacy and liquidity and further possible restrictions on institutional size, activity and capital quality. From bank shareholders' perspectives, such reductions in returns point towards the need for caution and restraint in the adoption of new regulations, but this may in turn impede the adoption of socially optimal levels of regulation.

Barrell, Davis, Karim and Liadze (2010) show that revisions to capital adequacy, albeit agreed internationally, would result in some countries' banking systems requiring more extra capital than others' which were healthier and less volatile prior to the crisis, if an objective of reducing risk across the OECD is to be achieved. The UK would be one such banking system and the consequent rise in the cost of capital could lower the international competitiveness of UK banks and be detrimental to future investment. We discuss this point further in the next section.

As regards structural reform, the Governor of the Bank of England is mentioned by the House of Commons Treasury Committee (2009) as recognizing the benefits in terms of stability that would be achieved by the separation of traditional and investment banking, but he also points out the difficulties in achieving this in practice: returns on heavily regulated retail banks' equity would fall below those of less regulated wider banks and investors would shift funds accordingly.

Clues to the eventual structure of UK financial markets can be found in the latest policy initiative by the Conservative-Liberal Democrat coalition, which has formed the Future of Banking Commission. The Commission aims to consider the views of the banking industry, academics, regulators, the government and the public, and to forward these to the Chancellor for incorporation into final regulations. Their initial proposals[20] (Future of Banking Commission 2010) include the use of 'living wills' (Recovery and Resolution Plans) detailing the mechanisms by which a bank in difficulties will ensure its continuance without jeopardizing systemic stability. This will be partially achieved by ensuring separate balance sheets and liquidity funding for core banking activities so that deposits and the payments system are ring-fenced from risky investment banking activities by the firm.

The Future of Banking Commission also intends to complement living wills by calling for 'safe haven' accounts that are 100% guaranteed because funds are invested in safe assets. Market discipline of banks is to be strengthened by raising the status of depositors above that of bond holders in the event of bankruptcy, so that the latter have more incentives to monitor the banks. The report also unambiguously calls for structural reforms to separate core and investment banking activities so that depositors are protected, moral hazard in the presence of taxpayer guarantees is reduced and the 'too big to fail' problem is minimized. Although the Commission recognizes that the separation of activities may not in itself prevent bank failure (as in the case of Northern Rock), it hopes that in combination with improved capital and liquidity standards UK banks will be more stable in future.

The impact of macroprudential regulation

An emerging consensus, particularly following the sub-prime crisis, is that there is a need to complement microprudential regulation, concerned with firm-level stability, with macroprudential regulation, which promotes systemic stability. The latter considers both the overall tightness of regulatory policies and whether they should vary over the cycle. However, international consensus on the next generation of regulations will be influenced by the diverse levels of regulatory tightening required by players in the international banking arena. Adhering to revised capital and liquidity standards may be more costly for the UK banking system relative to other Anglo-Saxon banking systems such as France and Germany, partly because the UK banking system holds much less liquidity than other OECD banking systems, but also because the UK economy is more volatile and crisis-prone than other major EU economies.

As also discussed in section one, Barrell, Davis, Liadze and Karim (2010a, 2010b; Barrell, Davis, Karim and Liadze 2010) derived a stable early warning system for banking crises in OECD economies. They found that the most important macroprudential indicators are two banking sector 'robustness' variables: unweighted capital adequacy and liquidity, and two real economy 'vulnerability' variables: residential real estate prices and the current account. Having identified these policy instruments Barrell, Davis, Karim and Liadze (2010) estimated the changes to capital and liquidity standards that would be required to restore systemic stability in 14 OECD economies, including the UK. Their results suggest that the UK banking system would have to increase its capital and liquidity buffers substantially more than most other OECD banking systems in order to reduce crisis risk to a given level. So, for example, using maximum crisis risk over 1998–2008 as a benchmark to determine desirable levels of capital and liquidity, the UK needs 6 percentage points more liquidity and capital to reduce crisis risks to 1% per annum, whereas for France it is 5%, Germany 3% and Italy 2%. Barrell, Davis, Karim and Liadze (2010) note that an international agreement that imposed an average rise in capital to attain the 1% crisis level would mean 3.7% more capital across the

OECD as a whole. The UK would either have to impose higher charges via its domestic regulation, or become effectively undercapitalized relative to the rest of the OECD, imposing externalities on other countries. The former would appear more likely. Although it is not clear how these ratios would translate into micro-level bank adjustments, it is inevitable that banks will pass some of these additional costs on to customers via increased spreads. Given the already depressed prospects for UK investment discussed in section two, this may affect productivity substantially.

The revised capital and liquidity standards are likely to test the competitiveness and business models of many UK banks. The new standards which are currently undergoing calibration are expected to be implemented by the end of 2012, by which time it is possible that much of the monetary support to the financial system will have been withdrawn, while wholesale funding needs will be sizeable. A significant change to the UK's financial architecture is thus possible, with weaker, inefficient banks disappearing to leave a more concentrated banking system. This, in turn, will put more banks in the 'too big to fail' category and will challenge regulators further.

Further pressures on unprofitable banks may emerge if rules on the quality of regulatory capital are revised according to current debates. There is widespread consensus in the regulatory policy community that Tier 2 capital as defined in the Basel Capital Adequacy Agreement is unsatisfactory. Turner (2009) expressed concerns that Tier 2 is only useful to protect creditors in failure (gone concern), but does not give the right incentives to banks' ongoing operations (going concern). From a regulatory point of view, this implies capital adjustments should be biased towards holding more equity capital, which for unprofitable, smaller banks could be costly.

In the context of reforms proposed by the Basel Committee on Banking Supervision (which will be embedded into Basel III), the Bank of England (2010b) identifies two channels by which UK banking capital will have to increase. These will have different impacts on banks' operations. The first type of increase will be in response to the Capital Requirements Directive (CRD 3) as part of EU legislature which will make operational the Basel Committee's requirements. This directive is expected to have a moderate impact on banks' existing Tier 1 capital ratios, especially since the Basel Committee will defer the adoption of this component to the end of 2011. The expectation is that the transition period will allow banks to adjust their portfolios to be able to meet the new requirements without rationing credit to real sectors.

However, European banks will face an additional layer of capital adjustments instigated by Basel III. These will be transmitted by revisions to the existing Capital Requirements Directive (CRD 4) of the EU Commission. If implemented immediately, these adjustments would have a significant impact on UK banks' operations: major banks' core Tier 1 capital ratios would fall short by 4%, whereas the CRD 3 implies a shortfall of below 2%. Hence, to minimize the loss of real output from frictions in credit availability, the Bank of England (2010b) suggests the timing of any implementation should be conditional on the state of the economy, a proposal that accords with the views of the FSA.

Calculations of the impact of increased capital on economic out-turns are quite variable. Barrell *et al.* (2009) suggest that reforms introduced solely in the UK gradually should have a long-run impact of around –0.1% on GDP per percentage point increase in required capital and liquidity. The Financial Stability Board (2010) has comparable median predictions for individual countries. Barrell, Holland and Karim (2010) show that the effects are much lower than –0.1% if all countries move together to tighter regulation—around –0.03% or lower per percentage point increase in liquidity and capital. This is because when all OECD countries act together, the initial impact is to lower investment and raise saving. Real interest rates fall as a result. As equity markets reflect the discounted value of future profits and the discount rate has fallen the equity price rises and the cost of equity finance falls. These two effects offset about two-thirds of the output costs we identified when the UK acted alone. Certain industry bodies suggest much more severe impacts, but their neutrality is in doubt.

Recently, in recognition of the procyclical amplification of systemic risks during the sub-prime episode, BIS (2010b) proposed a macroprudential framework that embodies a countercyclical capital structure so that bank losses during downturns are better absorbed. The House of Commons Treasury Committee (2010) welcomes the implementation of countercyclical provisioning as a means of reducing volatility in the supply of credit to the private sector. However, Barrell, Davis, Karim and Liadze (2010) did not find evidence of procyclicality being driven by GDP or credit per se; rather it is the risky lending practices to which GDP growth contributes alongside behavioural factors which contribute to risk build-up during the upturn. These are indicated by factors such as asset prices and current account balances. Hence provisioning based on GDP or credit cycles may not adequately address systemic risk—and penalize 'benign' upturns.

The UK's position on whether rules or discretion should dominate revised policies is also subject to criticism. The Bank of England (2009b) suggests that discretionary leeway in the enforcement of domestic regulation is necessary, arguing that it is difficult to design rules-based systems that survive through time. Nevertheless, Barrell, Davis, Karim and Liadze (2010) show that it is possible to institute rules for capital adequacy that respond to property prices.

The regulatory changes discussed above suggest that a turbulent change to the UK banking system is possible. However, it is interesting that from the point of view of the banking sector, the imminent regulatory changes and the tax to be imposed on the banking system were not the most important concerns in May 2010 (Bank of England 2010b). Banks were more worried about sovereign risk exposures, the level of public debt and the potential risks arising from an economic downturn. However, the banking sector did place risks associated with regulatory changes above risks arising from both property price declines and increases in household and corporate defaults. Given the outlook for investment and financial conditions as well as the housing market, as discussed in sections two and one, respectively, it remains to be seen whether this ranking of risk by the banking community will remain the same.

Conclusions

Following this review of UK monetary, banking and financial policies in recent years, we note that in the run-up to the crisis, a key underlying issue was that macroprudential surveillance failed to predict the depth of the crisis, and although some concerns were expressed, no policy action was taken (partly reflecting lack of macroprudential levers). During the crisis, interest rate easing may have been delayed unduly, while the quantitative easing policy could have been more effective had it focused on private sector assets, and the bank rescue strategies focused too little on the implications for competition. Exit strategies are still in the offing, but it is essential that they be well designed to avoid risks of inflation and moral hazard on the one hand, and renewed recession and credit rationing on the other. The risk of prolonged low interest rates, for example in causing atrophy of funding markets, also has to be taken into account.

A successful return to growth requires the financial sector and economy to function well together, e.g. in respect of the housing market, investment and banking/financial market conditions, including impact of likely regulatory reforms. For example, given the importance of the UK housing market as a store of household wealth, recent trends in residential property prices have negative implications for households' and banks' balance sheets. Corrections to over-valued property prices have begun and corresponding weakness in consumption is likely, with wider impacts on growth. The level of defaults and non-performing loans associated with negative equity in residential property may cause problems for UK bank balance sheets in the medium term.

In addition, the increased risk aversion of banks towards non-prime borrowers has continued to reduce the availability of credit to the real sector, which is likely to generate further negative effects on UK growth. The UK banking system may also face problems due to its exposure to the commercial property market, since commercial property prices are on a downward trend and indebtedness of property firms is high. UK banks themselves are also concerned with their counterparties' exposures to sovereign risk. Furthermore, the overall macroprudential risks faced by banks are making it harder for UK banks to access wholesale funds. Meanwhile, the proposed costly changes to regulatory capital will raise the cost of credit, albeit with a major benefit of reducing the risk of future crises. These issues suggest the scope for the UK economy's return to growth may become increasingly restricted in the coming years, to the extent that it relies on credit finance.

Notes

1 In the authors' words, 'the finding of a single structural break may be questionable. The financial crisis entered its most intense phase in September 2008

with the collapse of Lehman Brothers and associated events; steep reductions in UK policy rates began in the following month. Since these events are excluded from a 15% trimmed sample, we also ran the Quandt-Andrews test with trimming rate of 5%; in this case two structural breaks were detected, in October 2008 and again in April 2007. There are too few observations on the post-Lehman period in our sample (13) to permit estimation of a separate policy rule in this period'.

2 The haircuts vary with maturity and credit/liquidity quality. While they can be varied by the Bank, in April 2008 they ranged from 1% for open market eligible and G10 sovereign paper under three years to maturity, to 22% for residential mortgage-backed securities (RMBS), covered bonds and credit card ABS with 10–30 years' maturity.

3 The advice was probably wrong since the same EU legislation applied in Germany and the IKB bank was secretly saved. Equally, as discussed later, the UK authorities behaved differently in 2008 under the same EU legislation.

4 Such confidentiality can help to prevent knowledge of lender of last resort support from giving rise to panic, a rise in borrowing costs or a loss of reputation to the bank in receipt of lender of last resort.

5 Further difficulties arose thereafter for the UK authorities owing to the lack of a special insolvency scheme for banks in that country. This difficulty was resolved in the Banking Act also.

6 NAO (2009) commented that the indemnity for the Bank of England's emergency support to RBS and HBOS was not reported to Parliament, as would normally be expected under long-standing procedures put in place by the Treasury to control the use of public money. This indemnity would normally have been notified to Parliament as a contingent liability before it was granted.

7 This proved a structural weakness because much of the funding for securitizations came from other banks or from overseas. The sub-prime crisis in the USA hit the demand for UK securitizations directly. Suspicions arose about the real level of risk of highly rated securities as a result of the high rate of default on the loans underlying US sub-prime collateralized debt obligations (CDOs). This led to a 'buyers' strike' also for UK securitizations, notably by US banks.

8 The Undertakings for Collective Investment in Transferable Securities (UCITS) Directive governs the management and marketing of investment funds intended for retail investors within the EU.

9 See the next footnote for an FSA response.

10 Other elements to the planned changes are as follows: first, all regulated entities must have adequate liquidity and must not depend on other parts of their group to survive liquidity stresses, unless permitted to do so by the FSA. Second, there will be a new systems and controls framework based on the recent work by the Basel Committee on Banking Supervision (BCBS) and the Committee of European Banking Supervisors (CEBS). Third, there will be a system of quantitative individual liquidity adequacy standards (ILAS) for each institution based on a firm being able to survive liquidity stresses of varying magnitude and duration. Fourth, a new framework for group-wide and cross-border management of liquidity is to be introduced, allowing firms, through waivers and modifications, to deviate from self-sufficiency where this is appropriate and would not result in undue risk to clients. Fifth, a new reporting framework for liquidity is introduced, with the FSA collecting detailed, standardized liquidity data at an appropriate frequency so the FSA can monitor both firm-specific and market-wide developments in terms of liquidity-risk exposures.

11 Based on four commonly used UK house price indices: Nationwide, Halifax, Communities and Local Government (CLG) and Land Registry, as cited in ONS 2009a.

12 ONS 2009b strikes a note of caution with this interpretation since long-term relationships between house prices and earnings may be unstable due to changing influence of economic fundamentals such as interest rate regimes.

13 Investment Property Databank.

14 Percentage change over the period June 2007 and July 2009.

15 Between August 2008 and May 2010.

16 Whilst the amount of external debt held by individual economies is known (see, for example, chart 2.3, Bank of England 2010b), the exact exposures of individual banks to different sovereign risks are less transparent.

17 Based on average five-year senior credit default swap premia (weighted by assets) for banks with assets exceeding $100 billion, see chart 2.7, Bank of England 2010b.

18 According to the Bank of England (2010b), the peak in liquidations that occurred during the last quarter of 1992 manifested nine quarters after the first period of negative growth.

19 That said, Barrell, Holland and Liadze (2010) show that the contribution of financial services to UK productivity growth was only 0.2% a year.

20 Available from commission.bnbb.org/banking/sites/all/themes/whichfobtheme/pdf/commission_report.pdf.

References

Bank of England (2007), *Financial Stability Report*, April, London: Bank of England.

——(2008a) 'The Development of the Bank of England's Market Operations, Consultative Paper', London: Bank of England.

——(2008b) 'Financial Stability Report, October 2008', London: Bank of England.

——(2009a) 'Quantitative Easing Explained', Bank of England, www.bankofengland.co.uk/monetarypolicy/assetpurchases.htm.

——(2009b) 'The Macrofinancial Environment', Section 1, *Financial Stability Report*, December.

——(2010a) 'Agents' Summary of Business Conditions', August.

——(2010b) 'Financial Stability Report', June.

Barrell, R. and D. Holland (2010) 'Fiscal and Financial Responses to the Economic Downturn', *National Institute Economic Review* 211: R51-R62.

Barrell, R., D. Holland and D. Karim (2010) 'Tighter Financial Regulation and its Impact on Global Growth', *National Institute Economic Review*, July.

Barrell, R., D. Holland and I. Liadze (2010) 'Accounting for UK Economic Performance 1973-2009', NIESR Discussion Paper No. 359.

Barrell, R., E.P. Davis, T. Fic, D. Holland, S. Kirby and I. Liadze (2009) 'Optimal Regulation of Bank Capital and Liquidity: How to Calibrate New International Standards', FSA Occasional Paper no. 38, October.

Barrell, R., E.P. Davis, I. Liadze and D. Karim (2010a) 'Bank Regulation, Property Prices and Early Warning Systems for Banking Crises in OECD countries', *Journal of Banking and Finance* 34: 2255-64.

——(2010b) 'The Impact of Global Imbalances: Does the Current Account Balance Help To Predict Banking Crises in OECD Countries?' NIESR Discussion Paper No. 351.

Barrell, R., E.P. Davis, D. Karim and I. Liadze (2010) 'Calibrating Macro-prudential Standards', NIESR Discussion Paper No. 334.

Basel Committee (2010) 'Countercyclical Capital Buffer Proposal', Basel Committee, Basel: Bank for International Settlements.

BIS (2008) 'BIS Quarterly Review December 2008', Basel: Bank for International Settlements.

——(2010a) '80th Annual Report', Basel: Bank for International Settlements.

——(2010b) 'Countercyclical Capital Buffer Provision', Consultative Document, Basel Committee on Banking Supervision, Bank for International Settlements.

Dale, S. (2010) 'QE – One Year On', remarks at the CIMF and MMF conference, Cambridge entitled 'New Instruments of Monetary Policy – the Challenges', 12 March.

Davis, E.P. (2009a) 'Financial Stability in the United Kingdom: Banking on Prudence', OECD Economics Department Working Paper no. 717.

——(2009b) 'The Lender of Last Resort and Liquidity Provision – How Much of a Departure is the Sub-prime Crisis', paper presented at the LSE Financial Markets Group conference on the Regulatory Response to the Financial Crisis, 19 January.

——(2011) *From crisis to kingdom – Exploring the approaches of economics and theology to the global financial crisis and its aftermath*, Cascade Books, forthcoming.

Davis, E.P. and Karim, D. (2008) 'Could Early Warning Systems Have Helped to Predict the Sub-prime Crisis?' *National Institute Economic Review* No. 206.

Davis, E.P. and H. Zhu (2009) 'Commercial Property Prices and Bank Performance', *Quarterly Review of Economics and Finance* 49: 1341–59.

Demirgüç-Kunt, A. and E. Detragiache (2005) 'Cross-Country Empirical Studies of Systemic Bank Distress: A Survey', IMF Working Papers 05/96, International Monetary Fund.

ECB (2010) 'Financial Stability Review', June, European Central Bank.

Federal Open Market Committee (2009) Press Release – FOMC Statement, www.federalreserve.gov/newsevents/press/monetary/20090318a.htm.

Financial Stability Board (2010) 'An Assessment of the Long-term Economic Impact of Stronger Capital and Liquidity Requirements', August, Basel.

FSA (2007) 'Financial Risk Outlook, 2007', London: Financial Services Authority.

——(2008) 'Strengthening Liquidity Standards', Financial Services Authority Discussion Paper, No. 08–22, London.

Future of Banking Commission (2010) 'The Future of Banking Commission', United Kingdom.

Gagnon, J., M. Raskin, J. Remache and B. Sack (2010) 'Large-scale Asset Purchases by the Federal Reserve: Did they Work?' Federal Reserve Bank of New York, Staff Report No. 441.

George, E. (1994) 'The Pursuit of Financial Stability', *Bank of England Quarterly Bulletin* February: 60–66.

Goodhart, C.A.E. (2010) 'Money, Credit and Bank Behaviour, the Need for a New Approach', *National Institute Economic Review* 214, October: F73–F82.

Haldane, A. (2010) 'The $100 Billion Question', comments given to the Institute of Regulation and Risk, Hong Kong, 30 March.

HM Treasury (2009) 'UK International Financial Services – the Future', UK: HM Treasury.

——(2010) 'Discussion Paper on Non-Bank Lending', UK: HM Treasury.

IMF (2008) 'Global Financial Stability Report, October 2008', Washington, DC: International Monetary Fund.

——(2009) 'Europe: Securing Recovery', Regional Economic Outlook, World Economic and Financial Surveys, October, Washington, DC: International Monetary Fund.

——(2010a) 'Exiting from Crisis Intervention Policies', Washington, DC: International Monetary Fund.

——(2010b) 'Resolving the Crisis Legacy and Meeting New Challenges to Financial Stability', Global Financial Stability Report, April, Washington, DC: International Monetary Fund.

IPD (2010) 'IPD Index Statement', Investment Property Databank, May.

Joyce, M., A. Lasaosa, I. Stevens and M. Tong (2010) 'The Financial Market Impact of Quantitative Easing', Bank of England Working Paper No. 393.

King, M. (2008) 'Monetary Policy Developments', speech to the Leeds Chamber of Commerce, 21 October.

——(2009) 'Treasury Committee Opening Statement, UK Parliament, 24 June, www.bankofengland.co.uk/publications/other/treasurycommittee/ir/tsc090624.pdf.

Klyuev, V., P. de Imus and K. Srinivasan (2009) 'Unconventional Choices for Unconventional Times, Credit and Quantitative Easing in Advanced Economies', IMF Staff Position Note SPN/09/27.

Lenza, M., H. Pill and L. Reichlin (2010) 'Monetary Policy in Exceptional Times', *Economic Policy* April: 295–339.

Martin, C. and C. Milas (2010) 'Financial Stability and Monetary Policy', Working Paper 05/10, University of Bath.

Meier, M. (2009) 'Panacea, Curse, or Nonevent? Unconventional Monetary Policy in the United Kingdom', IMF Working Paper No. WP/09/163.

Miles, D. (2010) 'Interpreting Monetary Policy', speech at Imperial College, London, 25 February.

NAO (2009) 'Maintaining Financial Stability Across the United Kingdom's Banking System', report by the Comptroller and Auditor-General, National Audit Office, December.

ONS (2009a) 'Recent Developments in the UK Housing Market', *Economic & Labour Market Review* Vol. 3, No. 8, August, UK: Office for National Statistics.

——(2009b) 'The Housing Market and Household Balance Sheets', *Economic & Labour Market Review* Vol. 3, No. 9, September, UK: Office for National Statistics.

Treasury Committee (2008) 'The Run on the Rock', House of Commons Treasury Select Committee Report, UK Parliament, London.

——(2009) 'Banking Crisis: Dealing with the Failure of UK Banks', Seventh Report of Session 2008–09, House of Commons, United Kingdom.

——(2010) 'Too Important to Fail – Too Important to Ignore', Ninth Report of Session 2009–10, House of Commons, United Kingdom.

Tucker, P. (2008) 'A Protracted "Peacetime"', remarks at the Chatham House Conference on 'The new financial frontiers', London, 29 April.

——(2009) 'The Repertoire of Official Sector Interventions in the Financial System: Last Resort Lending, Market-Making, and Capital', remarks at the 2009 International Conference: Financial System and Monetary Policy Implementation, Bank of Japan, 27–28 May.

Turner, A. (2009) 'A Regulatory Response to the Global Banking Crisis (The Turner Report)', London: FSA.

Wadhwani, S. (2008) 'Should Monetary Policy Respond to Asset Price Bubbles? Revisiting the Debate', *National Institute Economic Review*, 2008.

9 Disease and cure in the UK

The fiscal impact of the crisis and the policy response

Rowena Crawford, Carl Emmerson and Gemma Tetlow

Introduction

The financial crisis and its associated economic effects have had a large, adverse impact on the estimated size of the structural (i.e. 'recovery-resistant') budget deficit, in addition to the increase in government borrowing that is thought to reflect the temporary impact of the recession on tax receipts and public spending. While there are good reasons for government borrowing to be allowed to increase when the economy is weak—and particularly when monetary policy is already very loose and its effectiveness in stimulating aggregate demand is considerably more uncertain than usual—it is also important that those financing this borrowing remain confident that it will be reduced over time.

In this paper we discuss the official diagnosis of the 'disease' in the UK's public finances (section two) and the 'cure' for this malady that has been announced by the Government (section three). The likely impact of the medicine—higher taxes, lower welfare payments and lower spending on public services—on household incomes and on spending on public services is also discussed (section three).

If the latest official forecasts are correct, the cure should be sufficient to return the UK's public finances to a sustainable footing within four years. Whether investors in UK government debt and the general public believe this to be the case depends on public confidence in official fiscal forecasts and confidence in the coalition Government's ability to deliver painful tax increases and spending cuts. Confidence in fiscal forecasts and stated fiscal targets has been knocked in recent years by the perception that politicians have 'moved the goalposts' to suit their own ends. The new Government's solution to this lack of public confidence in official forecasts has been to outsource the forecasting process to an independent Office for Budget Responsibility (OBR). We assess the merits of this in section four. Section five concludes.

Section two: disease—how have the financial crisis and associated recession affected the UK's fiscal position?

Prior to the financial crisis and recession, the then Chancellor Alistair Darling's official forecasts in the Budget of March 2008 suggested that UK government borrowing was fairly low and was expected to reduce further over the following few years. As Figure 9.1 shows, the official measure of public borrowing used by the UK Treasury (known as public-sector net borrowing, PSNB) was projected to be 2.9% of national income in 2008–09:[1] 0.2 percentage points of this was believed to represent cyclical borrowing, with the UK economy thought at that time to be operating very slightly below its sustainable level. Thereafter, PSNB was forecast to fall to 1.3% of national income by 2012–13, principally reflecting planned increases in public spending that were lower than expected growth in the economy. On the Maastricht Treaty definition, this implied a deficit of 3.2% of national income in 2008–09 (slightly above the level consistent with the Stability and Growth Pact), falling to 1.6% of national income by 2012–13.

By the time of the March 2011 Budget, the situation had deteriorated markedly, with actual borrowing having come in at 6.7% of national income in 2008–09, and with the OBR forecasting that borrowing would more likely than not remain above 3% of national income until 2014–15. Some of the increase in borrowing in 2008–09 and 2009–10 reflected the active fiscal stimulus measures adopted by the Labour Government in an attempt to limit the length and depth of the recession, while much of the fall in borrowing from 2010–11 onwards reflects policies to increase tax rates and cut public spending over the next few years to bring down borrowing. The remainder of this section sets out the 'disease'—how government borrowing would have evolved in the absence of active policy decisions—and the next section

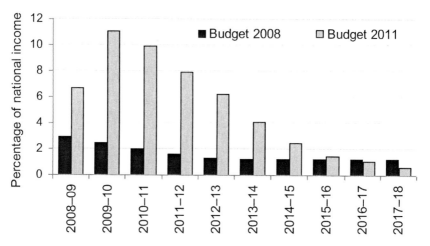

Figure 9.1 Changing forecasts for government borrowing
Note: For the purpose of the Budget 2008 numbers in this figure, we have assumed that the economy was expected to return to trend output (i.e. output gap equal to zero) in 2013–14, while we assume for the purposes of the Budget 2011 figures that the economy returns to trend output in 2017–18, as forecast by the OBR (see paragraph 5.22 of Office for Budget Responsibility 2011). Source: Authors' calculations using HM Treasury 2008a; Office for Budget Responsibility 2011

examines the (already implemented and proposed future) 'cure'—the discretionary policy measures taken to shore up the public finances by reversing this permanent damage.

Taking the OBR's latest official forecasts for borrowing (published in March 2011), and adjusting them for the estimated direct impact of all fiscal policy measures announced since Budget 2008 (before the impact of the crisis became apparent in the fiscal projections), provides an indicative assessment of how the financial crisis affected the public finances and what the outlook for borrowing, and consequently debt, would have been if there had been no fiscal policy response to the crisis or recession.

The results of this exercise are presented in Figure 9.2, which shows what borrowing would now be forecast to be for each year between 2008–09 and 2017–18 if there had been no discretionary policy action announced since Budget 2008. The darkest blocks show the level of borrowing forecast for each year by Mr Darling in his March 2008 Budget (as also shown in Figure 9.1). The mid-shade blocks show the additional borrowing that the OBR estimated in its March 2011 *Economic and Fiscal Outlook* (EFO, which accompanied the March 2011 Budget) has resulted from the financial crisis and which cannot be explained by the usual impact on public borrowing of temporary weakness in the economy—in other words, the extra structural borrowing. This amounts to 6.1% of national income in 2010–11, falling back to 5.9% (or £91 billion in 2011–12 terms) by 2014–15.[2] Finally, the pale blocks show the OBR's estimates of the additional temporary borrowing incurred while the economy is expected to be operating below its sustainable level. While productive assets (labour and capital) are being underutilized, tax

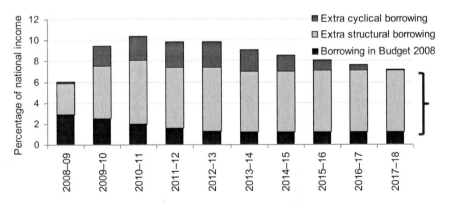

Figure 9.2 Disease—official borrowing forecasts, less the direct impact of post-crisis discretionary policy changes

Note: For the purpose of this figure, we have assumed that—as forecast by the OBR in March 2011—the economy returns to trend output (i.e. the output gap equals zero) in 2017–18.

Source: Authors' calculations using HM Treasury 2008a, 2008b, 2009a, 2009b, 2010a, 2010b, 2010c, 2011; Office for Budget Responsibility 2010c, 2011

revenues are temporarily depressed and demands on public spending are higher; this results in so-called cyclical borrowing. In 2010–11 the OBR estimates that this cyclical component of borrowing amounted to 2.5% of national income, and some additional cyclical borrowing is expected to persist until the economy returns to its trend level of output (that is the level of economic activity that is sustainable in that it is consistent with both stable inflation and employment). The OBR's view in March 2011 was that this would happen in 2017–18.

We can think of the structural hole caused by the crisis as having two components:

- First, the Treasury estimated in the March 2010 Budget that the UK's productive potential would be permanently lower than it had been expecting in Budget 2008. Specifically, in the March 2010 Budget, the Treasury's view was that, by the third quarter of 2010, the UK's productive potential would have fallen 5.25% below the levels it was forecasting for that point prior to the crisis; the Treasury's view was that this loss of potential would be permanent thereafter. Of this reduction, 4.75 percentage points was thought to have come from a fall in output per worker; the remaining 0.25 percentage point was from a fall in the size of the labour force, arising from lower net inwards migration than had previously been expected. The OBR's assessment of trend output is more pessimistic: by the start of 2015, their central estimate is that trend output will be a further 2.25% below the projection that underpinned Mr Darling's March 2010 public finance forecasts.[3] A total reduction in trend output of 7.75% would permanently cost the Exchequer around 5.4% of national income (or £83 billion in 2011–12 terms) a year in lost revenues and higher spending.
- Second, there is a further permanent loss to the Exchequer of about 0.5% of national income (or £6 billion in 2011–12 terms), predominantly reflecting changes in price levels. These changes in price levels feed through into lower future revenues and higher future spending relative to nominal national income. The OBR forecast in its March 2011 EFO that stock prices, house prices and economy-wide prices (as implied by the GDP deflator) would remain permanently lower than had been forecast in Budget 2008.

Lower-than-anticipated asset prices feed through into weaker public finances because revenue from stamp duties, capital gains tax and inheritance tax are affected. Changes in the price level can also affect the outlook for spending. One particular reason why lower-than-anticipated price levels have fed through into a permanent weakening of the public finances (in the absence of policy action) during the current crisis relates to the way in which the Treasury plans public spending. The 'no policy change' forecasting assumption for spending is to assume, for the period covered by an existing Spending Review, that plans for cash spending by departments (that is, spending on public services) are adhered to and that thereafter some particular real-terms growth rate (that is, growth over and above any growth in the GDP deflator) occurs. The Spending Review preceding the financial crisis had set plans for the years 2008–09 to 2010–11. Because of lower than expected inflation through to 2010–11, the Treasury's cash spending plans for 2010–11 (set in the October 2007 Comprehensive Spending Review) turned out to be more generous in real terms (and relative to the size of the economy) than initially anticipated. Given the 'no policy change' forecasting assumption, in the absence of any 'discretionary policy action', this higher level of real-terms spending in 2010–11 (the base year) would have fed through into higher real-terms spending for evermore. Thus lower-than-anticipated inflation would have fed through into a permanent increase in public spending.

Figure 9.2 suggests that had the government announced no new tax increases or spending cuts since Budget 2008, public-sector borrowing would have been forecast to be 7.1% of national income (or about £109 billion a year in 2011–12 terms) even after the economy had recovered from recession (although the implied path for debt—see Figure 9.7—suggests that it would lead to a bigger increase in borrowing through subsequent increases in debt interest spending). This compares with the government's plans before the financial crisis, which implied that borrowing would stabilize at about 1.2% of national income (or £19 billion in 2011–12 terms).

The outlook for public-sector revenues and spending in the absence of any discretionary policy action since Budget 2008 is shown in Figure 9.3. The amount of revenue yielded by the UK tax system is generally related to the level of national income, and so while the crisis lowered the forecast productive potential of the economy, revenues as a share of national income were relatively unaffected—forecast to fall from their pre-crisis level of 38.6% of national income to 36.9% by 2015–16. Tax revenues would not be forecast to regain their previous share of national income in the absence of policy changes for two reasons: first, because the financial sector, which is relatively profitable and therefore pays relatively more tax than other industries, is not expected to comprise as large a share of total output in future as it had before the crisis; second, because, as discussed above, property and equity prices are now forecast to be lower than was expected pre-crisis.

Public spending increased sharply as a share of national income during the crisis as the decline in the productive potential of the economy meant that the cash spending plans set up to 2010–11 accounted for a much larger share of national income than originally planned, as discussed above. Spending as a share of national income would fall only very gradually in the absence of any discretionary policy changes since, at the time of Budget 2008, the 'no-change' policy assumption for public spending was that it would grow at 1.8% a year in real terms from 2011–12 until at least 2014–15.

Assessing how much of the current huge budget deficit is structural and permanent, as distinct from cyclical and temporary (i.e. the decomposition shown in Figure 9.2), is not straightforward and is likely to be even more uncertain

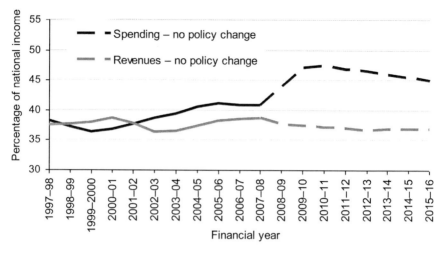

Figure 9.3 Disease official spending and revenue forecasts, less the direct impact of post-crisis discretionary policy changes

Note: Figures for spending and revenues from 2008–09 onwards under 'no policy change' assume that no additional policy measures had been implemented after those announced in Budget 2008.

Source: Historic figures for spending and revenues are from HM Treasury, Public Finances Databank, www.hm-treasury.gov.uk/psf_statistics.htm. Figures for 2008–09 onwards under 'no policy change' are authors' calculations using figures from HM Treasury 2008a, 2008b, 2009a, 2009b, 2010a, 2010b, 2010c, 2011; Office for Budget Responsibility 2010c, 2011

in the aftermath of a financial crisis. Unsurprisingly, the Treasury's views have changed significantly over the past two years, and the views of the new OBR are again different from what the Treasury believed in the past. Figure 9.4 shows what the estimated size of the effect of the financial crisis on the public finances—that is, the additional structural borrowing—has been at the time of each of the various Budgets and Pre-Budget Reports (PBRs) since March 2008.

The November 2008 PBR—published in the immediate aftermath of the collapse of Lehman Brothers and the intensification of problems in the financial sector—initially estimated that the permanent effect of the crisis on government borrowing would be to increase the structural deficit by 3.2% of national income (or about £49 billion in 2011–12 terms). However, by the time of the Budget in April 2009, the Treasury had revised up this estimate to 6.4% of national income (or £99 billion) instead. This reflected an increase in the Treasury's assessment of the permanent loss of productive capacity in the UK economy (from 4% to 5%), further falls in the price of assets between November 2008 and April 2009 (which reduced future expected revenues) and a projected lower level of economy-wide inflation in 2009–10 and 2010–11 (which boosted real-terms plans for central government spending on public services in 2010–11 and thereafter, as described above).

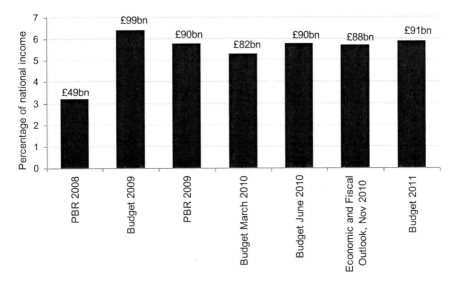

Figure 9.4 Disease—estimated size from different vintages of official forecasts
Source: Authors calculations using HM Treasury 2008a, 2008b, 2009a, 2009b, 2010a, 2010b, 2010c, 2011; Office for Budget Responsibility 2010c, 2011

The estimate in the December 2009 PBR was somewhat smaller, at 5.8% of national income (or £90 billion in 2011–12 prices). While economic growth was actually weaker than expected between Budget 2009 and the 2009 PBR, the public finances performed largely as expected and it was therefore the Treasury's assessment that the lower economic growth represented a greater cyclical rather than permanent downturn in the economy, meaning that there was greater scope for a fall in cyclical borrowing. The estimates of structural deficit were also helped by two other factors: first, growth in the stock market far exceeded the previous forecast, boosting forecasts for revenues from stamp duty on share transactions, capital gains tax and inheritance tax; second, economy-wide inflation in 2009–10 and 2010–11 was no longer expected to be as low as forecast at the time of the April 2009 Budget, which reduced the real value of the cash spending plans for 2010–11.

The estimate in the March 2010 Budget was smaller again (5.3% of national income or £82 billion). The economy and earnings were expected to grow slightly less quickly than previously thought (leading to reduced revenues and increased structural borrowing), but this was more than offset by higher than expected receipts in 2009–10 which were largely expected to persist into future years, and a reduction in forecast spending in 2010–11 (due in large part to lower than previously expected debt interest spending), which would then feed through into lower spending in future.

The OBR's June 2010 Budget estimate of the underlying permanent increase in the structural deficit seen since Budget 2008 was 0.5% of national income higher than the Treasury's March 2010 Budget estimate, at 5.8% of national income (or £90 billion in 2011–12 prices). The OBR's estimate was higher because they believed there was less spare capacity in the UK economy and, therefore, less scope for above-trend growth in the next few years than Mr Darling projected in the March 2010 Budget. Partially offsetting this, the OBR expected stronger underlying tax revenues (when considered as a share of national income).[4] The March 2011 EFO implied a further small upward revision in the OBR's assessment of the underlying increase in borrowing (to 5.9% of national income, or £91 billion).

The changes in the Treasury's estimates of the structural deficit over time, and the OBR's further revised picture of the situation, partly reflect the fact that there is great uncertainty about what has actually happened to trend output over recent years. In particular, both Budget 2009 and the June 2010 Budget contained revisions to the estimate of the structural deficit that happened because of a change in official view about the level of sustainable output of the UK economy. This caused them to change their assessment of how much of the observed levels of borrowing would be structural rather than cyclical. A commonly used measure of the amount of spare capacity in the economy is the output gap, which is the difference between the actual level of output and the assessed level of trend output. A large negative output gap implies that there is considerable spare capacity in the economy—that is, underutilized labour and capital—which could be brought back into full use, thus providing much scope for above-trend growth without generating inflationary pressures.

In the March 2010 Budget the Treasury estimated that the productive potential of the economy grew by almost 3.5% a year during the Labour Government's first term in office (1997 to 2001), then by just over 2.75% a year thereafter. When the crisis hit in mid-2007, trend growth fell to just over 1% for three years—in other words, a sharp fall in the growth rate of potential output between 2007 and 2010.[5] These assumptions implied a negative output gap of around 6% by the end of 2009.

One explanation put forward for this sudden loss of potential output was the effect of an increase in the cost of capital on the productive capital stock, but what if the productive potential of the economy did not go into sudden and unexpected decline in mid-2007, but rather the Government (amongst many others) consistently overestimated the potential of the economy in the good years, lulled into a false sense of security by global disinflation? In the June 2010 Budget the Treasury described what the output gap would have looked like under an alternative scenario, which assumes that the output gap at the end of 2009 was around 4% (as forecast by the OBR in the June 2010 Budget) and that prior to this the trend rate of economic growth had averaged 2.3% a year, which is the average growth in GDP in the UK over the last 50 years. This alternative version of history is also shown in Figure 9.5. Under this alternative scenario, the output gap follows a very similar pattern over the period from 1987 to 1997 to the series produced by the Treasury in the March 2010 Budget. However, the two series then diverge, with the alternative scenario

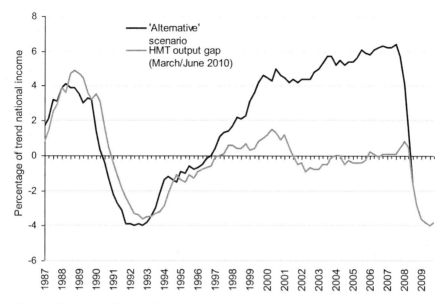

Figure 9.5 A bust without a boom?
Note: The output gap is the difference between actual national income and potential national income measured as a percentage of the latter, with a negative output gap indicating that the economy is operating below trend. Source: HM Treasury output gap shows the estimates from the HM Treasury 2010a for all quarters up to 2008 Q2, and from HM Treasury 2010b thereafter. The alternative scenario is taken from box 2.1, page 24, of HM Treasury 2010b, although similar analysis to this can be found in Chote 2009

suggesting that economic activity was operating above trend for the whole period administered by the Labour Government, reaching over 6% above potential by 2007. The true history of the output gap may lie somewhere between these two scenarios.

Under the alternative scenario the government's finances were being flattered by an unsustainable economic boom and thus the government should clearly, with the benefit of hindsight, have been running a much stronger fiscal position over the decade prior to the financial crisis. The headline figures for borrowing since 1970–71 and the June 2010 Treasury estimates of the structural budget deficit are compared, in Figure 9.6, to an estimate of the structural budget deficit that uses the alternative scenario for the output gap presented in Figure 9.5. Over the period from 1987 to 1997 the two measures of structural borrowing follow a very similar pattern, since the assumed output gap series (as shown in Figure 9.5) are fairly similar. Both series suggest that the peak of structural borrowing in the early 1990s was just under 6% of national income (and below the previous peak seen in the mid 1970s). From 1997 the series diverge: the alternative scenario implies that the economy was moving well above trend and therefore headline borrowing was understating the structural level of

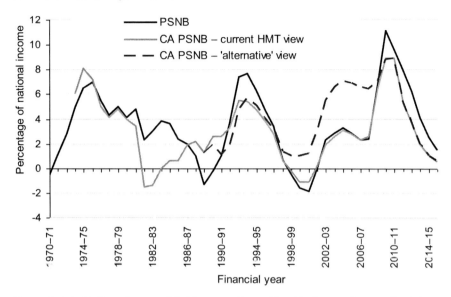

Figure 9.6 A hidden disease with 10 years of considerably looser than realized fiscal policy, 1999 to 2008?
Source: The headline PSNB and the current HM Treasury view of the structural budget deficit are taken from HM Treasury 2011. The alternative view applies the Treasury's methodology for cyclically adjusting (taken from HM Treasury 2008c) to the headline PSNB series using the alternative scenario for the output gap from box 2.1, page 24, of HM Treasury 2010b, which is shown in Figure 9.5.

borrowing. At its peak in 2006–07, the difference between the two estimates of structural borrowing reaches 4.3% of national income.

While it is easy, with the benefit of hindsight, to say that borrowing should have been lowered under such a scenario, it is unclear how easy that would have been to justify to the public at the time. Retail price inflation was sub-dued over the period rather than demonstrating the rapid inflation that would normally be expected to accompany such a boom. That the 'missing' boom seems to have manifested itself in asset and credit markets—rather than those for labour, goods and services—will have made it rather less obvious to obser-vers at the time. Had Gordon Brown—as Chancellor—chosen to run much tighter fiscal policy over this period, it is also plausible that the Monetary Policy Committee of the Bank of England would have responded with even lower interest rates in order to remain on track to meet their inflation target, off-setting the impact of the fiscal tightening on aggregate demand. Such a response may have inadvertently further fuelled asset price bubbles, for example in the UK housing market.

Such a fiscal tightening did not occur prior to the crisis. In the absence of any policy response at all, the financial crisis and associated recession would have resulted in a permanent increase in the structural deficit of 5.9% of national income (shown in Figure 9.2). The implications for debt are shown in Figure 9.7, which presents forecasts for the debt level based on the borrowing plans from Budget 2008 and the borrowing plans implied by the March 2011 Budget in the absence of any policy changes since Budget 2008. Without action, the financial crisis would have pushed the public finances onto an unsustainable path, with debt and debt interest payments rising remorselessly as shares of national income over the coming decades. The stock of national debt would exceed national income by the end of the decade and would have surpassed 200% of national income by the middle of the century. In fact, the consequences of leaving the structural deterioration in the public finances unaddressed would almost certainly be even more dramatic than

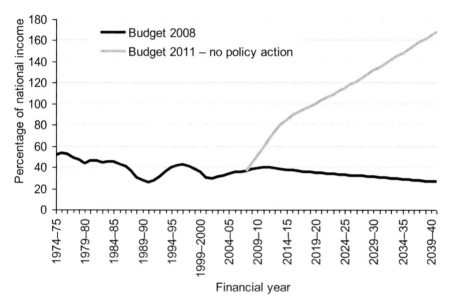

Figure 9.7 Disease—debt forecasts ignoring the direct impact of post-crisis discretionary policy changes

Note: Forecasts for debt levels assume that non-debt interest spending and revenues remain constant as a share of national income from 2017–18 onwards, while inflation is assumed to run at 2.7% a year and real growth in national income at 2.2% a year from 2017–18 onwards. Average nominal interest rates are assumed to rise from 4.1% (the level forecast in the March 2011 Economic and Fiscal Outlook for the end of the OBR's forecast horizon, 2015–16) to equal nominal GDP growth, of 4.9%, between 2017–18 and 2027–28. From 2027–28 onwards, nominal interest rates are assumed to equal nominal GDP growth. This implies that total net debt interest payments decline/rise as a share of national income as net debt falls/rises, which in turn implies a strengthening/ weakening of the current budget over time. The no policy action scenario assumes that no discretionary policy announcements were made after Budget 2008.

Source: Historical data are from HM Treasury, Public Sector Finances Databank, 26 April 2011, www.hm-treasury.gov.uk/d/public_finances_databank.xls. Forecasts are authors' calculations using figures from HM Treasury 2008a, 2008b, 2009a, 2009b, 2010a, 2010b, 2010c, 2011; Office for Budget Responsibility 2010c, 2011

Figure 9.7 suggests. This is because the debt projections in Figure 9.7 assume that the Government would be able to continue borrowing at interest rates that equal the rate of growth of nominal national income, still a relatively low rate historically, but investors would almost certainly take fright at such a scenario and demand higher rates to lend to the government, thus pushing up debt interest payments and increasing the rate of debt accumulation.

The key point is that it is the deterioration in the structural budget deficit that would drive debt onto an unsustainable path, not the temporary borrowing as a result of the recession or the Labour Government's short-term response to the crisis (discussed in section three), which added significant but one-off amounts to borrowing. Tackling this problem therefore required the Government to reduce the annual flow of borrowing in a lasting way—either by increasing tax revenues or reducing spending as a share of national income in each year going forwards—and not just to seek one-off reductions in the level of debt (for example through the sale of public-sector assets or through temporary tax rises or spending cuts). We now turn to the short-term and long-term policy response to the fiscal crisis.

Section three: cure—what is the direct impact on the UK's public finances of the fiscal policy action taken since the crisis began?

The fiscal policy response to the crisis can be thought of in two parts: first, the short-term stimulus measures designed to reduce the length and depth of the recession; and second, the long-term fiscal tightening designed to get the public finances back on a sustainable footing. Section three examines the direct impact on the overall public finances of all the fiscal policy measures announced since the financial crisis came to light. The same section examines what impact these measures had on household incomes and focuses on the impact on spending on public services.

The impact of the cure on the public finances

In response to the problems created by the crisis, the Labour Government announced a series of discretionary policy changes in the 2008 PBR, the 2009 Budget, the 2009 PBR and the March 2010 Budget. The response had two components: first, a short-term fiscal stimulus package, taking effect in 2008–09 and 2009–10, designed to mitigate the length and depth of the recession; second, a long-term fiscal tightening, starting in 2011–12 and increasing in size until 2016–17, which would permanently lower spending and increase taxes in order to reduce borrowing back to sustainable levels in the medium term.

As Figure 9.8 shows, the net direct effect of Labour's policy announcements after Budget 2008 was to increase government borrowing in 2008–09 and 2009–10. This was the result of the fiscal stimulus package, which included some tax giveaways (such as the 13-month reduction in the main rate of VAT

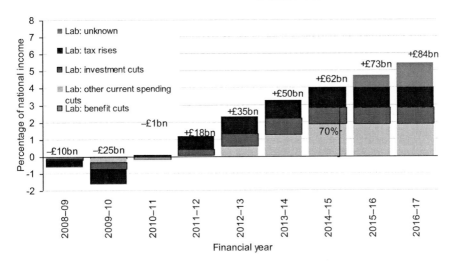

Figure 9.8 Cure—reduction in borrowing from discretionary policy changes announced
under Labour since Budget 2008
Note: Bars represent the planned fiscal tightening (reduction in government borrowing), decomposed into tax increases and spending cuts, with the spending cuts further
subdivided into benefit cuts, other current spending cuts and investment spending cuts.
£ billion figures show the net exchequer gain each year from the planned fiscal consolidation, in 2011–12 terms. Source: Authors' calculations using HM Treasury 2008a,
2008b, 2009a, 2009b, 2010a

from 17.5% to 15.0%) and some spending giveaways (such as the higher
benefit payments to pensioners and families with children in early 2009 and
the higher winter fuel payments to those aged 60 and over in winter 2009–10).
In 2010–11 the net effect of policy measures was negligible, with a net loos-
ening of just £1 billion.

From 2011–12 onwards, the policy announcements were expected to reduce
borrowing by an increasing amount each year until 2016–17. The path of the
fiscal tightening was front-loaded, with the additional discretionary tightening
added each year gradually declining from 1.5% of national income in 2010–11
(reflecting the removal of the bulk of the fiscal stimulus package) to 0.7% of
national income in 2015–16.

The Labour Government had set out in legislation two specific targets for
the reduction of borrowing in the medium term. The Fiscal Responsibility
Act 2010 committed the government to halving the overall budget deficit by
2013–14 from its 2009–10 level as a share of national income. At the time of
the March 2010 Budget, this would have required borrowing in 2013–14 to
be no higher than 5.8% of national income. The Fiscal Responsibility Order
2010 set out a second (more stringent, but more easily altered) target to reduce
borrowing to no more than 5.5% of national income in 2013–14. The forecasts set out by the Treasury in the March 2010 Budget implied that the
planned fiscal tightening would reduce borrowing to 5.2% of national income

by 2013–14, and so was slightly more ambitious than was necessary to achieve even the more binding of their two targets.[6]

Figure 9.8 also decomposes the Labour Government's planned fiscal tightening into tax increases and spending cuts, with spending cuts further decomposed into cuts to benefit spending, other cuts to current spending, and cuts to investment spending. The long-term impact of Labour's benefit changes was minimal (around a £0.3 billion giveaway), although whether this would have remained the case had they been re-elected in May 2010 is not known.[7] Cuts to other current spending and investment spending were much more significant, and increasing year on year from 2011–12 onwards. By 2014–15 70% of Labour's planned tightening was to come from cuts to public spending; cuts to investment spending were planned to provide one-third of these, a seemingly disproportionate share given that Budget 2008 forecast that investment spending in 2012–13 would account for just 6% of total spending.[8] The remaining 30% of the discretionary tightening was planned to come from tax increases. For the most part these were to be implemented in 2012–13, so the vast majority of the extra tightening planned for 2013–14 and 2014–15 was to be on the spending side.

The March 2010 Budget did not describe from where the additional tightening in 2015–16 and 2016–17 would come. It stated that investment spending would be spared from further cuts, but gave no indication of whether the remaining fiscal tightening would come from further cuts to current spending or increases in taxes. So the final composition of the tightening that would have occurred under Labour is unknown.

The new coalition Government (which took office in May 2010) chose to change the path of the fiscal tightening from what the Labour Government had planned. Specifically, it decided to tighten sooner—with some spending cuts announced for the 2010–11 financial year—and to tighten by more than Labour had planned. The decision to increase the overall size of the fiscal tightening was in part a response to the fact that the OBR's June 2010 forecast for structural borrowing was less optimistic than Mr Darling's March 2010 Budget forecast had been. Figure 9.9 shows the reduction in borrowing from all discretionary policy changes since Budget 2008, including those introduced since May 2010. Assuming the OBR's fiscal forecasts from the time of the March 2011 Budget are correct, the coalition Government's planned fiscal tightening should be sufficient to fill the 5.9% of national income hole in the public finances by 2014–15, and a year later to do so with 0.8% of national income to spare.

The new coalition Government has set itself a 'fiscal mandate' and a 'supplementary target'. The fiscal mandate is to have at least a balanced structural current budget by the end of the forecast horizon. In other words, after taking into account the ups and downs of the economic cycle, government receipts should be projected to be equal to, or to exceed, non-investment spending. The supplementary target is that debt should be falling as a share of national income in 2015–16. Given current (and indeed any plausible future)

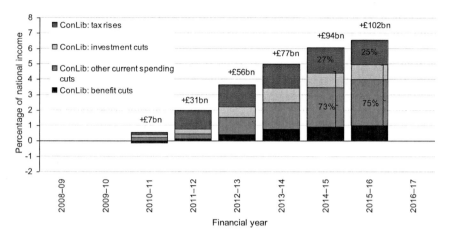

Figure 9.9 Cure—reduction in borrowing from discretionary policy changes announced
since Budget 2008 including the impact of measures announced since May 2010
Note: Bars represent the planned fiscal tightening (reduction in government borrowing), decomposed into tax increases and spending cuts, with the spending cuts further
subdivided into benefit cuts, other current spending cuts and investment spending cuts.
£ billion figures show the net exchequer gain each year from the planned fiscal consolidation,
in 2011–12 terms.
Source: Authors' calculations using HM Treasury 2008a, 2008b, 2009a, 2009b, 2010a,
2010b, 2010c, 2011; Office of Budget Responsibility 2010c, 2011

investment plans the first fiscal rule is the binding one. For example, if the
OBR's March 2011 forecasts prove correct to 2014–15, and if the structural
current budget was in balance in 2015–16 (rather than in surplus of 0.8% of
national income as the OBR forecasts), then investment spending would need
to exceed the projected 1.1% of national income by 1.9% of national income
for public-sector net debt not to fall.[9] The OBR's March 2011 EFO forecast
is actually for a 0.8% of national income structural current budget surplus in
2015–16, the last year of the forecast horizon. On the basis of past Treasury
forecasting errors and under the assumption of no further policy changes, the
OBR suggests that this gives the Government a 70% chance that a cyclically
adjusted current budget surplus will actually materialize in 2015–16.

Figure 9.9 decomposes the coalition's planned fiscal tightening into cuts to
benefit spending, cuts to other current spending, cuts to investment spending
and tax increases. The new measures introduced in the June 2010 and March
2011 Budgets amounted to a reduction in borrowing of 1.9% of national income
in 2015–16, in addition to what the Labour Government had planned for that
year; this amounts to £36 billion in 2015–16 terms, or £29 billion in current
(2011–12) terms. This changes the composition of the total tightening to 75%
from spending cuts and the remaining 25% from tax rises by 2015–16.[10] The
coalition's planned tightening therefore relies slightly more on spending cuts
than Labour's planned tightening did, at least by 2014–15.

Unlike the fiscal consolidation planned by the Labour Government, part of the fiscal consolidation is to be delivered by cuts to benefit spending; these are set to account for around 15% of the tightening by 2014–15. Investment spending is planned to contribute a smaller proportion of the total tightening than under Labour's plans (15.6%, compared to 23.7%), while other current spending cuts are planned to contribute 41.7%, compared to 50.4% under Labour's plans. However, since the coalition plan is to tighten faster and by more overall than the Labour Government planned, the total tightening in 2014–15 is greater. Therefore, as a share of national income the cuts to investment spending are around the same under the coalition plans as under Labour's plans, while the tax rises and the cuts to other current spending by 2014–15 are both more than one and a third-times as large as what was planned under Labour. However, Labour would have required greater additional spending cuts and/or tax increases after 2014–15 than the coalition Government, as their fiscal tightening was set to be more back-loaded.

In the absence of policy action since Budget 2008, as discussed in section two and shown in Figure 9.10, borrowing would have been left running at around 7% of national income. However, the combined effect of the measures announced since then (which was shown in Figure 9.9) has been sufficient,

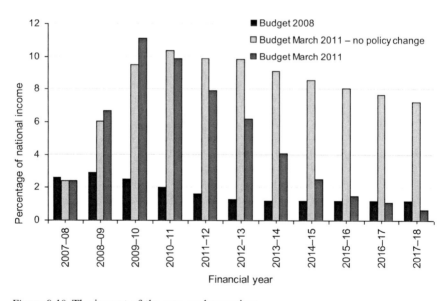

Figure 9.10 The impact of the ▮▮▮ ▮▮▮ ▮▮▮▮▮▮▮▮▮
Note: Bars represent the planned fiscal tightening (reduction in government borrowing).
Source: Authors' calculations using HM Treasury 2008a, 2008b, 2009a, 2009b, 2010a, 2010b, 2010c, 2011; Office of Budget Responsibility 2010c, 2011

according to the OBR's March 2011 EFO forecasts, to reduce borrowing substantially over the medium term: borrowing is forecast by the OBR to fall to just 1.5% of national income by 2015–16. This, along with the borrowing forecasts from Budget 2008, is also shown in Figure 9.10. Borrowing is now forecast by the OBR to have peaked at 11.1% of national income in 2009–10, with most of the rise being explained by the financial crisis and associated recession, but some (the difference between the two 'March 2011' bars) reflecting the direct impact of the fiscal stimulus package. Going forwards, the tax increases and, in particular, the cuts to implicit plans for public spending are forecast to reduce and, from 2016–17, more than cancel out, the increase in borrowing arising directly from the crisis. Current forecasts imply that the discretionary tightening will bring borrowing down to just 0.6% of national income by 2017–18.

The implications of the cure for public revenues and spending are shown in Figure 9.11. The fiscal stimulus package implemented by the Labour Government reduced tax revenues and increased spending as a share of national income, most notably in 2009–10 but also in 2008–09. The fiscal tightening planned by the coalition Government is forecast to be sufficient to increase revenues to 38.4% of national income by 2015–16, 1.6 percentage points higher than if there were no policy change since Budget 2008, and roughly the level seen in 2006–07. Public spending is forecast to fall much more sharply to 39.9% of national income by 2015–16, 5.0 percentage points lower than if there had been no policy changes since Budget 2008, and slightly higher than

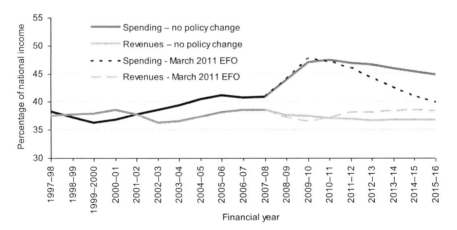

Figure 9.11 The impact of the cure on revenues and spending
Note: Figures for spending and revenues from 2008–09 onwards under 'no policy change' assume that no additional policy measures had been implemented after those announced in Budget 2008. Source: Historic figures for spending and revenues are from HM Treasury, Public Finances Databank, www.hm-treasury.gov.uk/psf_statistics.htm. Figures for 2008–09 onwards under 'no policy change' are authors' calculations using figures from HM Treasury 2008a, 2008b, 2009a, 2009b, 2010a, 2010b, 2010c, 2011; Office for Budget Responsibility 2010c, 2011

the level of spending seen in 2003–04. The emphasis of the fiscal consolidation plan on spending cuts rather than tax rises compensates for the asymmetric movements in spending and revenue that occurred during the crisis, and brings the levels of spending and revenues as a share of national income to around the levels seen in the pre-crisis years.

The implications of the planned fiscal tightening for debt are shown in Figure 9.12. This shows the same debt profiles as in Figure 9.7, plus a forecast for the path of debt once we include the policy action the coalition Government and the previous Labour Government have introduced since Budget 2008. The OBR's March 2011 forecast is that the planned fiscal policy action has been sufficient to bring debt onto a downward path by 2014–15, which confirms that the new coalition Government is on target to meet its supplementary target. However, under our assumptions for nominal GDP growth and interest rates, Figure 9.7 also shows that debt would not return to pre-crisis levels—i.e. below 40% of national income—until 2028–29.[11]

However, the 'Budget 2011' line makes the assumption that the primary balance—the difference between government spending (excluding debt interest payments) and government receipts—is constant as a share of national income beyond 2017–18. While this is one interpretation of current policy continuing unchanged, another interpretation would be to assume that there would be no further discretionary changes to taxation or spending. One factor that is likely to lead to changes in both receipts and spending without further discretionary policy change is the changing size, and age composition, of the UK population. Therefore, also shown in Figure 9.12 is the projected path of debt once the OBR's estimates of the future impact of projected demographic changes on the public finances are taken into account.

Demographic changes are projected to increase government borrowing in the future, as the 'baby-boomers' (those born in the aftermath of the Second World War) move into retirement and start to receive state pensions and place greater demands on the National Health Service (NHS). Assuming that no further tax increases or spending cuts are implemented to offset these estimated effects, public-sector net debt is still forecast to fall over the next couple of decades (and therefore the UK's public finances can still be said to be on a sustainable path), but debt is forecast to remain above pre-crisis levels (40% of national income) throughout the first half of this century.

The impact of the cure on household incomes

The large fiscal tightening by 2014–15 will have a significant effect on the well-being of households in the UK. Assessing which individuals will be affected by cuts to public service spending and exactly how large these impacts will be is an interesting question but hard to answer and we will not attempt that here.[12] However, more can be said about the direct impact on household incomes of many of the proposed changes to taxes and benefit payments. We describe here the direct impact on household incomes of the tax and benefit

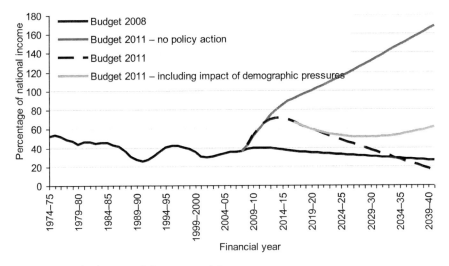

Figure 9.12 The impact of the cure on debt
Note: Forecasts for debt levels assume that non-debt interest spending and revenues remain constant as a share of national income from 2017–18 onwards, while inflation is assumed to run at 2.7% a year and real growth in national income at 2.2% a year from 2017–18 onwards. Average nominal interest rates are assumed to rise from 4.1% (the level forecast in the March 2011 Economic and Fiscal Outlook for the end of the OBR's forecast horizon, 2015–16) to equal nominal GDP growth, of 4.9%, between 2017–18 and 2027–28. From 2027–28 onwards, nominal interest rates are assumed to equal nominal GDP growth. This implies that total net debt interest payments decline/rise as a share of national income as net debt falls/rises, which in turn implies a strengthening/weakening of the current budget over time. The no policy action scenario assumes that no discretionary policy announcements were made after Budget 2008. The forecast including the impact of demographic pressures assumes that age-related spending increases between 2009–10 and 2039–40 evolves in the way forecast by the OBR in its November 2010 Economic and Fiscal Outlook, assuming a linear increase in age-related spending between each of the 10-yearly forecasts that they provide.
Source: Historical data are from HM Treasury, Public Sector Finances Databank, 26 April 2011, www.hm-treasury.gov.uk/d/public_finances_databank.xls. Forecasts are authors' calculations using figures from HM Treasury 2008a, 2008b, 2009a, 2009b, 2010a, 2010b, 2010c, 2011; Office for Budget Responsibility 2010c, 2011. Forecasts for age-related spending are from table 5.6 of Office of Budget Responsibility 2010c

changes that have been announced over the last few years, which reduce household incomes overall. Of course, it should be noted that the negative consequences for households in the UK of not attempting to raise taxes or to cut benefits, and thus not cutting government borrowing, would also be severe.

The set of tax and benefit measures announced since the crisis began are forecast to raise tax revenues by 1.7% of national income and reduce benefit spending by 0.9% of national income by 2014–15, thus reducing both government and household incomes by 2.6% of national income overall. The main tax-raising measures are: increased taxation of earned income (through increasing employee rates of National Insurance from April 2011) that will reduce the net incomes of those on above-average earnings; increases in fuel duties affecting motorists; a 2.5 percentage point increase in the main rate of VAT (from 17.5% to 20%) that will affect all consumers; and increases in income tax that will affect those with incomes above £100,000 a year. The main benefit cuts are: large cuts to housing benefit affecting many low-income renters; cuts to a benefit for disabled people affecting recipients who are now judged to be not sufficiently unhealthy; time-limiting receipt of the main contributory disability benefit for working-age people who are not deemed very unhealthy; cuts to tax credits affecting many families with children, clawing back child benefit from families containing a higher-rate income tax payer; a move to a lower measure of inflation for indexing most benefits (with the notable exception of the Basic State Pension which is to be indexed more generously) that will affect many benefit recipients including all families with children, many pensioners and those working-age individuals receiving unemployment or disability benefits; and a nominal freeze in the universal benefit available to families with children.

Exactly how individual households will be affected depends on factors such as their earnings, other income, spending, and which benefits and tax credits they receive. It is not possible to attribute the impact of some of the tax and benefit changes to individual households, as insufficient data are available, but Figure 9.13 shows the estimated distributional impact of those policies implemented since Budget 2008, which are due to come fully into effect between April 2010 and March 2015, that it is possible to attribute. It should be noted up front that there are three important caveats to this analysis:

- First, while all tax rises and benefit cuts will ultimately be reflected in lower household incomes, it is not possible to assign the impact of all of the reforms to households. For example, the reforms to corporation tax announced by the new coalition Government in the June 2010 Budget (cutting the main rate of corporation tax while making investment allowances less generous) will undoubtedly create some winners and losers but it would be very difficult to model which ones. Among the other reforms that it has not been possible to include in the analysis here are the net increases to capital gains tax announced in the June 2010 Budget; as these are likely to reduce the incomes of higher-income households by more than lower-income households, we probably overstate the regressivity of the June 2010 Budget by excluding this measure.
- Second, the losses from the 2.5 percentage point increase in the main rate of VAT will be highest as a share of current income for households with low levels of current income relative to their current levels of spending. Arguably, the amount that households spend might actually be a better measure of their lifetime resources than their current income: those households with relatively low incomes and relatively high spending are likely to include many households whose income is only temporarily low—for example,

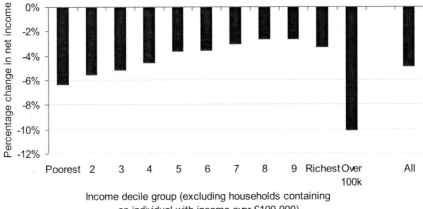

Figure 9.13 The impact of the cure on household incomes in 2014–15, by income decile
Note: Income decile groups are derived by dividing households into 10 equally sized
groups based on their disposable income, adjusted for family size using the McClements
equivalence scale. Assumes full take-up of means-tested benefits and tax credits. Excludes
most 'business taxes' (notably corporation tax and business rates, though not employer
National Insurance contributions) and capital taxes (notably inheritance tax, stamp
duties and capital gains tax). Excludes impact of Universal Credit.
Source: We are grateful to James Browne for providing this figure, which is based on
the analysis presented in Browne 2011

self-employed individuals who happen to have experienced a loss in the
current period. Ranking households by income and measuring the losses
as a share of income suggests that increasing the rate of VAT is mildly
regressive, whereas ranking households by spending and measuring the losses
as a share of spending rather than income gives the result that an increase
in the main rate of VAT is mildly progressive.[13]
• Third, the estimates assume that behaviour and pre-tax prices do not change
in response to the measures. While assuming that households' behaviour
would be unaffected is not realistic, it is not clear that incorporating such
responses would make the distributional analysis a better guide to the
impact on people's well-being. For example, those induced into paid work
are likely to incur additional effort. Assuming that pre-tax prices do not
alter will be more plausible in some cases than others and could affect the
distributional findings. For example, some of the cost of raising the main
rate of VAT by 2.5 percentage points could fall on shareholders or
employees rather than on consumers, while some of the cost of the cuts to
housing benefit could fall on landlords rather than on tenants.

For the purposes of this analysis, households that do not contain an individual with an income above £100,000 a year (98% of working-age adults) are
split into 10 equally sized deciles and arranged in Figure 9.13 with the lowest
income 10% on the left through to those with the highest incomes on the

right. The estimated impact on those households containing an individual with an annual income in excess of £100,000 a year is shown separately.

Overall, the measures that can be attributed to households are estimated to reduce net incomes by 5.0%. Across most of the income distribution (from the lowest income decile up to decile 8) the reforms are regressive—that is, the average loss measured as a share of income decreases as income increases. However, the impact on the incomes of the poorest 98% of the population is dwarfed by the average loss in net income for those households fortunate enough to contain an individual with an income of £100,000 a year or more, which stands at just over 10%. In the longer run the package of measures will be more progressive, as a major reform to working-age benefits announced by the new Government (known as the Universal Credit)—the impact of which is not included in Figure 9.13—will on average benefit those in the bottom half of the income distribution more than those in the top half.

The regressive impact over the majority of the income distribution of the package of reforms (with respect to current income) announced since the crisis began is because of the reforms that have been announced by the new coalition Government since the May 2010 election. Relative to the plans set out by the previous Labour Government, the coalition Government's new reforms are estimated to reduce current incomes of those lower down the income distribution by more, as a share of current income, than those who are further up the income distribution. This has offset all of the estimated progressivity of the package of post-crisis measures that was bequeathed to the new coalition Government by its predecessor—as shown by Browne and Levell (2010). In other words, the new coalition Government has revealed a preference for less redistribution through the tax and benefit system than the previous Labour Government had favoured.

The impact of the cure on public-service spending

Both the present coalition and previous Labour Government's planned reliance on reducing the growth of public spending as a way of cutting borrowing implied a very tight squeeze on public-service spending over the next few years. In fact, the latest forecasts for spending suggest that the period from 2010–11 to 2015–16 will, if implemented, be the longest sustained period of cuts to public-service spending since the end of the Second World War. Figure 9.14 shows the annual real increases in a broad measure of public service spending since 1949–50, and the six years of cuts that are currently planned by the coalition Government for 2010–11 to 2015–16. Public-service spending has not been cut in real terms for more than two consecutive years at any point since the Second World War. The next six years could also be the tightest six years over this period, with the average annual real cut to public-service spending (forecast to be 1.9%) surpassing the average annual real cut of 1.6% over the six years ending in 1981–82, which included both the early years of Margaret Thatcher's premiership and the period in which the

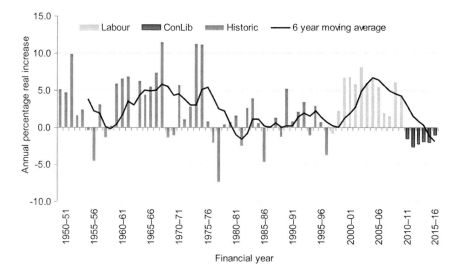

Figure 9.14 The impact of the cure on spending on public services
Note: Spending on public services defined as total public spending less spending on welfare benefits and gross debt interest.
Source: Historical data are from ONS series ANLY, ANLT, ANNW, ANNZ and ANLO from table 2.3C of Financial Statistics Freestanding Time Series Data, www. statistics.gov.uk/statbase/tsdtimezone.asp. Historic figures for the GDP deflator are from HM Treasury (www.hm-treasury.gov.uk/data_gdp_fig.htm). Forecasts are authors' calculations from supplementary table 2.24, of Office for Budget Responsibility 2011 and using GDP deflator forecasts from table 4.3, page 95, of Office for Budget Responsibility 2011

previous Labour Government attempted to comply with the International Monetary Fund's (IMF) austerity plan in return for having agreed a loan.

The spending allocations for individual public services for the years 2011–12 to 2014–15 were announced in the Spending Review of October 2010. The spending plans set out in this imply a cut to overall Departmental Expenditure Limits (DELs)—which broadly comprise spending by central government departments on the administration and the delivery of public services—of 12.2% in real terms over the four-year period.[14] (This is in addition to the cuts to spending in 2010–11 that were announced immediately after the coalition Government took office in June 2010.) The previous Labour Government was not explicit about its plans for spending on public services. However, the OBR's estimate in June 2010 was that the previous Labour Government's aspirations to cut public spending would have implied a 10.2% cut to DELs between 2010–11 and 2014–15, unless further cuts to welfare spending had been found.[15]

The pain has not been equally shared across the public services, however. As Figure 9.15 shows, some areas are to be cut much more severely than others, while a few (relatively small) areas will actually see large increases in

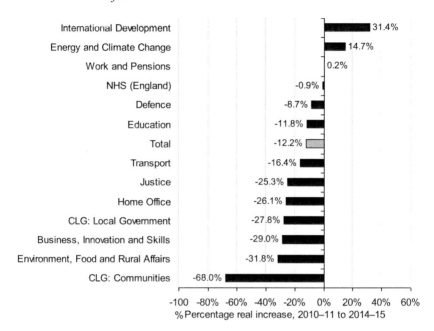

Figure 9.15 Planned spending changes, by department to 2014–15
Notes: Figures show the real-terms percentage change in the department's budget by 2014–15, from its 2010–11 level.
Sources: Authors' calculations using baseline (2010–11) spending plans set out in HM Treasury (2010c), cash spending in 2014–15 from HM Treasury (2011) and GDP deflators from OBR (2011).

spending. Overseas aid spending is to be increased sharply, in order to meet an international commitment to spend 0.7% of Gross National Income on aid. The NHS is also set to be relatively protected, although if implemented this would still be the tightest settlement for the NHS for 50 years.[16] As health spending comprises a large share (currently 27%) of overall public-service spending, affording the NHS this degree of protection from the cuts had significant consequences for the spending available for other areas. The Home Office and Ministry of Justice—which between them are responsible for the provision of policing, the courts and prisons—are to have their budgets cut by just over one-quarter in real terms. The largest cuts were imposed on the Communities budget of the Department for Communities and Local Government (CLG), reflecting in large part an intention to cut investment spending on social housing by 80%.

Overall, the cuts to spending on public services are intended to be relatively front-loaded, with 40% of the cut to be implemented in 2011–12. However, the time profile of the cuts differs across departments. The cuts to education spending, for example, are planned to be very front-loaded: 55% of the cut is to be delivered in the first year, with significant cuts to investment spending on schools. In contrast, the cuts to defence and transport spending are much more back-loaded, with most of the cuts not expected until 2013–14 and 2014–15. These differences in timing probably reflect the ease with which spending, in particular investment spending, can be adjusted quickly by different departments. For a longer discussion of the departmental spending plans, including differences between the decisions taken by the Scottish Parliament, the Welsh Assembly and the Northern Ireland Executive and those taken for England by the UK Government, see Crawford *et al.* (2011).

Section four: institutional reform: can we boost confidence that the patient will take the medicine?

In an attempt to enhance the credibility of its fiscal policy commitments, the coalition Government has set up an independent Office for Budget Responsibility.[17] This body has taken over responsibility for producing and publishing official economic and fiscal forecasts from Treasury ministers. The UK is one of a number of countries to have adopted such an independent fiscal council in recent years; Sweden, Canada, Hungary and Slovenia have also all created similar bodies over the last four years. These in turn follow the example of bodies such as the Central Planning Bureau (CPB) in the Netherlands and the Congressional Budget Office (CBO) in the USA.

Though the structure and remit of each of these bodies is slightly different, the broad aims are the same. Essentially, there is a concern that politicians are prone, or are perceived to be prone, to under-value the longer-term costs of borrowing—perhaps because of pressure from special interest groups or political short-termism—which causes them to allow excessive debt accumulation.[18] Even if politicians sign up to fiscal rules that theoretically constrain the amount of borrowing they are allowed to do (such as Mr Osborne's fiscal mandate and supplementary target mentioned above), the complex nature of economic and fiscal forecasting is such that the electorate find it hard to hold governments to account. If the electorate prefer less borrowing than politicians do, politicians have an incentive to produce optimistic fiscal forecasts to hide their intention to borrow excessively. (It is also possible that immediately after a change of government incoming ministers might have an incentive to produce deliberately pessimistic forecasts in order to increase the chance that the new government will be able to announce better than expected performance in subsequent budgets.)

Deviations from forecasts could indicate either that the initial forecasts were intentionally misleading or that unforeseen events occurred after the forecasts were produced. This in turn also has a cost for prudent governments: though they may be committed to maintaining sound public finances, they may struggle to convince the electorate and market actors of this, and so may not be fully rewarded for behaving virtuously. This was a key rationale behind Mr Brown's decision to place a lot of personal political capital on his pledge to meet two fiscal rules on becoming Chancellor in 1997: he wanted to convince others that he would not repeat the perceived mistakes of some previous Labour Chancellors.

Fiscal councils are intended to help improve scrutiny of the government's fiscal intentions by providing a transparent and independent assessment of the economic and fiscal position and forecasts. As Debrun *et al.* (2009) argue, 'A [fiscal council] could help reduce deficit bias, while leaving full discretion to the political representatives. FCs could contribute to greater transparency—a key prerequisite for the accountability of fiscal policy—and thereby raise the political cost of inappropriate uses of fiscal policy in terms of credibility of the policymakers.

By increasing transparency and credibility they can complement fiscal rules. The desire for this reform in the UK in part reflects that the fiscal promises of the previous Labour Government were undermined by the moving of the goal-posts that occurred just as one of Mr Brown's two fiscal rules (the golden rule) looked on course to be missed rather than met, and that fiscal forecasts reflected politically motivated wishful thinking rather than dispassionate professional judgement—notably in the run-up to the 2005 general election.

The remit of the OBR is to:[19]

- examine and report on the sustainability of the public finances;
- produce fiscal and economic forecasts, and provide an assessment of the extent to which the fiscal mandate has been or is likely to be achieved, on at least two occasions each financial year;
- prepare an assessment, at least once a year, of the accuracy of economic and fiscal forecasts previously prepared by it;
- prepare an analysis, at least once a year, of the sustainability of the public finances;
- examine the impact of decisions made by the Government on the sustainability of the public finances, but not examine alternative policy scenarios; and
- act objectively, transparently and impartially.

The OBR's funding allocation has been fixed, for the four years covered by the recent Spending Review (2011–12 to 2014–15), at £1.75 million a year. Having such certainty over funding is an important part of establishing an independent fiscal council. It is more likely that such a fiscal council will feel able to act—and will be perceived as being able to act—without let or hindrance from the Government if they are certain that comments that are detrimental to the Government will not lead to their funding being cut. The experience of the Hungarian Fiscal Council—which in 2010 was threatened with a nearly 99% cut in its budget, from 835.5 million forints to just 10 million forints—suggests that this risk can be all too real.[20]

The OBR in practice

The OBR produces forecasts for the economy and public finances using resources similar to those previously used by the Treasury. Importantly, the OBR has access to all the same data, expertise and models as the Treasury. The forecasting judgements are made by the three-person Budget Responsibility Committee (BRC), which comprises Robert Chote (Chairman), Stephen Nickell and Graham Parker. Previously such forecasting judgements were the responsibility of the Chancellor. The OBR is now charged with publishing these forecasts and the Chancellor can either accept them or, in theory, reject them and use his or her own.

Four OBR forecasts have been published since the general election in May 2010. The first two were a pre-Budget Report (in June 2010—preceding the Government's Emergency Budget) and a Budget forecast (accompanying the June 2010 Budget). Both of these were carried out by an interim OBR, with an interim BRC comprising Sir Alan Budd (Chairman), Geoff Dicks and Graham Parker. Since then, the permanent OBR has produced two *Economic and Fiscal Outlooks* (in November 2010 and March 2011).[21] In addition, they provided independent scrutiny and certification of the Government's costings of annually managed expenditure (AME) policies in the October 2010 Spending Review.

In the future it seems likely that the OBR will publish four types of analysis (all of which were previously published at least semi-regularly by the Treasury):

- Economic and fiscal forecasts, an assessment of the cost of any new policies, and a judgement on compliance with the fiscal mandate and supplementary target, at the time of the Government's spring Budgets.
- Economic and fiscal forecasts and a judgement on compliance with the fiscal mandate and supplementary target in the autumn. The Chancellor has reserved the right to announce new policy measures at this time, the costings of which would also need to be approved by the OBR.
- An annual long-term fiscal sustainability report, examining long-term pressures facing the public finances.
- An annual end of year fiscal report, examining how fiscal out-turns for the last financial year compared to previous forecasts.[22]

Most of the forecasts produced by the OBR are, like all economic forecasts, likely to prove to be inaccurate. Therefore, in order for the OBR to build its reputation they should take as much advantage as possible of the required end of year fiscal report to conduct and communicate detailed analysis of how and why outcomes deviated from the forecasts. Informing the public about the extent to which errors made in forecasts were unavoidable, due to the inherent nature of the task at hand, or were avoidable and therefore will not be repeated again, will be an important part of the OBR's role. This should help to increase confidence that the forecasts were not intentionally misleading, and that any lessons that can be learnt are being learnt. A regular timetable is also sensible.

Interaction between the OBR and the Government

The OBR is now the only government or parliamentary body with the resources to produce detailed economic and fiscal forecasts. This has the advantage of avoiding costly duplication of tasks. However, it has the cost that the Government—when deciding whether, and what, additional policy measures might be required—does not have its own forecasting model on which to draw. It will be necessary, therefore, for the Government to know what the OBR's forecasts are before they can decide exactly what policy measures they can or should implement—whether this is giving away extra money if the outlook improves, or announcing further tax increases or spending cuts if the OBR thinks that current policy is not consistent with meeting the Chancellor's fiscal mandate or expected fiscal sustainability. This exchange of information could happen in a number of different ways and there are advantages and disadvantages to each of them, from the OBR, the Government's and the public's perspectives.

At one extreme, the OBR could decide to have no private interaction with the Government at all. It would produce its forecasts independently and then make them publicly available, including stating whether current policy was consistent with the Chancellor's fiscal mandate. The Government could then decide what action to take in its next Budget. The advantage of this approach is that it would probably help maximize the appearance of independence for the OBR. There should be little suspicion that the OBR has been coerced by ministers into making suboptimal forecasting assumptions. However, there are at least two disadvantages.

- First, the Government would potentially be put in the position of the OBR stating publicly that fiscal policy was not consistent with meeting the fiscal mandate or with achieving expected fiscal sustainability before they had had a chance to decide how to deal with this problem. This is almost certainly undesirable from the Government's point of view but might also be undesirable for the country more generally if it led to periods of greater uncertainty about the stability of the UK's public finances.
- Second, this approach might lead to worse policy-making. As an example, suppose the Government were to decide—in light of the OBR's revised forecasts—that a 1% of national income fiscal tightening was required to reduce borrowing. The Government would have to adopt a package of measures which they thought likely to cut borrowing by this amount. However, without the ability to confer with the OBR and without any other official source of forecasting expertise, making such a decision would be difficult. It is quite possible that the OBR would then judge that the package actually raised more (or less) money than the Government was hoping for. This would be an undesirable situation for both the Government and the public.

The Swedish Fiscal Policy Council is one independent fiscal council that explicitly has no discussions with their government before publishing each annual report. Their head, Lars Calmfors, has argued that the same should be true of the OBR in the UK.[23] However, this *modus operandi* is perhaps facilitated by the fact that it is not responsible for producing economic and fiscal forecasts (this is done by other public bodies in Sweden), but considers only broader issues of fiscal sustainability.

An alternative option is to adopt a more consultative approach. This is essentially what the OBR has done so far. Under this model the OBR discusses its forecasts with the Chancellor; then the Government decides what—if any—policies to implement; then the OBR incorporates the impact of these policies into its forecasts, which are published at the same time as the policy announcements. One of the advantages of this approach is that one set of economic and fiscal forecasts can be published alongside the policy announcements at the time of each Budget. A clear advantage from the Government's point of view is that they are able to prepare and take action before the OBR makes any public statement. This approach should also aid policy-making by giving ministers access to better information about how the policies they are considering might affect the outlook for the economy and public finances before they finalize policy decisions.

However, the disadvantage is that these kinds of private consultations between ministers and the OBR could make the forecasting process less transparent. This, in turn, could potentially undermine at least the appearance of the OBR's independence. For example, it has been argued that regular meetings between cabinet ministers and officials at the CPB in the Netherlands are sometimes used to coerce the bureau into changing its analysis.[24] Many of the benefits that are derived from an independent fiscal council come from the increased transparency and credibility, which are argued to outweigh the additional costs of such a body. To lose these advantages would be a heavy price to pay, and the OBR will have to continue to ward against this danger; this was highlighted by debate around figures released by the interim OBR in summer 2010.[25] However, the risks of losing the perception of independence are probably outweighed by the potential gains in the quality of policy-making to be derived from the OBR holding meetings with ministers during the forecasting process. Therefore, a continuation of the model that has been adopted so far, whereby members of the BRC have held a limited number of meetings with ministers prior to the publication of forecasts, seems appropriate. However, to reduce any suspicions that these meetings might cause the OBR to be coerced into changing its judgements, the OBR should be as transparent as possible about what meetings have been held, and when and how all key assumptions made in their forecasts were decided upon.[26]

Increasing transparency

Macroeconomic forecasts

Instead of tasking the OBR with producing macroeconomic forecasts, the Government could instead have made use of the macroeconomic forecasts already being produced by the Bank of England—the existing, official body that is responsible for setting monetary policy but is independent of government. Some of the attractions and drawbacks of such an arrangement were discussed in the 2010 *IFS Green Budget*.[27]

As this option has not been chosen, there are now two sets of forecasts for the UK economy being produced by bodies that are official but independent of government. Those produced by the OBR will be used when deciding fiscal policy, while those produced by the Bank of England will be used by the Monetary Policy Committee when deciding on monetary policy. Understanding how and why these forecasts are different—or similar—may well be important for assessing how well co-ordinated are fiscal and monetary policy.[28] Analysis of these similarities and differences by experts both inside and outside these bodies has the potential to increase debate and understanding of which assumptions underlying the forecasts are most important or controversial, and thus could improve the quality of the macroeconomic forecasts produced.

Quite how much understanding of the differences and similarities between these forecasts will be possible will depend in part on how much detail on their forecasts and forecasting models the OBR makes publicly available. Thus far, they have published more detail than the Treasury previously did—for example, on some of the outputs of the macroeconomic modelling that are important inputs into the modelling of the public finances, listed below. This is a welcome development. They should continue to go further, for instance by providing more detail on their underlying forecasting models as well.

Fiscal forecasts

There have been a number of welcome increases in transparency that have accompanied the shift of fiscal forecasting from the Treasury to the OBR:

- To date, the OBR's publications have provided much more information on the economic assumptions underlying the fiscal projections than the equivalent documents previously produced by HM Treasury. For example, they now reveal key assumptions about corporate profits growth, earnings growth, and growth in property prices and the volume of transactions.
- The OBR has been responsive to requests for additional detail on their assumptions where this was not already provided in their publications.[29] Furthermore, to aid the perception of impartiality, they have adopted the policy of publishing responses to such requests at a fixed (pre-announced) time and date each month.
- The requirement that the OBR provide independent scrutiny of the Treasury's estimates of the 'direct' impact of individual Budget policy measures on the public finances,[30] has been associated with more detail being publicly provided by the Treasury of how these estimates have been reached.
- Previously the Treasury published forecasts for the public finances which built in an unquantified degree of 'caution'. That is, the forecasts were claimed not to be the Treasury's best central estimate but rather a slightly

pessimistic view. In contrast, the main forecasts of the OBR are central estimates. This then leaves the Chancellor to make the explicit policy decision over the extent of caution with which he or she wishes to aim to meet the fiscal target.

- The OBR explicitly takes uncertainty into account by also publishing 'fan charts' that provide some indication of the likelihood of alternative outcomes, in much the same way as the Bank of England does for its inflation and economic growth forecasts. The *Economic and Fiscal Outlooks* have also considered the sensitivity of the forecasts to several parameters and forecast the key fiscal aggregates under alternative economic scenarios.

All of these improvements are welcome. While so far OBR publications have omitted some information that was previously provided in similar Treasury publications, it appears that this has usually been through oversight rather than intentional omission. Experience to date suggests that if these gaps are drawn to the OBR's attention they will be remedied in future publications. However, in the realms of both macroeconomic and fiscal forecasting the OBR should make publicly available as much data, and as much detail on their models, as possible.

Consideration of alternative policy scenarios

The primary legislation that set up the OBR states that it 'may not consider what the effect of any alternative policies would be'.[31] In other words, the OBR is not allowed to publish an assessment of what the outlook for the economy and public finances would be under a different set of policies than those legislated by the Government (such as those presented in sections two and three of this chapter). One simple alternative policy scenario for which forecasts should certainly always be published alongside each significant fiscal event (such as Budgets) is that of no new discretionary measures. This would inform debate on the impact of the new measures on both the economy and the public finances.

There are also some other policy scenarios for which the OBR's consideration might aid public debate. The current remit forbids the OBR from commenting on the public finance implications of proposals made by other political parties (or indeed the individual parties that form the current coalition), and also from considering policies that the Government has mooted (for example, in speeches, green papers, white papers, legislation, manifestos and the coalition agreement) but not implemented.

This is in contrast to the CPB in the Netherlands, which does provide costings of other political parties' policies, as set out in their manifestos, before each election (and during negotiations over the formation of a new coalition government).[32] The advantage for the OBR of being prevented from considering opposition parties' policies is that it is less likely to be drawn into a political debate on the relative merits of alternative policy options. However, it may not be immune from this, as the current arrangement means that the Government will be able to have 'OBR-approved' costings for future policies that it has committed to in past budgets, but the opposition parties will not have this option open to them. The disadvantage for the public of the OBR being prevented from considering opposition parties' policies is that while existing policies are subject to intense scrutiny, the options with which they are presented at the time of general elections will not be, and so they will find it harder to make informed decisions. Moreover, in the run-up to a general election where it is widely believed that an opposition party is likely to form the next government, the fiscal plans of that opposition party are, arguably, more important for the sustainability of the public finances than those of the current government. Of course, Institute for Fiscal Studies (IFS) researchers—who are also independent of the Government and the opposition parties—and other bodies will continue to provide careful scrutiny of policy proposals, including, where possible, costings of new measures, but in at least some cases the OBR would have the advantage of having access to better data.

Overall, the OBR is a welcome innovation. The intention, and the practice to date, of promoting greater transparency of official economic and fiscal forecasts will aid scrutiny of the Government's compliance with their specific fiscal targets (discussed above). A better assessment of broader compliance with the longer-term objective of fiscal sustainability should also be aided by the OBR's future work programme. The OBR will need to work hard to maintain, and where possible enhance, its reputation as a politically independent body, particularly as quite considerable discussion and exchange of information may be required between the Treasury and the OBR in advance of the publication of its forecasts. There is a case for extending the remit of the OBR so that it is able to consider the impact on the economy and public finances of alternative policy options, at least in some limited circumstances such as the run-up to a general election.

Section five: conclusions

Following 10 years of relative fiscal stability, in 2008 the UK's public finances plunged deeply into the red. Public-sector net borrowing reached 11.1% of national income in 2009–10, a level unprecedented in peacetime. Figures from successive official forecasts for public borrowing suggest that much of this deterioration in the public finances (about 5.9% of national income, or £91 billion in 2011–12 terms) is expected to reflect permanently higher borrowing unless active steps are taken to cut it.

Many independent commentators (including those at the IFS) had expressed concern that the Government's fiscal forecasts prior to 2005 included an element of over-optimism. For this reason, we and others had called for additional fiscal tightening prior to the crisis but only of the order of approximately 1% of national income (or £15 billion in today's terms). There was no widespread call before 2008 for a fiscal tightening on the scale that would have been required to offset the size of permanent increase in public borrowing (5.9% of national income) that has now emerged.

This permanent increase in borrowing therefore seems likely to be explained by one (or both) of two possible factors. First, that the adverse consequences of recent (in particular, financial sector) developments truly have permanently and unexpectedly damaged the productive capacity of the UK economy. Second, that there was collective blindness to an unsustainable boom in the UK economy prior to 2008, perhaps with imported deflation masking domestic inflationary pressures (the traditional signal of economic over-heating), which instead showed up solely in the prices of assets such as housing.

Whether or not the higher level of structural borrowing could or should have been identified earlier, the challenge now facing the UK Government is the same. A substantial reduction in annual borrowing levels is required to return the UK's public finances to a sustainable path. The new coalition Government has set itself the task of eliminating the structural current budget deficit by 2015–16 and to have debt falling as a share of national income by the same point, though its current fiscal plans are actually rather more ambitious than this (and the first fiscal rule is, in practice, likely to be the binding one).

In order to achieve these goals the coalition Government has legislated for a package of tax increases (to bear about 25% of the strain of deficit reduction) and spending cuts (to deal with the remaining 75% of the problem). The package of tax increases and cuts to welfare benefits that has been announced is regressive across most of the income distribution. The most notable exception is those on the highest incomes who are bearing a particularly large share of the burden. However, it is harder to know how the substantial planned cuts to public service spending will impact on individuals.

Like many other countries, the UK Government has in recent years struggled to maintain credibility in its fiscal forecasts and stated fiscal objectives. Independent observers suspected that the previous Labour Government had in recent years used overly optimistic economic assumptions to flatter the public finance outlook and 'moved the goalposts' to make their fiscal rules easier to achieve. The fiscal consolidation challenge facing the new coalition Government is substantial and public credibility of the plans will be essential, not least in order to ensure that fiscal discipline is properly rewarded through more favourable borrowing terms for the UK Government. Therefore, the new Government has implemented a major reform to UK fiscal institutions—the introduction of an independent OBR—designed to boost people's confidence that the official forecasts are the best available and that the public finances can be expected to evolve as the Chancellor predicts. Its success will depend crucially on its ability to establish a reputation for political independence and high quality, transparent and clearly communicated, analysis. However, if it is successful, it could be effective in holding the government to account and increasing transparency, and thus trust in, official public finance forecasts.

Appendix: The 'debt falling' condition

Given that debt in $t+1$ is:

$$d_{t+1} = d_t \left(\frac{1+r}{1+g}\right) - ps_{t+1} \tag{1}$$

Where d_x = debt to GDP ratio in period x; r = nominal interest rate; g = nominal growth rate of GDP; and ps_x = primary surplus (as a share of GDP) in period x.

To fulfil the constraint $d_{t+1} < d_t$ requires:

$$d_t \left(\frac{r-g}{1+g}\right) < ps_{t+1} \tag{2}$$

Or alternatively, written in terms of PSNB:

$$d_t \left(\frac{g}{1+g}\right) > b_{t+1} \tag{3}$$

Where $b_{t+1} = -ps_{t+1} + i_{t+1}$; $i_{t+1} = d_t*(r/(1+g))$ = interest on outstanding debt paid in $t+1$ (measured as a share of $t+1$ GDP).

Under the OBR's forecasts published at the time of the March 2011 Budget, nominal growth in 2015–16 is 5.6%, with the average interest rate on government debt set to be 4.14%, and the debt level in 2014–15 at 70.5% of national income.

This implies that the minimum allowable primary balance in 2015–16 in order to fulfil the 'debt falling' condition is a deficit of 1.0% of national income. Assuming that the OBR's forecast for debt interest spending in 2015–16 (of 2.8% of national income) is correct, this would imply maximum allowable borrowing of 3.8% of national income in 2015–16 to fulfil the 'debt falling' condition.

Total borrowing is forecast by the OBR under current plans to be 1.1% of national income in 2015–16. If the forecasts to 2014–15 prove correct, then for debt not to fall in the following year the primary balance would need to be 2.7% of national income worse than forecast in 2015–16.

If the new coalition Government's first fiscal rule (of a balanced structural current budget in 2015–16) were met exactly, rather than with the 0.8% of national income margin currently forecast, this could explain up to 0.8% of national income of this higher primary deficit. The remaining 1.9% of national income higher borrowing would need to come from greater than forecast investment spending; this implies investment spending of 2.9% of national income compared to the projected 1.1% of national income.

Notes

1 Throughout this paper we use the term 'national income' to refer to gross domestic product (GDP)—that is, the market value of all final goods and services made within the UK in any year. In the UK fiscal years run from April to March; thus 2008–09 refers to the period from April 2008 to March 2009.

2 The small part of this additional 'structural' borrowing that is temporary rather than permanent reflects the OBR's view that the public finances will bounce back by more than would normally be expected given their forecasts for economic growth over this period.

3 See paragraph B.4, page 73 of Office for Budget Responsibility (2010a).

4 In particular, the OBR has assumed that the share of value-added tax (VAT) revenues to which the government believes it is entitled but which are not collected (known as the VAT gap) will remain constant over time as opposed to increasing as the Treasury previously assumed.

5 Source: Authors' calculations based on table B.2, page 155, of HM Treasury (2010a).

6 The OBR's pre-Budget forecast published in June 2010 (Office for Budget Responsibility 2010a) on the basis of the latest economic data at that time and assuming that policy followed the plans that had been announced by the Labour Government suggested that borrowing was actually set to be just 5.0% of national income in 2013–14. Of course, it is possible that the outlook would have been different had the Labour Government actually been re-elected, if, for example, debt interest rates had turned out to be different as a result.

7 Prior to the May 2010 general election all three main UK political parties were vague about the measures that they would implement, if elected, in order to bring the public finances back onto a sustainable path (Chote *et al.* 2010).

8 A discussion of the investment spending plans can be found in Emmerson (2009).

9 See Appendix A for more details.

10 For the previous year, 2014–15, the new measures split 80% spending cuts, 20% tax rises. The fall in share explained by tax rises between 2014–15 and 2015–16 is explained partly through continued cuts to public spending but also for the last in a series of cuts to the main rate of corporation tax being planned for April 2014, the fiscal impact of which will be largely felt in 2015–16.

11 In fact, in the June 2010 Budget the Treasury published their own illustrative figures suggesting that debt would not fall back below 40% of national income until after 2030. Source: chart 1.5, page 24, HM Treasury 2010b.

12 See O'Dea and Preston (2010, 2011) for a discussion of attempts to allocate the benefits of public service spending to individual households. Horton and Reed (2010) try to assess the distributional impact of the planned cuts to public service spending.

13 See figure 7.5, page 146, of Brewer *et al.* 2010.

14 Calculated using the baseline (2010–11) spending figures presented in HM Treasury 2010c, cash spending plans for 2014–15 from HM Treasury 2011 and forecasts for the GDP deflator from Office for Budget Responsibility (2011).

15 Source: Office for Budget Responsibility (2010a).

16 Despite the relative protection afforded to the NHS, upwards revisions to forecast inflation since the Spending Review mean that the cash spending plans set in the 2010 Spending Review no longer appear sufficient to meet the coalition Government's stated commitment to increase NHS spending by more than inflation each year.

17 See budgetresponsibility.independent.gov.uk and www.legislation.gov.uk/ukpga/2011/4/contents/enacted for details.

18 A number of previous papers have discussed the reasons behind excessive government debt accumulation and the arguments for independent fiscal councils. For a useful summary see Calmfors 2010.

19 This is taken from the Budget Responsibility and National Audit Act 2011 (www. legislation.gov.uk/ukpga/2011/4/contents/enacted).

20 *Wall Street Journal*, 22 November 2010, 'Hungary to disband Fiscal Council', blogs.wsj.com/new-europe/2010/11/22/hungary-to-disband-fiscal-council.

21 See Office for Budget Responsibility 2010a, 2010b, 2010c, 2011.

22 The OBR did publish a comparison of the Treasury's forecasts for 2009–10 with the latest estimated out-turn in November 2010. See Office for Budget Responsibility 2010d.

23 www.guardian.co.uk/commentisfree/2010/jul/28/how-its-done-in-sweden.

24 Bos and Teulings 2010, cited in Calmfors 2010.

25 See www.guardian.co.uk/commentisfree/2010/jul/14/office-for-budget-responsibility-editorial.

26 Alongside both the November 2010 and the March 2011 *Economic and Fiscal Outlooks*, the OBR published a log of all contacts that had been made between the OBR and ministers. This is quite a high degree of transparency. However, repeating such an exercise may be more difficult in cases where there is more interaction between the OBR and the Treasury, as might be required if the Government were considering a substantial package of new policy measures (such as those implemented in the June 2010 Budget).

27 See Chote, Emmerson, Sibieta and Tetlow 2010.

28 For example, in November 2010 both the OBR and the Bank of England published new forecasts for GDP growth. The Bank's forecast was for cumulative real GDP growth to be about 0.5 percentage points higher over the next three years—2011 to 2013—than the OBR forecast. The OBR's forecast for growth in the Consumer Price Index (CPI) was also lower than the Bank's up to the end of 2012, but higher thereafter. Sources: Bank of England, *Inflation Report: November 2010*; Office for Budget Responsibility 2010c.

29 A variety of supplementary information has already been made available on the OBR's website, budgetresponsibility.independent.gov.uk/publications.html.

30 The Treasury estimates the cost or yield of firm and final policies. These costings take into account direct behavioural effects on the tax base to which the policy is applied and the base of closely related taxes. In the case of benefit reforms, these costings take into account the effect of interactions with other benefits. For further detail of the Treasury's methodology, see HM Treasury, *Budget 2010 policy costings*, www.hm-treasury.gov.uk/d/junebudget_costings.pdf. For a detailed discussion of alternative methods for costing policies, see Adam and Bozio 2009.

31 Budget Responsibility and National Audit Act 2011, www.legislation.gov.uk/ukpga/2011/4/contents/enacted.

32 See www.cpb.nl/en/what-does-cpb-do.

References

Adam, S. and A. Bozio (2009) 'Dynamic Scoring', *OECD Journal on Budgeting* Vol. 9, No. 2: 99–124.

Brewer, M., J. Browne, A. Leicester and H. Miller (2010) 'Options for fiscal tightening: tax increases and benefit cuts', in R. Chote, C. Emmerson and J. Shaw (eds), *The IFS Green Budget: February 2010*, London: Institute for Fiscal Studies, www.ifs.org.uk/publications/4732.

Browne, J. (2011) *Personal tax and benefit changes*, presentation at IFS post-Budget 2011 Briefing, www.ifs.org.uk/publications/5524.

Browne, J. and P. Levell (2010) *The distributional effect of tax and benefit reforms to be introduced between June 2010 and April 2014: a revised assessment*, Briefing Note 108, London: Institute for Fiscal Studies, www.ifs.org.uk/publications/5246.

Calmfors (2010) *The role of independent fiscal policy institutions*, www.finanspolitiskar adet.se/download/18.64075cf012c96962a7d800012034/Underlagsrapport+9+2010+C almfors.pdf.

Chote, R. (2009) *A bust without a boom? IFS Observation*, April, www.ifs.org.uk/public ations/4513.

Chote, R., C. Crawford, C. Emmerson and G. Tetlow (2010) *Filling the Hole: How do the Three Main UK Parties Plan to Repair the Public Finances? IFS Election Briefing Note EBN12*, www.ifs.org.uk/publications/4848.

Chote, R. and Emmerson, C. (2010) *The first cut, IFS Observation*, May, www.ifs.org. uk/publications/4924.

Chote, R., C. Emmerson, L. Sibieta and G. Tetlow (2010) 'Reforming UK fiscal institutions', in R. Chote, C. Emmerson and J. Shaw (eds), *The IFS Green Budget: February 2010*, London: Institute for Fiscal Studies, www.ifs.org.uk/publications/4732.

Crawford, R., C. Emmerson, D. Phillips and G. Tetlow (2011) 'Public spending cuts: pain shared?', in *The IFS Green Budget: February 2011*, London: Institute for Fiscal Studies, www.ifs.org.uk/budgets/gb2011/11chap6.pdf.

Debrun, X., D. Hauner and M.S. Kumar (2009) 'Independent Fiscal Agencies', *Journal of Economic Surveys* Vol. 23, No. 1: 44–81.

Emmerson, C. (2009) *Chronic underinvestment? IFS Observation*, June, www.ifs.org.uk/ publications/4554.

HM Treasury (2008a) *Budget 2008*, HC 388, March, London: The Stationery Office, webarchive.nationalarchives.gov.uk/20100407010852/http://www.hm-treasury.gov.uk/ bud_bud08_index.htm.

——(2008b) *Pre-Budget Report 2008*, Cm 7484, November, London: The Stationery Office, webarchive.nationalarchives.gov.uk/20100407010852/http://www.hm-treasury. gov.uk/prebud_pbr08_index.htm.

——(2008c) *Public Finances and the Cycle*, Treasury Economic Working Paper No.5, November, London: HM Treasury, webarchive.nationalarchives.gov.uk/20100407010 852/http://www.hm-treasury.gov.uk/prebud_pbr08_publicfinances.htm.

——(2009a) *Budget 2009*, HC 407, April, London: The Stationery Office, webarchive. nationalarchives.gov.uk/20100407010852/http://www.hm-treasury.gov.uk/bud_bud09_ index.htm.

——(2009b) *Pre-Budget Report 2009*, Cm 7747, December, London: The Stationery Office, webarchive.nationalarchives.gov.uk/20100407010852/http://www.hm-treasury. gov.uk/prebud_pbr09_index.htm.

——(2010a) *Budget 2010: securing the recovery*, HC 451, March 2010, London: The Stationery Office, webarchive.nationalarchives.gov.uk/20100407010852/http://www. hm-treasury.gov.uk/budget2010_documents.htm.

——(2010b) *Budget 2010*, HC 61, June, London: The Stationery Office, www.hm-treasury. gov.uk/junebudget_documents.htm.

——(2010c) *Spending Review 2010*, October, London: The Stationery Office, www.hm-treasury.gov.uk/spend_index.htm.

——(2011) *Budget 2011*, HC 451, March, London: The Stationery Office, www.hm-treasury.gov.uk/2011budget.htm.

Horton, T. and H. Reed (2010) *Don't forget the spending cuts! The real impact of Budget 2010*, www.touchstoneblog.org.uk/wp-content/uploads/2010/06/FINAL-Dont-forget-the-spending-cuts.pdf.

O'Dea, C. and I. Preston (2010) *The distributional impact of public spending in the UK*, 2020 Public Services Trust, www.ifs.org.uk/publications/5234.

——(2011) *Measuring the distributional impact of public service cuts*, in *The IFS Green Budget: February 2011*, London: Institute for Fiscal Studies, www.ifs.org.uk/publica tions/5234.

Office for Budget Responsibility (2010a) *Pre-Budget Forecast: June 2010*, London: Office for Budget Responsibility, budgetresponsibility.independent.gov.uk/d/pre_budget_forecast_140610.pdf.

——(2010b) *Budget forecast: June 2010*, London: Office for Budget Responsibility, budgetresponsibility.independent.gov.uk/d/junebudget_annexc.pdf.

——(2010c) *Economic and Fiscal Outlook: November 2010*, London: Office for Budget Responsibility, budgetresponsibility.independent.gov.uk/economic-and-fiscal-outlook-november-2010.

——(2010d) *Past Forecasting Performance: November 2010*, London: Office for Budget Responsibility, budgetresponsibility.independent.gov.uk/category/topics/forecast-performance.

——(2011) *Economic and Fiscal Outlook: March 2011*, London: Office for Budget Responsibility, budgetresponsibility.independent.gov.uk/economic-and-fiscal-outlook-march-2011.

10 The government's strategy for sustainable growth

Dave Ramsden

Over the pre-crisis decade, developments in the UK economy were driven by unsustainable levels of private-sector debt and rising public-sector debt. The pattern of unbalanced growth and excessive debt was revealed by the financial crisis and has helped create exceptional economic and fiscal challenges.

This chapter explains how the imbalances developed, and sets out the action the Government is taking: to tackle the fiscal position, through carrying out a comprehensive deficit-reduction plan; to reform financial regulation; and reform the supply side though *The Plan for Growth*, providing conditions for sustainable, balanced and private sector-led growth.

Unsustainable growth

In recent years, economic growth in the UK has been underpinned by the accumulation of unsustainable levels of private-sector debt and rising public-sector debt.

Figure 10.1 highlights the rise in private-sector debt in the UK. Households took on rising levels of mortgage debt to buy increasingly expensive housing, while by 2008 the debt of non-financial companies reached 110% of gross domestic product (GDP). Within the financial sector, the accumulation of debt was even greater. By 2007 the UK financial system had become the most highly leveraged of any major economy.

While rising debt was an international phenomenon, it was more pronounced in the UK than in most other countries. It has been estimated that the UK has become the most indebted country in the world (McKinsey Global Institute 2010).

The unsustainable accumulation of private debt contributed to inflated property bubbles, with property prices rising steeply in the decade preceding the financial crisis (see Figure 10.2). This trend was particularly clear in the prices of residential property, which in 2007 were four and a half times as high as in 1987.

As the Office for Budget Responsibility (OBR) has stated, over the past decade the UK household sector has, in aggregate, been a net borrower, with the sum of household consumption and investment exceeding income. Over

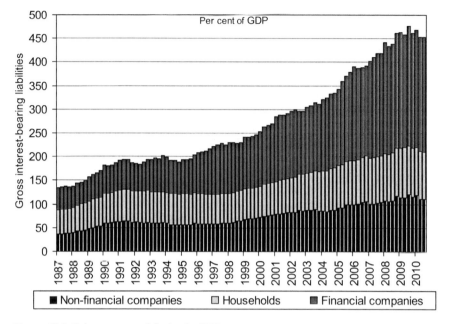

Figure 10.1 Private-sector debt in the UK
Source: Office for National Statistics

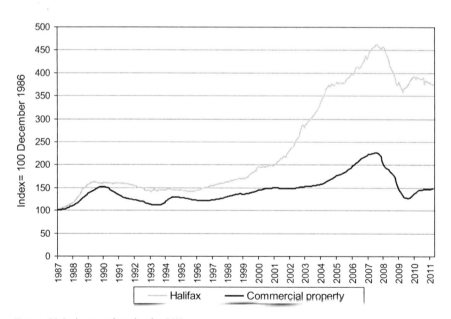

Figure 10.2 Asset prices in the UK
Source: Halifax and Investment Property Databank

this period 'households increased their residential investment spending—effectively borrowing money to purchase increasingly expensive houses' (Office for Budget Responsibility 2010: 41).

Increasing reliance on debt-financed consumer and government spending and on the financial sector also drove growing imbalances elsewhere in the UK economy. From 2001 onwards public spending grew steadily as a share of the economy and a structural deficit began to emerge. According to the Organisation for Economic Co-operation and Development (OECD), by 2007 the UK had the largest structural budget deficit in the G7 (OECD 2011). Public- and private-sector borrowing relied on finance from abroad. The UK's current account went from near balance in 1997 to a deficit of more than 3% of GDP by 2006, which was, in absolute terms, the third-largest in the world. The current account deficit was around 2.75% of GDP in 2007, a figure that was flattered by a 2.25% surplus on trade in financial services.

Between 1997 and 2007, government consumption increased from 18% to 21% of GDP, while business investment fell from 11.75% to 10.25% of GDP (see Figure 10.3). The recession has only compounded these imbalances, with government consumption accounting for 23.5% of GDP in 2009 and business investment falling over 25% from its peak, to trough at just 8.75% of GDP.

Between 2002 and 2007 there was a near tripling of UK bank balance sheets[1] and the UK financial system had become the most highly leveraged of any major economy in 2007. As a result, the UK was particularly vulnerable to financial instability and was hit hard by the financial crisis. The loss of

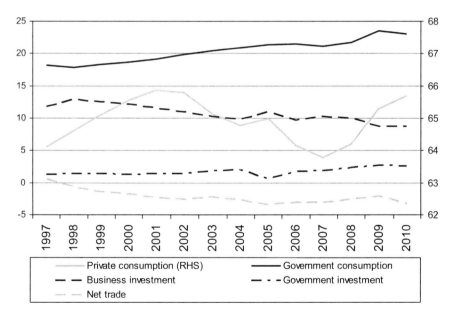

Figure 10.3 Shares of nominal GDP
Source: Office for National Statistics

confidence and withdrawal of credit that followed precipitated the deepest and longest recession since the Second World War: output fell just under 6.5% according to the Office for National Statistics (ONS). More than one-quarter of the GDP per capita growth in the pre-crisis decade to 2007 was reversed during the financial crisis and recession of 2008 and 2009.

Public-sector imbalances

In addition to the trend described within the private sector, imbalances in the public sector also built up over a number of years. In the UK a property boom and unsustainable profits and remuneration in the financial sector in the pre-crisis years drove rapid growth in tax receipts. The spending plans set out in the 2007 Comprehensive Spending Review were based on these unsustainable revenue streams, and on assumptions about trend economic growth that were later revised down significantly.[2]

The level of UK economic activity in current prices (money GDP) is estimated to be around 10% lower in 2010–11 than it was forecast to be at Budget 2008. In other words, the economy is now around 10% smaller than it was forecast to be only three years ago, reducing the resources available for government spending.

As tax receipts fell away during the crisis, the persistent gap between spending and revenue widened, with total public spending rising to around 47.5% of GDP by 2009–10.

Figure 10.4 later in this chapter shows both the persistent gap between spending and revenue in the pre-crisis years, and the dramatic widening of that gap in more recent years, the result of which has been to leave the UK with one of the most rapidly deteriorating fiscal positions of any major economy. This unsustainable fiscal position is a key vulnerability, reinforcing the case for urgent action to put the UK's public finances back on a sustainable footing.

This vulnerability is exacerbated by the interaction between the fiscal position and the UK's large financial sector. As the International Monetary Fund (IMF) has noted, 'any renewed turbulence in sovereign debt markets could trigger an adverse feedback loop between sovereign debt markets and the financial sector, inflicting major damage on the recovery' (IMF 2010a: 11). This paper goes on to summarize the domestic reforms being undertaken to counter such risks; including action to tackle the budget deficit but also radical reforms to the financial regulatory framework. Domestic reforms in the financial services sector are, moreover, complemented by an historic set of international reforms agreed by the Seoul, Republic of Korea G20 meeting in November 2010.

Role for government

Given the challenges set out, there is a need for the UK to move away from unbalanced growth reliant on a narrow range of sectors, unsustainably high

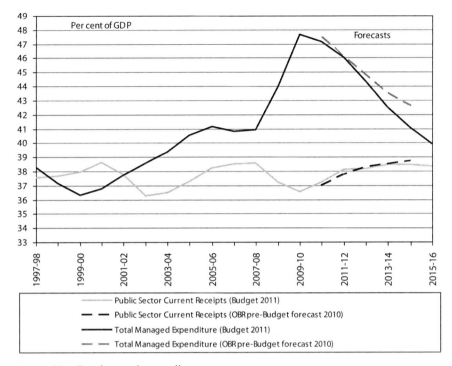

Figure 10.4 Receipts and expenditure
Source: Office for Budget Responsibility and Office for National Statistics

government spending and an unsustainable accumulation of private debt, which inflated asset prices and ultimately paved the way into the banking crisis and sharp falls in output.

The Government's economic policy objective is to achieve strong, sustainable and balanced growth that is more evenly shared across the country and between industries. The Government has announced action to meet this objective. Providing the right macroeconomic conditions will help correct the imbalance between the public and private sectors that built up over a number of years, underpinning a sustainable recovery.

Government policy has an important role to play in supporting the necessary rebalancing toward sustainable, private sector-led growth and minimizing risks to the recovery. The Government has set out a strategic policy response to the UK's exceptional economic and fiscal challenges:

- fiscal policy will bring the public finances back under control over the medium term, addressing the largest budget deficit in the UK's post-war history. It is essential to mitigate downside risks from rising public debt, promote stability and provide businesses with the confidence they need to invest;

- monetary policy will ensure price stability, and thereby support wider economic stability;
- reform of financial-sector regulation will help to prevent the build-up of systemic risks and ensure financial stability, a pre-requisite for sustainable growth; and
- microeconomic policies will drive growth and position the UK at the forefront of the global economy, to meet the Government's ambitions to: create the most competitive tax system in the G20; make the UK the best place in Europe to start, finance and grow a business; encourage investment and exports as a route to a more balanced economy; and create a more educated workforce that is the most flexible in Europe.

The Government has been clear that it is committed to delivering deficit reduction, while continuing to ensure economic recovery. The historically high level of public borrowing risked undermining fairness, growth and economic stability in the UK. A plan was therefore needed to accelerate deficit reduction and bring debt as a share of the economy under control in order to restore sustainability to the public finances. Tackling the budget deficit is essential to:

- reduce the UK's vulnerability to further shocks or a loss of market confidence, which could force a much sharper correction;
- underpin private-sector confidence, supporting growth and job creation over the medium term;
- help keep long-term interest rates down, helping families and businesses through the lower costs of loans and mortgages;
- keep debt and debt interest paid by the Government—and ultimately the taxpayer—lower than would otherwise have been the case; and
- avoid accumulating substantial debts to fund spending that benefits today's generation at the expense of tomorrow's, which would be irresponsible and unfair.

The OBR's Pre-Budget forecast (Office for Budget Responsibility 2010a) in June 2010 showed that without further action to tackle the deficit: public-sector net borrowing would remain at 4% of GDP in 2014–15; the structural deficit would be 2.8% of GDP and the structural current deficit still 1.6%; and public-sector net debt would still be rising in 2014–15, to 74.4% of GDP, with debt interest payments set to reach £67 billion in that year.

Fiscal policy and framework reform

As a consequence of unsustainable public finances and the need to provide the right macroeconomic conditions to underpin a sustainable recovery, the Government has set out a comprehensive set of policies to bring the public finances back under control.

The Government's Budget in June 2010 delivered additional consolidation plans on top of those set out by the previous Government. These plans totalled £40 billion a year by 2014–15, £32 billion of which were spending reductions. The remaining £8 billion are the net effect of changes to tax policy, including the increase in value-added tax (VAT).

When combined with the policies and assumptions set out by the previous Government, and adjusted for the results of the Spending Review, the total consolidation in this Parliament amounts to £80 billion of spending cuts by 2014–15 and a further £30 billion of tax increases. Approximately three-quarters of the planned consolidation is to be delivered through lower spending in 2014–15, with the proportion attributable to spending rising further in 2015–16.

The major contribution to the consolidation from public-spending reductions, rather than tax increases, is consistent with OECD and IMF research, which suggests that fiscal consolidation efforts that largely rely on spending restraint are more successful in supporting growth.[3] Tax measures are an effective tool for reducing the deficit quickly and supporting consolidation, allowing for phased reductions in public spending.

Therefore, the Government's fiscal consolidation plans have been designed with growth and fairness in mind, as far as possible:

- protecting the most productive public investment expenditure;
- avoiding punitive increases in tax rates on capital and labour; and
- reforming the welfare system to reward work.

Budget 2011 reaffirmed the Government's commitment to fiscal consolidation by announcing a set of measures which had a neutral effect on the public finances with all costs of discretionary policy decisions being met by measures to raise revenue.

As a result of the Government's fiscal strategy, spending is now projected to fall from 47.5% of GDP to under 40% of GDP by 2015–16, and receipts are expected to rise from 36.5% to 38.5%. The structural deficit is forecast to be reduced by 8.4 percentage points, from 8.9% of GDP in 2009–10 to 0.5% in 2015–16 (Office for Budget Responsibility 2011).

These plans to accelerate deficit reduction and consolidate the UK public finances, returning them to a sustainable path, are underpinned by significant reform to the UK's fiscal policy framework.

At June Budget 2010 the Chancellor announced the Government's forward-looking fiscal mandate to achieve cyclically adjusted current balance by the end of the rolling five-year forecast period. Given the OBR's pre-Budget forecast and the projection of rapidly rising debt, the fiscal mandate was also supplemented by a target for public-sector net debt as a percentage of GDP to be falling at a fixed date of 2015–16, ensuring that the public finances are restored to a sustainable path.

The fiscal mandate, supplemented by the target for debt, will guide fiscal policy decisions over the medium term, ensuring that the Government sets plans consistent with accelerating the reduction in the structural deficit so that debt as a percentage of GDP is restored to a sustainable, downward path.

The fiscal mandate is based on:

- the current balance, to protect the most productive investment expenditure; and
- a cyclically adjusted aggregate, to allow some flexibility at a time of economic uncertainty.

The choice of a five-year rolling forecast period for the fiscal mandate, supplemented by the fixed date for the debt target, reflects the exceptional environment in which the Government must address the fiscal challenge. They are designed to ensure that fiscal consolidation is delivered over a realistic and credible timescale. Once the public finances are closer to balance, the period over which the deficit target must be achieved could safely be shortened in order to create a tighter constraint. In addition, once the exceptional rise in debt has been addressed, a new target for debt as a percentage of GDP will be set, taking account of the OBR's assessment of the long-term sustainability of the public finances.

In order to enhance the credibility of the Government's fiscal policy and fiscal mandate, the new OBR was established in May 2010. The OBR will produce the official economic and fiscal forecasts and also assess the Government's fiscal policy against the likelihood of achieving the fiscal mandate.

The creation of the OBR introduces independence, greater transparency and credibility to the economic and fiscal forecasts on which fiscal policy is based. The establishment of the OBR places the UK at the forefront of institutional reform internationally and the IMF has advocated the benefits of such a model (IMF 2007). The OBR has been welcomed by international bodies including the European Commission, the OECD and the IMF, which stated that 'the establishment of a new independent OBR is a welcome step toward strengthening the budget process' (IMF 2010b: para. 9).

For June Budget 2010, the independent OBR operated on an interim basis under the chairmanship of Sir Alan Budd. In its pre-Budget forecast, published on 14 June 2010 (Office for Budget Responsibility 2010a) in advance of the June Budget, the OBR transparently laid out the full scale of the fiscal challenge. This included the OBR's judgement that the level of trend output and rate of trend growth were lower than assumed by the previous Government in its March 2010 Budget forecast, such that the projected trend output at the start of 2015 was around 2.5% below that implied by the assumption used for the March Budget public finances forecast. The OBR also produced its first Budget forecast on 22 June 2010, on the basis of the measures the Chancellor announced in June Budget 2010.

Legislation to place the OBR on a permanent, statutory footing received Royal Assent on 22 March 2011. In September 2010 the Chancellor appointed Robert Chote as the first permanent chair of the OBR, with his appointment approved by the Treasury Select Committee. In October 2010 Graham Parker and Professor Stephen Nickell were appointed as permanent members of the OBR's Budget Responsibility Committee (BRC).

The permanent OBR produced its first economic and fiscal outlook on 29 November 2010 and its first Budget forecast on 23 March 2011.[4] Taking into account the consolidation programme announced by the Government, at Budget 2011 the OBR forecast that the economy was continuing to grow across the forecast period to 2015–16.

As well as the official forecasts of the economy and public finances, the Budget Responsibility and National Audit Act 2011 also requires the OBR to make an assessment of whether the Government is on course to achieve its fiscal mandate and supplementary target for debt.

Taking account of uncertainty, the OBR's judgement is that the policies the Government has set out are consistent with a greater than 50% chance of achieving the Government's fiscal mandate. It is also the OBR's assessment that the Government's policies have a greater than 50% chance of meeting the target for debt in 2015–16 (Office for Budget Responsibility 2011).

As the OBR highlights,[5] all forecasts are subject to uncertainty and this applies in particular to economic and fiscal forecasts at the present time. Recognizing this, the Government has set policy to achieve a surplus on the cyclically adjusted current budget so that moderate shocks can be absorbed should they arise. The OBR's central forecast (Office for Budget Responsibility 2011) is for the fiscal mandate to be achieved in 2014–15, one year early. The forecast also shows the debt target being achieved a year early, in 2014–15.

As part of the Stability and Growth Pact (SGP) framework in the European Union (EU), the UK Government currently has an Excessive Deficit Procedure recommendation to reduce the Treaty deficit below 3% of GDP by 2014–15. The consolidation plans are also consistent with reducing the Treaty deficit below 3% of GDP by 2014–15 and placing the Treaty debt ratio on a downward path from 2014–15.

Regulation of financial system

The global financial crisis and recession have also shown the enormous cost associated with the loss of financial stability and have highlighted its importance as a necessary pre-condition for economic growth.

The Government has an objective to put a regulatory system in place that strengthens the resilience of the financial system to the long-run benefit of the economy. The reforms agreed by the Basel Committee and endorsed by the G20 address a number of the key weaknesses in financial regulation highlighted by the crisis and will substantially increase financial stability.

The Basel III reforms will be implemented in the EU through changes to the Capital Requirements Directive. Full, consistent and non-discriminatory implementation of these new international standards will help minimize the risks of regulatory arbitrage and the fragmentation of international financial markets, and ensure the long-run stability of the financial system.

In addition, the review of the Market in Financial Instruments Directive (MiFID) and European Market Infrastructure Regulation (EMIR) will provide the opportunity to further strengthen the financial system through improved transparency and investor protection, ensuring that markets remain resilient in the face of new technological developments and reforms to the market for over-the-counter derivatives.

Previously, the UK's 'tripartite' regulatory system made three authorities— the Bank of England (the Bank), the Financial Services Authority (FSA) and the Treasury—collectively responsible for financial stability. The Government believes that this system failed in a number of important ways: (i) to identify the problems building up in the financial system; (ii) to take steps to mitigate them; and (iii) to deal adequately with the crisis when it first broke.

The Government has therefore put forward proposals to overhaul the UK's financial regulatory framework, fulfilling the Coalition Government's commitment to provide the Bank of England with control of macroprudential regulation and oversight of microprudential regulation. The Government will abolish the tripartite structure and the FSA will cease to exist in its current form. The Government intends to create:

- a Financial Policy Committee (FPC) in the Bank of England;
- a new Prudential Regulation Authority (PRA) as a subsidiary of the Bank; and
- an independent business regulator, the Financial Conduct Authority (FCA).

The FPC will be responsible for protecting financial stability by improving the resilience of the financial system and by enhancing macroeconomic stability by addressing imbalances through the financial system. The Government will provide the FPC with control of macroprudential tools to ensure that systemic risks are dealt with.

The previous approach to financial regulation largely ignored the crucial interactions that financial firms have with each other and the wider economy, with devastating consequences. Under that framework, even institutions that appeared in good health before the crisis came close to collapse. Macro-prudential regulation aims to deliver financial stability by looking at the financial system as a whole, rather than individual institutions in isolation. It focuses on systemic risks and explores how financial markets interact with the wider economy. So, as well as enhancing financial stability, macroprudential policy should also encourage wider economic stability.

The PRA will have responsibility for supervision of individual firms subject to prudential regulation. Its objective will be to promote the stable and prudent operation of financial firms. It will also implement the FPC's decisions on the use of macroprudential tools in relation to firms. This will ensure that macroprudential regulation of the financial system is co-ordinated effectively with the microprudential regulation of individual firms, and that a new, more judgement-focused approach to regulation of firms is adopted so that business models can be challenged, risks identified and action taken to preserve stability.

By placing firm-specific prudential regulation under the auspices of the Bank, the Government will bring together responsibility for macroprudential and microprudential regulation in a single institution. There will no longer be a gap in which responsibilities are unclear and regulatory powers uncertain.

Regulation of conduct within the financial system—including the conduct of firms towards their retail customers and the conduct of participants in wholesale financial markets—will be carried out by a dedicated, specialist body with focused and clear statutory objectives and regulatory functions. The FCA will have the objective of promoting and enhancing confidence in the UK financial system.

This will benefit not only consumers and wholesale markets, but will also enhance financial stability. By identifying potentially significant consumer protection or market integrity issues and bringing them to the attention of the FPC—on which its chief executive will sit—the FCA will ensure that such risks are not only identified, but dealt with as quickly as possible.

These reforms will ensure that financial firms are responsibly managed and regulated. The greater stability and resilience of the financial services industry will not only benefit the sector itself, but also the wider economy. The Government will bring forward legislation to put this new architecture in place at the end of 2011.

Sustainable growth

Over a number of years, the UK's economy became unbalanced, and relied on unsustainable public spending and rising levels of public debt. For economic growth to be sustainable in the medium term, it must be based on a broad-based economy supporting private-sector jobs, exports, investment and enterprise.

Spending Review 2010 put public spending on a sustainable footing, demonstrating how the Government is delivering its plans to reduce the deficit and support macroeconomic stability. To protect the most productive public-sector investment, the Government increased the capital Spending Review envelope from that set out in Budget 2010. To ensure that capital spending is focused on the projects that deliver the highest economic returns, the Government, for the first time, undertook a fundamental review of capital spending plans across the public sector, analysing the economic value of around 250 projects and programmes, taking into account existing contractual commitments. The Government prioritized spending that helps to deliver outcomes that support growth.

In October 2010 the Government also published the UK's first ever National Infrastructure Plan setting out the infrastructure that the UK needs and how the Government will support some £200 billion-worth of public- and private-sector investment over the next five years to deliver it. This estimate is based on aggregating individual planned investments that have been publicly declared in both the public and private sectors. The majority of investment will be in transport and energy, with investment in the energy sector almost doubling between 2010 and 2015.

In November 2010 Chancellor George Osborne and Business Secretary Vince Cable announced the Growth Review, calling on business and industry to challenge government departments on the measures they are taking to remove barriers to growth and investment. The Growth Review process worked with business on an intensive programme reporting back at Budget 2011.

The Growth Review initially focused on two elements. First, structural reform priorities that can benefit the whole economy in: planning; competition; trade and investment; regulation; access to finance; corporate governance; and low carbon.

Second, removing barriers in sectors where there are clear opportunities for growth and where Government can make a difference, starting with the following sectors: construction; retail; health care and life sciences; professional and business services; advanced manufacturing; digital and creative industries; space; and tourism.

Building on the Government's action to restore economic stability and prioritize growth-enhancing spending, *The Plan for Growth*, published alongside Budget 2011, announced measures to achieve four overarching ambitions for the British economy:

- to create the most competitive tax system in the G20;
- to make the UK the best place in Europe to start, finance and grow a business;
- to encourage investment and exports as a route to a more balanced economy; and
- to create a more educated workforce that is the most flexible in Europe.

The Plan for Growth set out a range of measures to support these ambitions. For example, the Government will:

- reduce the main rate of corporation tax by a further 1% beyond the reductions announced in June Budget 2010. From April 2011 the rate will be reduced to 26% and by 2014 it will be reduced to 23%;
- drop existing proposals for specific regulations which would have cost business over £350 million a year;
- introduce a powerful new presumption in favour of sustainable development, so that the default answer to development is 'yes';
- reform the Enterprise Investment Scheme (EIS) and Venture Capital Trusts, including raising the rate of EIS income tax relief to 30% from April 2011;
- invest an additional £100 million in science capital development in 2011–12 and £200 million of new funding for rail projects;

- establish 21 new enterprise zones;
- fund an additional 80,000 work experience places for young people, ensuring up to 100,000 places will be available over the next two years, and fund up to 50,000 additional apprenticeship places over the next four years; and
- expand the university technical colleges programme to establish at least 24 new colleges.

Conclusion

Unbalanced growth and excessive debt accumulation in the UK, contributed to the exceptional economic and fiscal challenges that the Government is now acting to address. The economic policy objective is to achieve strong, sustainable and balanced growth that is more evenly shared across the country and between industries.

The Government's first priority is bringing the public finances back under control, by accelerating the reduction of the structural deficit, bolstered by fiscal framework reform. This involves the creation of the new independent Office for Budget Responsibility and setting of the new, forward-looking fiscal mandate.

Policy, alongside regulatory reform, will also have an important role to play in minimizing the risks to the recovery and supporting the rebalancing of the UK economy. The Government is placing an increased emphasis on enhancing the UK's competitiveness. Essential elements will involve a stable macroeconomy, competitive tax system and removal of barriers to business.

Notes

1 Speech by Mervyn King, Governor of the Bank of England, at the Lord Mayor's Banquet for Bankers and Merchants of the City of London at the Mansion House, 16 June 2010.
2 For example, the March 2010 Budget estimated that trend growth between mid-2007 and mid-2010 would average just under 1%, as a result of the financial crisis (and for trend growth to return to 2.75% beyond mid-2010)—compared to a central assumption of 2.75% a year assumed at the 2007 Comprehensive Spending Review. The OBR's forecast at June Budget 2010 was based on the judgement that the current level of trend output was lower still than assumed in the March Budget. See 'box 1.4: Output gap assessment' of HM Treasury 2010.
3 See IMF 2009; OECD 2007.
4 See Office for Budget Responsibility 2010b, 2011.
5 See HM Treasury 2010; Office for Budget Responsibility 2010b.

References

HM Treasury (2010) *Budget 2010*, available at cdn.hm-treasury.gov.uk/junebudget_com plete.pdf.

IMF (2007) *Code of Good Practices on Fiscal Transparency*, available at www.imf.org/external/np/pp/2007/eng/051507c.pdf.

——(2009) *UK Article IV Consultation; May 2009*, available at www.imf.org/external/np/ms/2009/052009a.htm.

——(2010a) *World Economic Outlook – Recovery, Risk and Rebalancing*, available at www.imf.org/external/pubs/ft/weo/2010/02/index.htm.

——(2010b) *UK Article IV Concluding Statement*, available at www.imf.org/external/np/ms/2010/092710.htm.

King, M. (2010) *Speech at the Lord Mayor's Banquet for Bankers and Merchants of the City of London at the Mansion House*, available at www.bankofengland.co.uk/publications/news/2010/052.htm.

McKinsey Global Institute (2010) *Debt and deleveraging: The global credit bubble and its economic consequences*, McKinsey.

OECD (2007) *OECD Economic Outlook No.81*, OECD.

——(2011) *OECD Economic Outlook No.89*, OECD.

Office for Budget Responsibility (2010a) *Pre-Budget Forecast; June 2010*, available at budgetresponsibility.independent.gov.uk.

——(2010b) *Economic and Fiscal Outlook; November 2010*, available at budgetresponsibility.independent.gov.uk.

——(2011) *Economic and Fiscal Outlook; March 2011*, available at budgetresponsibility.independent.gov.uk.

Index